Global Blockchain Governance

Global Blockchain Governance

Who Regulates the Regulators?

Tarek Omraneh

Mindful Pages

Published in 2026

ISBN: 9789374594148 (PB)
ISBN: 9789374596715 (eBook)

Published by

Mindful Pages
Imprint of Alpha Editions LLC
312 W. 2nd St #1834
Casper, WY 82601, USA

Content

Introduction

A single line of code can move billions across borders while regulators debate definitions once crafted for cheques and courthouse ledgers. A teenager with a laptop can summon a global market in seconds, yet a government minister seeking to update a securities rule must convene committees, draft consultations, and wait for parliamentary cycles to turn. The world now transacts at machine speed, but legitimacy still travels by diplomatic pouch. This mismatch between the velocity of markets and the rhythms of governance is not a footnote to our present era; it is the defining tension that will shape the next century of economic and political authority. Blockchain systems expose that tension with unusual clarity, not because they are exotic or esoteric, but because they place power in places our institutions were never designed to look.

One might imagine this story beginning in a gleaming data centre or a start-up's glass-walled office. But its roots stretch into older rooms. Picture a colonial official in the nineteenth century assessing a ledger of trade receipts from a territory he has never visited. He trusts the entries not because he knows the merchants, but because the ledger carries the stamp of an institution recognised by others who matter. Today, replace the official with a compliance officer in Frankfurt and the ledger with a public blockchain explorer, and the continuity becomes obvious. What changes is not the need for trust but the machinery that produces it. And in this shift, it is no longer clear who the ultimate arbiter is:

the state whose laws frame economic life, the corporation whose platform mediates access, or the decentralised protocol whose consensus rules determine what counts as valid. This book examines the contested frontier where these claims collide.

The urgency is not merely technological. It is civilisational. Every society in history has been shaped by the infrastructures through which value, identity, and obligation travelled. The empires of the ancient world were built on roads and waterways that determined who could tax, who could trade, and who could flee. The modern nation-state grew alongside banking networks and printing presses that allowed administrators to reach across mountains and oceans. Today, the most consequential infrastructure is intangible: algorithms that sequence transactions, oracles that certify facts, and bridges that move assets between realms. These systems now mediate financial stability, political dissent, criminal activity, philanthropy, and everyday savings. They are not merely technical artefacts; they are constitutional in their effects. And like all constitutions, they are shaped by the interests, fears, and imaginations of those who steward them.

What makes blockchain governance uniquely revealing is that its lines of authority are rarely where they initially appear. A protocol may claim decentralisation, yet depend on a multisignature wallet controlled by five individuals in one jurisdiction. A corporation may claim neutrality, yet its user interface silently filters which "decentralised" options are visible. A state may publish rules that purport to regulate global markets, yet its reach ultimately depends on the willingness of foreign platforms to comply. Power migrates through code, contracts, and social norms, often disguising itself as mere implementation detail. This book offers a method to see that movement clearly: a way to trace how control is exercised, how legitimacy is constructed, and how conflicts between competing authorities are resolved or left to fester.

The central metaphor of this book is the triangulation of power—state, corporation, and protocol—each claiming a different kind of sovereignty. States draw authority from territory, law, and the promise of public order. Corporations govern through user experience, infrastructure control, and the subtle pressures of market dependence. Protocols derive power from consensus mechanisms that, at least in theory, treat all participants as equal peers. Yet none of these spheres can escape the influence of the others. States need platforms to implement oversight. Corporations need jurisdictions to anchor their operations. Protocols, despite their rhetoric of autonomy, rely on human stewards whose decisions are shaped by political and economic reality. The most consequential disputes in blockchain governance lie not within any one domain, but in the spaces between them.

Consider the question that animates policymakers worldwide: who regulates a stablecoin? The issuer may sit in one country, the reserve custodian in another, the end users in dozens more. The code that enforces redemption rules may be deployed on a public blockchain that no authority can unilaterally alter. A regulator might attempt to police the issuer, only to discover that the real gatekeeper is an API provider or a wallet interface that determines which assets appear in default views. Meanwhile, a decentralised community might believe it sets the rules through on-chain votes, yet find that corporations shape those votes through delegation markets or governance campaigns. To analyse such a landscape requires abandoning simple categories. It requires looking at the choreography itself: who influences which outcomes, under what constraints, and with what forms of accountability.

This book offers a structured framework for doing exactly that. Each chapter illuminates a different facet of blockchain governance, but the themes interlock. The first examines the tension between code, courts, and consensus—three systems of rule-making that operate in parallel but answer to different constituencies. Later chapters explore how standards become more powerful than statutes, how corporations act as regulators through their infrastructure choices, how states assert sovereignty across borders, and how decentralised communities attempt to legitimise their own authority. Rather than presenting fragmented debates, the book shows how they form a coherent architecture of power.

Historians have long observed that governance rarely adapts to technological change at the pace one might expect. When the printing press spread across Europe, it took generations for laws, institutions, and social norms to stabilise around its implications. Yet blockchain systems cannot afford such indulgence. They operate in markets of immense liquidity, with actors capable of exploiting gaps in real time. A protocol flaw can liquidate positions across continents in minutes. A sanctions designation can freeze assets, not by court order, but by the decision of a single front-end maintainer. A regulatory ambiguity can drive billions in capital flows towards jurisdictions that barely understood their own newfound attractiveness. The stakes are immediate, and the consequences borderless.

At the heart of this book lies a recurring question: what does legitimacy mean in a world where authority is both decentralised and fragmented? Traditional political theory binds legitimacy to processes—elections, courts, public debate. Corporate governance relies on shareholder rights, fiduciary duties, and commercial incentives. Protocol governance invokes transparency, predictability, and resistance to capture. Yet blockchain systems scramble these categories. A protocol might be entirely transparent yet deeply plutocratic. A company might offer remarkable user safeguards while claiming no editorial power. A government might possess clear statutory authority yet lack any practical means to enforce it. Governance becomes a puzzle of overlapping claims, where each actor asserts its own vision of what fairness, safety, or neutrality should entail.

The motif that threads these tensions together is the idea of settlement—both financial and political. In finance, settlement determines whose claim is final. In governance, settlement is the moment when argument yields to rule. Blockchains have accelerated financial settlement to extraordinary speed, yet political settlement remains as slow as ever. Whether this gap narrows or widens will shape not only the evolution of digital assets but the future distribution of global power. Some foresee a world of increasing centralisation as states and corporations tighten control in response to crises. Others envision a more pluralist landscape where diverse communities, protocols, and jurisdictions negotiate coexistence rather than impose uniformity. This book does not predict which path will prevail. Instead, it equips readers to understand the forces that push systems in one direction or another.

The stakes are not abstract. They affect ordinary lives in ways that often go unnoticed. When a diaspora worker sends money home through a stablecoin, the infrastructure beneath that transfer determines exposure to fees, censorship, and financial surveillance. When a small business manages supply-chain data on a permissioned ledger, its economic fate hinges on contractual clauses buried in a consortium agreement. When a protest movement uses blockchain tools to coordinate, its resilience depends on the governance of the interfaces it relies upon—interfaces that can be modified, restricted, or deactivated by a handful of decision-makers. Blockchain governance, in other words, is not a niche concern for technologists or investors. It is a matter of public significance woven into the daily acts of moving value, proving identity, and asserting agency.

The chapters that follow will examine these dynamics with the depth and specificity they demand. They will map hidden power structures, interrogate the narratives that surround decentralisation, and dissect the points where technical design becomes political choice. They will show, with clarity rather than cynicism, how real authority operates beneath the rhetoric. Yet the aim is not merely to reveal problems; it is to provide readers with a durable method of analysis. Markets will evolve, standards will shift, and laws will be revised, but the framework offered here—a way to see authority in the interplay of code, institutions, and communities—will remain applicable long after today's headlines fade.

As we stand at this frontier, pressing questions emerge. Who decides when a protocol should pause in an emergency? Whose interpretation of risk determines whether an asset may circulate across borders? How can communities claim meaningful voice when financial power accumulates in the hands of a few? What happens when public authorities depend on private infrastructure that they do not fully control? And crucially, who regulates the regulators in a world where the regulators themselves are increasingly heterogeneous—some public, some private, some algorithmic?

This book does not promise comfort. It offers clarity. And with clarity comes the ability to make informed choices—choices about which infrastructures we rely on, which standards we adopt, which institutions we strengthen, and which forms of authority we challenge. In tracing these lines of power, the chapters ahead invite readers to look beyond the surface of code or policy, and to recognise the deeper contest shaping the governance of the digital age.

The paradox remains: markets settle at machine speed, but legitimacy still travels slowly, burdened by history, politics, and human judgement. Whether that gap becomes a fault line or a foundation depends on how we understand it today. This book is an invitation to engage with that challenge, to read the dissonance with sharper eyes, and to navigate the emerging landscape with a sense of agency rather than resignation. The transformation underway is not inevitable. It is governed—by choices, by structures, by people. And those who grasp the mechanics of that governance will shape the next chapter of global order.

Chapter 1
The New Jurisdiction: Code, Courts, and Consensus

The trouble began, as it often does in the blockchain world, with a vote that everyone assumed would be decisive. Holders of a major stablecoin had overwhelmingly approved an on-chain proposal to adjust reserve management—a change that, in theory, would signal the will of the community in its purest form. Yet the next morning, the issuer quietly announced that the alteration could not be implemented. A global payments platform had updated its terms of service overnight: assets with the proposed configuration would no longer meet the criteria for listing. The protocol's vote remained visible, immutable, unchallenged. And utterly irrelevant. In that moment the fiction of a single authority dissolved. The on-chain community had spoken, but the corporation had vetoed through interface control, and the regulators, catching the scent of systemic risk, began to take an interest. It felt less like a dispute between stakeholders and more like three sovereignties colliding in real time.

Stand at that crossroads long enough and a pattern emerges. States claim authority through statute and territory; corporations govern through infrastructure and interfaces; protocols declare themselves neutral systems where consensus, not hierarchy, ordains truth. Each insists it is the rightful arbiter. Each operates with its own tools of compulsion or persuasion. And each is only fully intelligible when one examines not just its claims but the frictions at their boundaries. Blockchain systems reveal those frictions with unusual sharpness because they expose, rather than obscure, what is usually taken for granted: that authority is never singular, and legitimacy is always contested.

This chapter begins with that recognition. There is no single jurisdiction in blockchain governance. Instead, there are overlapping regimes, each asserting a different language of power—legal, commercial, algorithmic—and each capable of shaping the same transaction simultaneously. What makes this terrain fascinating is not the clash itself but the choreography. A regulator's definition of a "digital asset" may ripple through compliance departments, modify platform rules, and compel protocol upgrades. A corporation's backend API may enforce a sanctions list that no court has examined. A community's vote may redefine a system parameter, only for its implementation to be filtered by custodial gateways that consider the change too risky. Authority migrates, sometimes subtly, sometimes with dramatic force, through channels that traditional governance theories struggle to describe.

Yet the tension is far from new. History is filled with moments when multiple authorities coexisted uneasily: medieval cities balancing royal decrees with merchant guild customs; colonial administrations interacting with local religious courts; multinational companies negotiating with governments over extraterritorial influence. What distinguishes blockchain systems is the speed and clarity with which these contests unfold. There is no dusty archive to pore over, no centuries-long evolution from custom to decree. The conflicts are timestamped on public ledgers, embedded in API documentation, listed in GitHub repositories, and captured in regulatory circulars that update with dizzying frequency. If the nineteenth century belonged to parliaments and courts, and the twentieth to international organisations and corporate multinationals, the twenty-first is marked by an additional category of institutional actor: the protocol.

To study this new jurisdiction is to recognise the distinctive nature of each claim to authority. States derive theirs from coercion, legitimacy, and historical continuity. Corporations derive theirs from infrastructure control and user dependence. Protocols derive theirs from predictability and automated rule enforcement. But none of these claims operate in isolation. They are constantly entangled. A token may be *property* in a statutory sense, a *permission* in a platform sense, and a *state variable* in a protocol sense. A stablecoin may be backed by reserves that are legally custodial, commercially integrated into platform risk models, and technically reliant on upgrade keys held by individuals in a particular legal system. When these domains align, the system feels orderly. When they drift, the contradictions become acute.

One of the most revealing sites of this entanglement is protocol design. Token mechanics often masquerade as neutral engineering choices—parameter settings, multisig configurations, fallback modules. But look closely and the legal DNA is unmistakable. Property rights surface in transfer restrictions and recovery processes. Contract theory appears in upgrade frameworks and fee structures. Fiduciary concepts emerge in treasury mandates and security council duties. When a protocol gives a small committee the power to pause the system in emergencies, it mirrors the discretionary powers of administrative agencies. When a token's redemption rights bind issuers to specific behaviours, the protocol is writing a quasi-contract. And when governance delegates significant authority to technocratic experts, it is recreating the familiar tension between democratic participation and specialist oversight. Code becomes a jurisdiction not because it replaces law, but because it embeds its own version of law—sometimes intentionally, often unconsciously.

But design is only part of the story. Surrounding every protocol is a theatre of compliance. Some actors perform gestures towards regulation—blacklists that cannot propagate through forks, disclosures that no one reads, attestations that lack enforcement mechanisms. Others exercise genuine control: custodians who can freeze assets; interface providers who can block access; validators who can halt a chain. The challenge for observers is to determine which actions shape reality and which merely signal virtue. A government announcement that an asset is illegal may mean little if platforms decline to enforce it. Conversely, a minor update to a platform's risk engine can make an asset effectively unusable, even if no law has changed. Understanding power in this context requires asking a simple but ruthless question: who can actually do what? Who can halt a transaction, compel a change, or prevent one? Who has the practical capacity to enforce—not hypothetically, not rhetorically, but in the live system?

Network effects add a further layer of complexity. They turn behaviour into regulation long before statutes intervene. A token that is technically permissible may be functionally excluded because major exchanges decline to list it, custodians refuse to support it, or wallet standards do not recognise it. Conversely, a design pattern that gains liquidity may become unavoidable, shaping norms across jurisdictions regardless of policymakers' intentions. When liquidity pools reward particular types of assets, they do not merely influence trading—they create incentives that cascade through project design, disclosure practices, and governance structures. Standards operate as silent regulators: APIs that define what counts as compatible; messaging protocols that determine how compliance is automated; formats that dictate how risk is expressed. Each of these channels establishes obligations without any legislative text. Authority, once the exclusive preserve of parliaments and courts, now emerges from adoption curves and coordination dynamics.

This chapter explores these tensions as a way of setting the stage for the deeper examinations that follow. It does not attempt to resolve the contradictions between code, courts, and consensus, because those contradictions are themselves the key to understanding the new jurisdiction. Instead, it invites the reader to examine the seams. What happens when a protocol declares a rule immutably binding, yet a corporation rewrites access conditions unilaterally? What happens when a state issues a prohibition that cannot be enforced without cooperation from actors it does not control? What happens when liquidity locks communities into governance structures they would otherwise reject? These are not theoretical questions. They shape the everyday functioning of markets, the stability of financial systems, the protection of users, and the limits of state power.

The stakes are immense. If the claims of states, corporations, and protocols continue to collide without coordination, the result will be systemic fragility masked by superficial compliance. If one claim dominates the others, the result may be stability—but at the cost of neutrality, innovation, or democratic legitimacy. The more promising path lies in understanding the interplay itself: how authority is built, contested, and sometimes surrendered; how legitimacy is earned, tested, or lost; how systems adapt when competing jurisdictions cannot be reconciled. This chapter provides the conceptual grounding to navigate that terrain.

As you move forward, you will see why the cliffs between these authorities matter more than any single actor's intentions. You will see how a small design choice can change the balance of power between nations and networks. You will see why the rhetoric of decentralisation often conceals centralised chokepoints, and why seemingly rigid laws bend when they encounter distributed systems. And you will see, with increasing clarity, that the central ambiguity in blockchain governance—who rules, and by what right—cannot be answered within any one framework. It can only be traced in the interactions themselves.

What follows is not a map of chaos but a taxonomy of power. By the end of this chapter, the phrase *new jurisdiction* will no longer feel like a metaphor. It will feel like an accurate description of the contested, dynamic, and profoundly consequential arena in which states, corporations, and protocols negotiate the boundaries of authority. And it will become clear why understanding this negotiation is not optional for anyone seeking to navigate, regulate, or participate in the systems that now mediate global economic life.

Three Claims to Authority

In February 2022, Circle, the issuer of the stablecoin USDC, discovered that technical governance was only one layer of the hierarchy it operated within. A community-led proposal to adjust how certain on-chain reserves were managed had gathered clear majority support on Ethereum. Yet the practical implementation stalled when Coinbase, headquartered in San Francisco, updated its risk controls and declined to support the altered asset in its primary retail interface. The on-chain vote stood untouched, a public expression of token-holder intent. But the behaviour that mattered—redemptions, listings, user flows—gravitated instead towards the platform's revised policy. This quiet mismatch between public consensus and private infrastructure exposed a deeper geometry of power: state-sanctioned companies, global platforms, and decentralised protocols all claiming the authority to decide what counts as valid, safe, or legitimate. One system stamped truth onto a ledger; another mediated access; a third held the legal licence without which neither could operate. And there was no referee capable of adjudicating the conflict.

The motif that threads through this subchapter is simple: who decides? Not in the abstract, but in concrete behaviours—whether transactions settle, whether assets circulate, whether rules bind. The friction between these claims to authority is rarely visible until a crisis or contradiction forces it into the open. Yet the architecture behind each claim is built long before any dispute arises, through laws, infrastructure choices, and protocol parameters that encode assumptions about power. As in all constitutional arrangements, what matters is not who speaks the loudest, but whose decisions actually shape outcomes.

States typically anchor their claim through sovereignty—law backed by coercive capacity. Corporations assert their authority through platform rules—terms of service, interface design, and infrastructure control that govern how users interact with systems. Protocols rely on consensus—automated procedures that define validity and finality. Each form of authority has internal logic, procedural rituals, and sources of legitimacy. But in decentralised finance and digital asset markets, their jurisdictions overlap so tightly that disentangling them is essential for understanding how governance truly functions.

The first claim—state authority—appears straightforward. Legislatures define categories such as property, contract, and rights; regulators implement oversight; courts resolve disputes. Yet the application of these powers in distributed systems is never neat. When the Financial Conduct Authority in the United Kingdom issued guidance on stablecoins in January 2021, its definitions conditioned how custodians, exchanges, and payment firms behaved. Transactions that moved freely on-chain came to be filtered by institutional risk models shaped by the regulator's stance. The law did not alter the protocol, but it recalibrated the behaviour of the intermediaries through which most users accessed it. Sovereignty, in this context, acted not by rewriting code but by modulating incentives, obligations, and liabilities.

Protocol designers often imagine themselves outside this legal frame. They speak of *consensus* as a separate jurisdiction: the chain is final because the network agrees it is final. Yet consensus rules do not float above the world. They are executed by participants with legal identities, subject to taxation, litigation, and physical constraint. In June 2020, when the Steem blockchain saw a contentious fork after disputes involving its largest token holder, the protocol's rules executed reliably. But the ensuing power struggle was shaped by legal realities: accounts were connected to identifiable individuals, some of whom faced threats of litigation; exchange operators located in particular jurisdictions chose which fork to support. The consensus mechanism recorded the blocks, but it did not decide the legitimacy of the outcome. The actors did, guided by their regulatory environments and commercial obligations. The motif returns: who decides?

Between these poles stand corporations whose authority is subtler and often more consequential. They govern through infrastructure: default RPCs, custody arrangements, device permissions, transaction queues, risk engines. Their authority is enacted not through proclamations but through code updates and policy toggles. When Binance, operating from multiple jurisdictions but with significant presence in Dubai (2023), delisted certain privacy-focused tokens in response to European regulatory pressure, it didn't matter that the underlying protocols continued to function. What mattered was that millions of users lost immediate access. Platform rules, operationalised through listings and interfaces, became a form of regulation more immediate than any statute.

To understand the substance of these claims, it helps to examine how they collide. Consider a stablecoin issuer facing contradictory obligations: a community governance vote instructs it to alter reserve management, but a platform's terms prohibit the resulting asset from circulating. The issuer must choose which authority to satisfy. A purely technical reading would favour the on-chain instruction; a purely legal one would prioritise regulatory compliance; a commercial reading would consider the platform's role in maintaining liquidity. Each choice affirms one jurisdiction and suppresses another. And whichever authority the issuer obeys becomes, in practice, the one that governs.

Yet this tripartite structure is also marked by counter-examples that test its boundaries. Bitcoin, for instance, has operated since 2009 without a central issuer to negotiate these overlapping jurisdictions. There is no entity capable of altering its supply schedule or enforcing compliance on nodes distributed across continents. Its governance conflicts are internal: miners, developers, and users argue within a system structurally resistant to external compulsion. The 2017 blocksize dispute, centred around the activation of SegWit, illustrates this. The conflict pitted miners aligned with certain commercial interests against a broader user base advocating protocol change; the resolution emerged from a combination of user-activated soft forks and market preferences rather than regulatory decree. But the limitation of this counter-example is equally instructive. Even Bitcoin depends on corporate gateways—exchanges, custody providers, wallet developers—that remain highly sensitive to state and platform rules. Its protocol claims autonomy; its ecosystem reveals entanglement.

At the heart of these entanglements lies the quiet motif of *settlement*. States aim for legal settlement: a final decision enforceable across their jurisdiction. Protocols aim for technical settlement: a block accepted by the network's consensus. Corporations aim for commercial settlement: transactions that clear through systems they control. These settlements exist simultaneously, sometimes reinforcing one another, sometimes cutting across each other. The failure to distinguish which form of settlement applies in any given dispute leads to confusion about where ultimate authority resides.

To see how these layers interact, consider the October 2021 NFT takedown notices issued by OpenSea, then based in New York. Certain creators received messages stating that works had been removed due to intellectual property complaints. On-chain, nothing had changed: the tokens existed exactly as before. But for most users, the removal from the interface made the artworks effectively inaccessible. A legal complainant triggered a corporate enforcement action that reshaped the practical meaning of ownership in a system often described as decentralised. The claim of sovereignty operated through corporate filters long before protocol logic mattered.

Conversely, protocols can resist both corporate and state influence when their design embeds constraints sufficiently deep. Zcash's privacy features, launched by the Electric Coin Company in October 2016, are a case in point. While exchanges in South Korea delisted the asset in 2019 in response to regulatory concerns, the protocol's core privacy guarantees remained intact. Users who retained custody and operated through compatible wallets maintained access to shielded transactions. Here, corporate rules filtered availability, but they could not rewrite or diminish the protocol's functionality. The protocol's claim to authority survived by limiting the points where external actors could intervene.

A third example illustrates the uneasy hybridity of these structures. In March 2023, MakerDAO faced governance debates around diversifying its collateral, including proposals to increase holdings of U.S. Treasury bills. Token holders voted to approve a range of changes. Yet implementing these changes required coordination with regulated custodians, including those operating in the United States, subject to national securities and banking rules. The protocol's autonomy was bounded by the institutions holding the real-world assets. On-chain consensus bestowed legitimacy; off-chain regulation dictated feasibility. Authority became a negotiation rather than an assertion.

These examples converge on a central insight: authority in blockchain systems is situational. No actor commands unqualified power. The potency of each claim depends on context—liquidity location, custody pathways, user habits, regulatory appetite, and the architecture of specific protocols. Sovereignty matters when regulators can reach identifiable intermediaries. Platform rules matter when users rely on custodial interfaces. Consensus matters when network participants coordinate without central choke points. The balance shifts from moment to moment, event to event, upgrade to upgrade.

This situational quality also explains why network effects often overshadow legal or technical design. When an exchange listing determines liquidity, its listing criteria effectively become a regulatory standard. When wallet developers adopt specific naming schemes or transaction previews, they implicitly designate which assets feel safe or comprehensible. Behaviour follows friction. A state may declare an asset permissible, but if liquidity pools lack depth or platforms decline support, the rule is hollow. A protocol may declare upgrades final, but if validators dissent, forks can splinter the asset's legitimacy. The system acquires its structure not through edict but through coordination.

For professionals navigating this field, the challenge is not merely to recognise each claim to authority, but to observe the choreography between them. Who sets defaults? Who maintains choke points? Who commits code? Who signs custody agreements? Who writes enforcement notices? These actions, more than any constitutional claim, reveal where effective power resides.

The subchapter ends with the tension it began with: a simple but persistent question. When state law, platform rules, and consensus instructions collide, which authority should a rational actor heed if they wish their decision to matter in the real world? The answer is never stable. It is discovered—through behaviour, through settlement, through the quiet but decisive choices that underpin every transaction.

When Law Meets Protocol Design

In June 2016, the engineers behind The DAO watched their screens in disbelief as ether drained from the smart contract they had championed. The bug was technical, but the fallout was legal, economic, and political. The Ethereum Foundation, based primarily in Zug, faced a decision whose consequences would echo for years: intervene through a hard fork to restore funds, or treat the exploit as final under the protocol's own rules. Vitalik Buterin, then twenty-two, argued publicly that the fork represented a form of emergency governance akin to a court issuing equitable relief. Opponents claimed it violated the principle of code determinism. The chain split; markets diverged; and users discovered that protocol parameters—block heights, fork mechanics, upgrade keys—were not apolitical artefacts. They were instruments of judgement. The motif that persists through this subchapter is simple: *a rule written in code can still behave like law.*

The DAO incident showed something deeper than a vulnerability. It showed how design choices embed doctrines familiar to legal historians—property, contract, fiduciary duty—translated into variables and state transitions. The visible behaviour was the fork itself, executed through miners committing to new blocks. The underlying tension was the legal question refracted through protocol design: who decides what restitution looks like? And how is responsibility allocated when the system's stewards possess powers that resemble the discretion of administrators rather than the neutrality of machines? These questions did not perish with that crisis; they recurred as protocols became more complex, reserves more diverse, and governance more formalised.

Property rights appear first, often silently. In December 2020, the UK Jurisdiction Taskforce declared that cryptoassets could constitute property under English law. The statement influenced how custodians structured their systems: they measured control by mapping private keys to responsibility matrices and operational limits. Meanwhile, on-chain property took a more granular form. ERC-721 tokens, popularised by CryptoKitties in Vancouver in late 2017, encoded ownership as a field in a contract. The visible behaviour—users transferring tokens—was underpinned by a design choice: the contract could prevent or enable transfers, freeze tokens, or redirect them under special conditions. Each parameter reflected a policy. A freeze function mirrored the equitable doctrine allowing courts to restrain dealings with disputed assets. A non-fungible structure mimicked the common law differentiation between chattels and fungible goods. The legal concept shaped the technical design, which in turn shaped user expectations.

Contract theory surfaces just as prominently. A token's behaviour is, in effect, a set of commitments: how fees apply, how upgrades occur, how supply changes. These commitments operate like contractual terms, with predictable consequences when breached. In September 2022, the Merge shifted Ethereum to proof-of-stake. The visible behaviour was validator attestation; the contractual analogue was the change in obligations borne by participants. Validators committed stake as performance security, akin to consideration. Slashing penalties enforced behaviour as strictly as any liquidated damages clause. The design encoded risk allocation. When a validator misconfigured a client and suffered a slashing event, the protocol imposed consequences with the finality of an automated arbitrator. The implication was clear: technical configurations had metamorphosed into contractual duties, and failure to meet them triggered remedies without negotiation.

Fiduciary principles enter the scene whenever upgrade keys or pause functions exist. A multisignature wallet controlling emergency actions is not just a convenience; it is an office, with obligations that resemble those of trustees. When Compound Labs discovered a malfunction in its reward logic in September 2021, executives debated whether to use the paused-guardian key held in California to intervene. They ultimately declined, on the reasoning that governance, not administrators, should resolve the matter. The visible behaviour was restraint. The underlying principle was closer to fiduciary caution: those with discretionary power should act only when necessary and with a clear mandate. The analogy becomes more pronounced when guardians manage insurance funds, treasury assets, or upgrade pathways. Their decisions distribute risk, opportunity, and harm. They act as stewards, even if the system describes them as signers.

These doctrines—property, contract, fiduciary duty—become most vivid when protocols confront external legal demands. In October 2022, after the U.S. Treasury's Office of Foreign Assets Control sanctioned Tornado Cash, major infrastructure providers adjusted their systems accordingly. Infura blocked RPC requests to certain addresses; Circle froze USDC associated with those addresses; and GitHub temporarily removed repositories belonging to the protocol's developers. The visible behaviours—API errors, frozen balances, restricted repositories—mapped directly onto legal doctrines. Circle acted as a custodian with obligations under financial sanctions law. GitHub behaved like a platform responding to compliance risk. The protocol itself continued functioning, but only for users who engaged through tools outside the corporate perimeter. The motif returns: code executes, but law allocates responsibility and risk.

Two additional examples reveal how deeply law permeates protocol design. In August 2020, Yearn Finance introduced the YFI governance token with the explicit declaration that it would have "zero pre-mine, zero founder allocation." This design decision, made in Switzerland by developers working across time zones, was not merely ideological. It signalled that the protocol sought to avoid the appearance of an unregistered securities offering. The visible behaviour was radical transparency: token distribution based solely on participation. The legal analogue was a structural distancing from issuer profit expectations. Meanwhile, in November 2021, Arbitrum's Optimistic Rollup included a challenge window parameter that allowed observers to contest invalid transactions. The parameter was technical, timed in minutes, yet it functioned as a quasi-procedural safeguard analogous to administrative review. Anyone could lodge a challenge; the system enforced it. Procedure, encoded.

A counter-example tests the contours of these mappings. Bitcoin, designed in 2008 by the pseudonymous Satoshi Nakamoto, contains no upgrade keys, no pause function, and no privileged actors. Its governance is cautious to the point of paralysis. Changes require rough consensus across globally distributed developers, miners, and users. The visible behaviour is stability bordering on immutability. The legal analogue is closer to customary law than administrative discretion. There is no steward with fiduciary obligations; no operator capable of freezing assets; no upgrade committee empowered to intervene. Yet even Bitcoin cannot escape legal influence. When China restricted mining operations in Sichuan in June 2021, hash power relocated, confirming that physical jurisdiction still shapes network behaviour. The limitation does not invalidate Bitcoin's claim to autonomy; it reveals that protocol design can minimise legal entanglement but never eliminate it.

For systems where entanglement is greater, the implications are profound. Parameter settings become policy positions. An upgrade delay can resemble regulatory forbearance. A pause function, when exercised, becomes a quasi-judicial act. The choice to use—or refuse to use—these tools determines not just system safety, but the distribution of power among stakeholders. Protocols that centralise emergency authority empower stewards but risk regulatory classification as centrally managed enterprises. Protocols that disperse such authority enhance resilience but may struggle to respond when real harm unfolds. The visible behaviour—timely patches or prolonged uncertainty—becomes a diagnostic of embedded governance values.

The quiet motif of *the key* helps unify these threads. Who holds the key? Who can commit code? Who can halt execution? Who can alter state? In law, the holder of the key—literal or metaphorical—is often the responsible party. In protocols, the same logic applies. The upgrade key becomes the office of stewardship. The pause key becomes a duty of care. The treasury key becomes a fiduciary instrument. The system may describe these as technical roles, but user expectations reveal their deeper significance. A user who deposits into a liquidity pool assumes that stewards will not arbitrarily drain it. A validator who stakes millions of pounds assumes that penalties will be applied consistently. A guardian who signs an emergency transaction assumes responsibility for the consequences. These assumptions mirror centuries of legal practice.

Protocols that ignore these parallels may find themselves facing unexpected consequences. In March 2023, the U.S. Commodity Futures Trading Commission filed a complaint against the decentralised derivatives protocol Ooki DAO, arguing that its governance structure did not insulate participants from liability. The visible behaviour prompting the action was token-holder voting on risk parameters and margin levels. The legal interpretation was that such actions constituted participation in an unregistered trading facility. Policy embedded in parameters was treated as regulatory conduct. Whether one views the complaint as overreach or coherence, the implication is clear: legal systems will interpret protocol design through their own frameworks, regardless of how decentralised a system claims to be.

The melding of law and protocol design also shapes user behaviour. Consider the metric of upgrade participation. When only a fraction of token holders vote on critical changes—as occurred in several DeFi governance proposals in 2021 and 2022—developers must decide whether to delay, override, or accept the outcome. Low turnout resembles a flawed shareholder vote. High turnout resembles democratic mandate. The patterns matter. They determine whether stewards feel empowered to act or compelled to defer. The system's governance quality becomes visible not in rhetoric but in participation rates, quorum thresholds, and dispute outcomes.

Yet the relationship is not deterministic. Protocols can intentionally design against legal entanglement. They can minimise privileged keys, automate dispute resolution, or rely on local execution that reduces dependency on identifiable intermediaries. These choices, however, reduce flexibility. A protocol that removes its pause function removes its capacity to intervene during a crisis. A protocol that disperses authority may find itself fragmented in moments requiring coordination. A protocol that embeds stringent procedural timelines may struggle to adapt to novel threats. The design choices never sit outside politics; they constitute politics.

The tension, as always, lies in the trade-off between discretion and neutrality. A protocol with expansive emergency powers risks behaving like an administrative agency without oversight. A protocol with none risks creating brittle systems where harm spreads before action is possible. States face the same tension. So do corporations. The alignment or misalignment between these layers determines how crises unfold and who bears loss.

As this subchapter closes, the unresolved question remains pointed. When protocol parameters embed policy—sometimes consciously, sometimes by accident—who should decide whether discretion is exercised, withheld, redesigned, or removed entirely? The answer determines not only the character of a system's governance but the legitimacy of the authority that underlies it.

Compliance Theatre vs Real Control

In August 2022, the U.S. Treasury's Office of Foreign Assets Control sanctioned Tornado Cash, naming the protocol's GitHub repositories and several Ethereum addresses. Within hours, Circle, the issuer of USDC based in Boston, froze tokens linked to the sanctioned accounts. A day later, Infura, headquartered in New York, began blocking RPC requests routed through its infrastructure. The visible behaviour—frozen balances and blocked calls—suggested decisive enforcement. Yet when developers in Amsterdam continued to operate local nodes, Tornado Cash contracts executed without interruption. The blacklist existed, but the forkless propagation that authorities expected did not arrive. The paradox was immediate: the dramatic gestures came from organisations acting at the perimeter, but the locus of real control remained inside the network's architecture. Some users were halted; others were not. The difference lay not in the sanction itself but in who held the switches that actually mattered.

The motif running quietly through this section is *the switch*—the ability to halt, list, or seize. Not the rhetoric of control but the instrument. Compliance theatre thrives where gestures substitute for switches; real control thrives where switches actually change behaviour. The Tornado Cash episode revealed how institutions can appear authoritative through public announcements while their influence disperses once transactions travel beyond the reach of custodians or standardised interfaces. The Treasury listed addresses. Platforms complied. But the protocol's state machine continued precisely as coded.

The distinction between gesture and enforcement is most visible when examining what platforms can commit. In September 2020, BitMEX, operated from Seychelles, restricted withdrawals after facing charges from the U.S. Department of Justice. The visible behaviour—paused withdrawals—was unambiguous control. Users felt it immediately: balances remained immobile until administrators restored the system. The switch existed, and the operator held it. Yet compare this with the dozens of protocols that published blacklists after incidents or alleged exploits in 2021 and 2022. In many cases, the blacklist lived only in a front-end repository or an analytics dashboard. Forks ignored them; local clients bypassed them. The gesture signalled vigilance, but behaviour barely changed. The switch did not exist.

This difference shapes the credibility of institutions involved. When the Monetary Authority of Singapore issued guidance in January 2022 warning retail investors against high-volatility cryptoassets, several exchanges headquartered in the city-state removed marketing materials and geofenced promotions. The visible changes—disappearing ads and altered landing pages—demonstrated compliance. Yet trading volumes barely shifted for users with offshore accounts. The platform's perimeter adapted, but the underlying protocols remained untouched. The gesture responded to domestic regulatory pressure; the switch sat elsewhere.

A second example illustrates how control can be asserted through listings rather than law. In March 2021, Kraken delisted Monero for users in the United Kingdom, reflecting concerns from the Financial Conduct Authority. The visible outcome was immediate: UK-based customers could no longer trade or withdraw the asset through the exchange. But Monero's network in London did not halt. Nodes continued to validate transactions. Users running their own wallets retained full functionality. The listing change altered liquidity pathways but could not seize or freeze assets held locally. The switch affected access, not possession. That difference matters: one is commercial discretion; the other is coercive control.

A counter-example tests these boundaries. In December 2021, after a vulnerability was discovered in the BadgerDAO front end, attackers extracted tens of millions in assets by manipulating the interface. The protocol's smart contracts were not flawed. The exploit targeted the corporate layer. Yet when the multisig controllers executed the emergency pause, they halted contract interactions across the system. Here the switch lived inside the protocol itself, not merely at the interface. Users saw deposits freeze, withdrawals stop, and governance actions suspended. The visible behaviour demonstrated genuine control. But it also revealed a limitation: emergency powers centralised in a small multisig committee introduce risk comparable to regulatory discretion. The tension between safety and decentralisation becomes unavoidable.

These contrasting cases converge on the core insight: gestures rely on narrative; control relies on operability. A protocol may publish a blacklist, but if forks can discard it or if local clients ignore it, the action becomes symbolic. Conversely, a platform may avoid theatrical measures but still wield immense power via its custody infrastructure, where a single keystroke can freeze millions in assets. These distinctions matter because they determine how users interpret signals of authority. If a system repeatedly performs gestures without impact, participants learn to discount warnings. If, instead, interventions consistently alter behaviour, expectations shift. Compliance theatre erodes confidence; real control reshapes incentives.

The difference can be measured in three behaviours: who can halt transactions, who can list or delist assets, and who can seize or freeze balances. Each behaviour carries a metric. Halting becomes visible through block production stoppage or paused contract execution. Listing becomes visible through liquidity changes and trade volumes. Seizure becomes visible through altered balances or restricted withdrawals. These metrics allow observers to distinguish performance from enforcement without relying on rhetoric.

The quiet motif of *the switch* reappears when examining cross-jurisdictional tensions. In November 2022, the European Union finalised elements of its Markets in Crypto-Assets Regulation (MiCA). Among the provisions were rules governing stablecoin issuance and reserve reporting. Exchanges operating in Paris or Berlin prepared to implement new disclosures and risk filters. But those changes had little effect on users interacting directly with DeFi protocols through self-hosted wallets. The EU could influence platforms within its territory; it could not alter protocol mechanics outside its jurisdiction. The switch was bounded by geography. Compliance theatre might dress itself as universal, but its enforcement mapped tightly to borders.

The same dynamic surfaced when Coinbase, headquartered in San Francisco, published its "Transparency Reports" in 2020 and 2021. Authorities requested information on thousands of accounts across multiple jurisdictions. Coinbase complied by handing over data. Yet the reports also recorded what the exchange could not do: it could not reverse on-chain transfers or seize non-custodial assets. The visible behaviour—account-level reporting—marked genuine legal compliance. The invisible limitation—no access to self-custodied keys—marked the boundary of actual control. Between these two edges lies the space where theatre grows: announcements that imply greater authority than systems permit.

Consider, too, how audits function. A smart-contract audit by Trail of Bits or CertiK—named firms with offices in New York and Singapore—examines code, flags vulnerabilities, and recommends mitigations. The visible behaviour is publication of a report. The gesture signals diligence. But unless developers commit fixes, users enable safeguards, and governance adopts recommendations, the audit does not control anything. It becomes compliance theatre: an artefact of effort rather than an instrument of enforcement. Real control appears only when systems integrate these recommendations into running code.

Yet there are cases where compliance measures do work precisely because the architecture funnels authority. In January 2021, the New York Attorney General reached a settlement with Tether and Bitfinex regarding misstatements about reserves. Under the agreement, both companies committed to regular attestations and reserve disclosures. The visible behaviour—published reports, altered corporate structures—resulted from legal pressure. The architecture of a centrally issued stablecoin allowed direct regulatory influence. Unlike decentralised protocols, central issuers hold custody and operational switches. They can be compelled. The limitation is clear: this control does not extend to autonomous systems without equivalent chokepoints.

The coexistence of these examples leads to a broader implication. Enforcement efficacy depends on where chokepoints reside. Systems anchored to custodial intermediaries lend themselves to regulatory command. Systems anchored to self-executing code resist indirect gestures but expose users to other risks: bugs, malicious governance actions, or coordination failures. Compliance theatre emerges when institutions try to exert influence without access to these chokepoints. Real control emerges when institutions—or sometimes private actors—operate the switches baked into infrastructure.

A second motif helps illuminate this interplay: *the perimeter*. Institutions attempt to reinforce the perimeter through sanctions lists, interface restrictions, jurisdiction-specific guidelines, and onboarding controls. But the perimeter is porous. When Uniswap Labs, based in New York, restricted access to certain tokens on its interface in July 2021, users in London quickly switched to aggregators or local front ends. The gesture influenced corporate risk posture; it did not alter the protocol's peer-to-peer exchange functionality. The perimeter shifted, not the core. This pattern repeats whenever enforcement acts at the level of interfaces rather than infrastructure.

These tensions sharpen when liquidity is at stake. In May 2022, during the collapse of TerraUSD, several platforms briefly disabled trading pairs to contain volatility. The action—unilaterally toggling markets—reflected genuine power. Yet the protocol underlying Terra continued to process transactions, even as its value spiralled. The switches acted on markets, not the ledger. The result was partial control: markets slowed, but the chain raced toward instability. Compliance theatre was not the issue here; rather, it was fragmented authority. Some switches existed, others did not.

What, then, distinguishes theatre from substance? It is not intention. It is not rhetoric. It is not public messaging or documentation. It is whether an action changes what users can do. A blacklist that cannot propagate does not halt anything. A disclosure that no actor reads changes nothing. A warning without enforcement is a narrative, not a constraint. Real control is behavioural. It appears in blocked withdrawals, halted blocks, frozen balances, or delisted markets. It appears when users must change behaviour because the system leaves no alternative.

The unresolved tension sits at the centre of this chapter's question: if only some actors hold real switches, yet many perform compliance gestures, how should professionals map authority in a system where visibility can mislead? The test remains stark. Who can halt? Who can list? Who can seize? And when those answers diverge across states, corporations, and protocols, which actor's decision will determine the next crisis?

Network Effects as Regulation

In June 2017, the founders of Bancor travelled to Zug to celebrate the successful launch of their token sale, only to discover that a far less visible event now governed their fate. Binance, then newly headquartered in Shanghai, added the BNT token to its order books. No regulator compelled the listing, no statute required disclosure, yet trading volumes surged and liquidity pooled around the exchange's depth charts. A single commercial decision, executed without fanfare, reshaped the project's governance priorities for months. The team drafted new disclosures, issued risk statements, and modified contract parameters not because law demanded it, but because the liquidity gravity exerted by one platform dictated what counted as credible. The listing was a switch. Liquidity followed the switch.

Network effects act with the quiet force of tide. No proclamation announces their arrival; users simply move. When enough movement concentrates in one venue, one standard, or one interface, behaviour shifts. And when behaviour shifts, governance shifts with it. This subchapter's motif, returning gently through the narrative, is *gravity*—the pull that liquidity and standards exert long before any authority raises a pen. Gravity regulates.

What makes network effects distinct from formal regulation is their immediacy. They require no enforcement notices, no binding orders, no statutory text. They appear instead in visible behaviours: volumes consolidated in an exchange's order book, liquidity pooled around one bridge rather than another, developers committing to a dominant standard because interoperability demands it. Each action is rational in isolation; together they create a centre of mass that acts like a rule.

This becomes clear when observing how standards emerge. The ERC-20 token standard, published by Fabian Vogelsteller and Vitalik Buterin in November 2015 in the public GitHub repository of the Ethereum Foundation, was not issued by any authority. Yet within a year, dozens of projects in Berlin, Singapore, San Francisco, and Seoul adopted it simply because exchanges and wallets recognised it. The visible behaviour was straightforward: tokens using ERC-20 were easier to trade, store, and integrate. The effect was policy-like. Projects that deviated faced questions about safety and compatibility. Those that conformed gained access to deeper liquidity and broader tooling. A design choice became a de facto regulatory instrument.

A second example shows the same pattern through different mechanics. When Uniswap launched its v2 architecture in May 2020, from the Labs office in New York, its automated market maker model offered predictable slippage curves and transparent pool mechanics. Liquidity migrated rapidly. By late summer, dozens of DeFi projects designed their token economics around Uniswap pool incentives. The visible behaviour—developers configuring initial liquidity pools, investors routing trades through the protocol—was driven by the gravitational pull of existing volume. The implication was unmistakable: Uniswap's pool structure shaped token design more directly than any disclosure rule issued by a financial authority. Incentives codified in an AMM governed project behaviour.

Yet not all systems succumb to gravitational dominance. A credible counter-example comes from the Bitcoin ecosystem. Despite the emergence of dominant custodians and exchanges, Bitcoin's core protocol has resisted the formation of a single liquidity centre that dictates design choices. The SegWit activation dispute in 2017 demonstrated that user and miner coalitions could defy commercial platforms when upgrading the protocol. Nodes in London, Tokyo, and Toronto signalled support for the user-activated soft fork even after certain major companies opposed it. Here, decentralised coordination overcame liquidity concentration. The limitation is important: network effects regulate more softly in systems where users operate full nodes and where design transitions require broad consensus. The counter-example does not negate the principle; it shows that architecture and norms can modulate the gravitational pull.

Where architecture is more permeable, gravity asserts itself quickly. Exchange listing rules operate as regulatory surrogates. When Coinbase, headquartered in San Francisco, formalised its "Digital Asset Framework" in 2018, projects hoping for a listing adapted their disclosures accordingly. Teams published security audits, risk statements, and governance charters. They clarified treasury holdings and sometimes restructured token allocations. Users never read the framework in large numbers, but volume responded to listings, and projects responded to volume. The order book—its depth, its spread, its throughput—acted as the enforcement mechanism. Behaviour changed without a law changing.

A second case reveals how liquidity centres can rewrite norms across borders. In December 2020, after South Korea's Financial Services Commission tightened reporting requirements, several Korean exchanges delisted privacy coins. The consequence was not local. Because those exchanges held significant liquidity for assets like Zcash and Dash, developers in Berlin and Denver adjusted communication strategies, emphasising compliance features and governance transparency to reassure other platforms. The delisting in Seoul altered narratives far beyond its jurisdiction. A local decision reshaped global behaviour, carried not by power but by gravity.

The motif of gravity returns when examining bridges and cross-chain standards. By 2022, Wormhole—developed in New York—had accumulated significant liquidity for moving assets between Solana, Ethereum, and several other chains. Its message format and validator set became the implicit standard for cross-chain interoperability. Projects integrating with Wormhole adopted its assumptions: message finality, signature verification, and delay parameters. No regulator mandated these parameters, and no consortium formalised them. Yet developers treated them as norms because the liquidity gravity of the bridge made alternative paths costly. The behaviour revealed the rule: to access liquidity, conform to its standards.

But gravity can mislead. It can concentrate risk as effectively as it concentrates value. When Curve's stable-swap pools, launched from Switzerland in 2020, became the dominant venue for stablecoin liquidity, dozens of protocols built dependencies around its pricing curves. The visible behaviour—protocols anchoring oracle feeds to Curve pools—seemed efficient. Yet the February 2022 de-pegging of certain assets exposed the fragility. Curve's pricing logic, optimised for shallow slippage, amplified instability when pools skewed. The gravitational pull had created a monoculture. Risk and liquidity moved together.

Network effects also shape governance participation. Protocols with high liquidity witness greater voter turnout because holders treat governance decisions as influential. A MakerDAO vote in March 2023, concerning collateral diversification, saw measurable participation because billions in value depended on collateral parameters. The behaviour—delegates debating risk, users staking tokens to vote—was propelled by the gravitational weight of the protocol. People commit where liquidity commits. The implication is structural: liquidity strengthens governance norms as much as governance norms try to shepherd liquidity.

Yet network effects do not always favour concentration. The rise of multi-chain wallets such as MetaMask, developed by ConsenSys in Brooklyn, showed that users gravitate to tools that minimise friction. This contributed to a broader distribution of activity across L2 networks in 2021 and 2022. By simplifying network switching, the wallet diluted the gravitational pull of any single chain. The behaviour—users bridging assets, experimenting with new networks, and adjusting RPC settings—revealed a limit to centralised gravity. Standards that distribute friction can distribute power.

Despite these nuances, the central dynamic remains consistent: liquidity forms the path of least resistance. Where liquidity flows, norms follow. And norms harden into rules. Developers measure depth charts before writing governance documents. Investors compare spreads before reading whitepapers. Users commit to interfaces that reduce cognitive load. Each behaviour reinforces the gravitational centre, making it even harder for alternatives to attract adoption without major differentiation.

The quiet motif of gravity appears again when considering oracles. Chainlink, founded in 2017 and headquartered in the Cayman Islands for corporate purposes while operating globally, became the dominant pricing oracle across DeFi by 2021. Projects integrated its feeds not because statute required it but because liquidity pools and lending protocols already trusted its accuracy. The behaviour—protocols calling Chainlink oracles for price data—created a feedback loop. The more systems relied on Chainlink, the more accurate its data became; the more accurate the data, the more systems integrated it. The gravitational pull of shared dependency turned a technical service into a quasi-regulatory role. A mispriced feed could liquidate positions across chains. The oracle's accuracy governed.

There is a temptation to treat network effects as background conditions—an economic fact rather than a governance mechanism. But the behavioural evidence is plain. When enough actors converge on a standard, deviation becomes expensive. When deviation becomes expensive, standards function as rules. And when rules emerge without formal authority, governance shifts to those who shape the standards themselves: exchange risk teams, wallet developers, bridge validators, liquidity providers.

The unresolved question sits at the heart of this dynamic. If gravity regulates without statutes, who—if anyone—should commit to moderating the gravitational centres when concentration grows too great? And what happens when the most powerful regulatory force in a decentralised system is not law, nor code, nor corporate policy, but the invisible pull of liquidity itself?

Chapter 2
Standards that Rule: How APIs Become Law

The engineers at a major European exchange still recall the moment their compliance dashboard lit up in December 2019. Without warning, a consortium of messaging-service providers—few of them household names—announced a new format for implementing the FATF "travel rule", the requirement that identifying information accompany cross-border transfers. No government had mandated this format, no legislature had debated it, and no court had reviewed it. Yet within forty-eight hours, exchanges in London, Frankfurt, and Zurich began rewriting their onboarding systems. Clients were asked for additional metadata; transfers that had cleared for years stalled behind new validation steps; risk teams adjusted scoring thresholds to reflect the consortium's framework. Nothing in statute had changed, but everything operational had. A private standard, adopted by enough infrastructure providers, had acquired the force of law. The API became the rulebook.

Moments like these reveal a peculiar truth of digital governance: power now resides as much in the interfaces that systems depend on as in the laws that governments write. A wallet's default network settings can narrow or widen a user's universe as effectively as any licensing regime. An oracle's price feed can shape trading behaviour more sharply than many investor-protection statutes. A bridge's validator set can determine which assets travel across networks and which remain stranded. These decisions, expressed through code and implemented at speed, govern not by proclamation but by design. Their authority grows with adoption. And adoption, like gravity, pulls everything into its orbit.

This chapter explores a world where standards become institutions and interfaces behave like regulators. It examines the actors whose fingerprints rarely appear in parliamentary records yet whose choices structure the possibilities of digital markets. They are the engineers who publish token standards on public repositories; the compliance architects who define messaging schemas; the wallet developers who decide which networks users see by default; the custodians who set withdrawal limits and token whitelists; the bridge operators who choose between permissionless openness and curated security. They do not claim sovereignty. They do not issue decrees. But they craft the protocols and pathways through which millions of transactions flow, and that is often enough to make their choices indistinguishable from law.

The motif running quietly through this chapter is *the hinge*: the small, often overlooked connection point that determines how two systems meet. A standard is a hinge. An RPC endpoint is a hinge. A message format is a hinge. A validator quorum is a hinge. Hinges decide what opens and what closes, though they are rarely the focus of public debate. In blockchain systems, hinges matter more than headlines.

The significance of private standards comes into sharp relief when tracing how they spread. The travel-rule messaging example showed how a coalition of service providers, not a government, set the practical requirements for global compliance. Yet this is hardly unique. In 2015, the ERC-20 token standard spread across the Ethereum ecosystem not because regulators endorsed it, but because wallets, exchanges, and developer tools chose to support it. Once enough liquidity accumulated, deviation became costly. The standard acquired a normative weight: if a token did not conform, users questioned its legitimacy; if developers deviated, platforms demanded explanations. This unspoken pressure, grounded in interoperability rather than law, shaped behaviours across continents.

The same structural force appears in more contemporary contexts. Consider how the default RPC settings in MetaMask governed user access to networks for years. Until 2022, most users relied on Infura's Ethereum endpoint, maintained in part from New York. When requests to certain sanctioned addresses were quietly restricted, users outside the affected jurisdictions experienced errors—not because Ethereum itself rejected their transactions, but because their default hinge refused to relay them. A single infrastructure setting regulated access more effectively than elaborate statutory frameworks. When users changed providers, the restriction dissolved. The hinge moved, and the rule changed with it.

Interoperability layers reveal a similar dynamic at larger scale. Bridges connecting networks make architectural choices that are, in truth, policy decisions: how large a quorum relays messages; how delays are handled; how disputes are resolved; which assets are admitted; which authorities maintain signing keys. These design choices determine which cross-chain transfers are possible, which are blocked, and which require trust in identifiable actors. When, in 2021 and 2022, several cross-chain protocols shifted from permissionless relayers to permissioned sets with named validators in response to systemic-risk concerns, they created implicit sanctions lists and behavioural constraints. These were not enacted through legislation. They were implemented through code, enforced by liquidity, and legitimated by platform adoption. Interoperability became governance.

Yet standards do not only regulate by enabling access; they regulate by making exit difficult. Forking—a core feature of decentralised systems—offers an escape route when governance fails or principles clash. But exit rights come with economic and social costs. When Bitcoin Cash split from Bitcoin in August 2017, or when Ethereum Classic held its ground after the 2016 fork, dissenters preserved a principle: the right to maintain an alternative version of the chain. But the cost of liquidity fragmentation became immediately apparent. Exchanges allocated separate tickers; wallets added new configuration files; custodians re-evaluated risk rules; liquidity thinned. Most users followed the gravitational centre. Exit remained possible, but expensive. Standards, interfaces, and liquidity pools regulated behaviour without the need for any authority to forbid fragmentation.

This chapter situates these dynamics in a broader historical pattern. Long before blockchain networks existed, private standards shaped economic life. In 1856, the International Telegraph Union—later the ITU—established standardised signalling conventions that effectively regulated cross-border communications. In the mid-twentieth century, ISO committees produced industrial and data standards that became mandatory in practice once enough manufacturers adopted them. And in the early internet era, the IETF's RFC process created norms that no government legislated but every major network respected. The pattern is consistent: wherever interoperability matters, and wherever coordination is costly, standards evolve into governance structures.

But blockchains extend this logic in unusual ways. Their openness allows anyone to propose a standard. Their composability ensures that a widely adopted standard can influence thousands of downstream applications. Their global reach makes local regulatory frameworks feel parochial when confronted with transnational infrastructure. And their liquidity concentration grants enormous informal authority to whichever venue, wallet, oracle, or bridge becomes the dominant hinge through which users act.

The deeper philosophical punch of this chapter is that private standards are neither inherently benign nor inherently dangerous. They are simply powerful. Their power comes from friction reduction: it is easier to integrate with existing APIs than to invent new ones, easier to follow a dominant messaging schema than to create bespoke compliance channels, easier to trust a dominant oracle than to maintain independent price sources. But ease is not neutrality. Ease channels behaviour. And behaviour, when aggregated across millions of transactions, becomes governance.

This raises uncomfortable questions for policymakers and developers alike. If private standards, rather than statutes, determine what is practically possible, should they be treated as public infrastructure? If a wallet or API provider can restrict visible networks or preferred tokens, is it exercising a form of administrative authority? If a messaging layer or bridge imposes procedural steps or validators, does it shape policy more directly than regulators? And if forking remains the ultimate escape valve, how meaningful is that escape when most liquidity stays anchored to the dominant version?

As you move deeper into this chapter, the hinges will come into sharper relief. You will see how messaging formats steer anti-money laundering compliance more effectively than legal definitions. You will see how a wallet's default RPC shapes what users perceive as "the network". You will see how bridges negotiate security and openness, producing governance consequences that extend far beyond their technical specifications. And you will see why the right to fork, though essential, does not erase the gravitational pull of liquidity, interfaces, and shared standards.

The questions that follow will not yield simple answers. They are not meant to. Instead, they open the intellectual space to examine a phenomenon that underpins the entire decentralised ecosystem: the transformation of private coordination choices into public-facing governance. The hinges through which systems connect have become the hinges through which authority flows. And understanding who designs them, who adopts them, and who depends on them may be the closest we come to understanding where power truly sits.

Private Standards, Public Outcomes

In December 2019, the Joint Working Group on interVASP Messaging Standards gathered in Geneva to review its draft specification for the "IVMS101" schema. The room was unremarkable—white walls, narrow tables, the kind of modest conference space shared by NGOs and trade associations alike. Yet the outcome was anything but modest. Within six months, major exchanges in London, Singapore, and New York had reconfigured their compliance workflows to match the schema's fields. Customer addresses were reformatted. Transaction metadata was reclassified. Transfers that once settled instantly now paused while systems checked whether counterparties could process the same data structure. No parliament had passed a law. No regulator had published a binding rule. A private messaging format—written by a coalition of technical specialists and compliance officers—had quietly redrawn the procedures governing cross-border transfers. Its adoption became the rule. Its fields became obligations. And its shape, once embedded in APIs and audit logs, operated with the force of law.

This is the hinge on which the subchapter turns: *a standard becomes an institution the moment enough systems depend on it.* The visible behaviour in Geneva was ordinary drafting. The governance effect was extraordinary: a schema that began as a voluntary alignment exercise rapidly acquired normative weight because service providers relied on it to interoperate. The motif that threads through the narrative—returning quietly in different forms—is *the mould*: once a standard sets the mould, everything poured through it takes its shape.

Standards wield influence because they align incentives rather than command obedience. A single data field, once accepted by enough custodians, becomes a checkpoint in every transaction. A particular ordering of attributes becomes the canonical language of risk teams. A version number inside an API header becomes the difference between a transfer clearing or failing. The power of standards lies not in coercion but in the friction they reduce: systems commit to the path that minimises cost, error, and delay.

To see this clearly, begin with a fact: interoperability demands shared formats. Show the effect: when the IVMS101 schema spread across exchanges in early 2020, transfers that could not support it were flagged, delayed, or rerouted. Name the driver: interVASP, a private industry body. Explain the mechanism: by defining how originator and beneficiary information must be represented, the standard became the de facto compliance benchmark. Implication: regulators and firms began assessing each other's compatibility by referencing a document no legislature had ever touched.

A second example reveals the same dynamic through different infrastructure. The ERC-20 token standard, proposed publicly on GitHub in November 2015, originated as a developer convenience. But once exchanges in Singapore and Hong Kong began using it to automate listing pipelines, its status transformed. The behaviour shifted: projects conformed to ERC-20 not to comply with law, but to meet exchange integration requirements. Name: the Ethereum Foundation. Explain: wallets, custodians, and analytics tools relied on ERC-20's predictable functions. Implication: adherence became a precondition for liquidity, which in turn shaped project governance. Standards regulated.

Even the less visible layers of the stack demonstrate the same moulding power. The FIX messaging standard in traditional finance—first published by Fidelity and Salomon Brothers in 1992—became mandatory not by statute but by ubiquity. Once brokers and exchanges aligned on FIX, new entrants who failed to adopt it faced prohibitive integration costs. Blockchain systems follow this historical pattern but accelerate it: adoption curves steepen because integration spreads through open repositories, not bilateral contracts. A schema uploaded at noon can influence hundreds of systems by nightfall.

The gravity of private standards becomes clearer when we observe their effect on risk assessment. A standard does not only define how information is structured; it defines what information *matters*. When a compliance API requires fields for jurisdiction of residence or wallet type, firms adjust onboarding to collect those fields. The behaviour—modifying forms, updating scripts, rejecting incomplete submissions—follows immediately. The mould hardens. Soon, regulators begin citing the emergent practices as evidence of "market norms," even though those norms began in private working groups. The hierarchy has inverted: private standards drive public reasoning.

A counter-example tempers the narrative. Bitcoin, with its minimal protocol-level standards, resists many forms of private standardisation. Its core protocol has no metadata schema, no KYC hooks, no embedded fields for identity. Nodes in Oslo, São Paulo, and Nairobi validate transactions without reference to external messaging formats. The mould remains loose. This architectural firmness—protocol minimalism—weakens the gravitational pull of private schemas. Yet even here, layer-two systems and custodial gateways reintroduce standardisation at the edges. Lightning implementations converge on specific message formats. Custodians adopt shared reporting templates to manage operational risk. The limitation therefore clarifies rather than contradicts the principle: protocol design can slow the rise of private standards, but it rarely halts them entirely.

Standards acquire their force through adoption, and adoption is measurable. Look at behaviour: which protocols exchanges support, which data formats custodians refuse to accept, which versions validators treat as canonical. Look at metrics: the percentage of transactions passing through services using a given schema; the proportion of wallets conforming to a standard interface method; the number of assets listed because they implement a familiar contract pattern. These metrics reveal that standards exert regulatory pressure not through punishment but through coordination.

This pressure shapes more than compliance workflows. It shapes governance itself. When a project anticipates that integration with major custodians requires particular message fields, it structures its smart contracts accordingly. When a wallet provider implements a default interface that only recognises specific token functions, it silently incentivises developers to follow the same conventions. The mould extends. A private decision about API ergonomics becomes a public constraint on design.

The motif reappears when examining cross-border effects. In 2021, several Asia-based exchanges aligned on a shared risk-scoring algorithm tied to address provenance. The algorithm required input data formatted according to proprietary analytics standards. Firms in London and Zurich updated their transaction-monitoring interfaces simply because most liquidity-providing partners expected the same fields. The visible behaviour—rewriting transaction parsers—reflected a deeper governance shift: one region's private standard reframed global assessment norms. The mould crossed jurisdictions long before law did.

These dynamics complicate the work of policymakers. A regulator may publish new guidance, but firms implementing private standards often move faster. When the Financial Crimes Enforcement Network in the United States opened consultation on travel-rule implementation in 2020, several U.S. exchanges had already aligned to private schemas shaped in Geneva and Singapore. The behaviour preceded the rule. By the time the consultation closed, a de facto framework governed cross-border transfers. Regulatory deliberation lagged behind infrastructural adoption.

But private standards also invite fragility. They centralise influence in groups that may lack formal accountability. A messaging schema may exclude certain attributes that minority jurisdictions deem essential. A token standard may encode assumptions incompatible with emerging security models. A reporting format may privilege the needs of large custodians over smaller operators. These choices, once widely adopted, are difficult to revise. The mould resists reshaping. Coordination costs rise.

A vivid instance of this fragility emerged when the original ERC-20 standard revealed ambiguities around token approvals and race conditions. The unintended behaviour—tokens inadvertently locked or double-spent—

stemmed from a design choice that had hardened into convention. Correcting the issue required either sweeping contract upgrades or the creation of new standards like ERC-777. Yet widespread migration proved slow because wallets, exchanges, and analytics tools were anchored to ERC-20. The mould became a constraint.

The persistence of private standards shows how power circulates through the network's connective tissue. Developers draft schemas. Platforms implement them. Users adapt. Over time, the schema becomes the expectation; the expectation becomes the rule; the rule becomes the baseline for assessing compliance and legitimacy. Public institutions respond to this baseline rather than define it. In effect, governance converges on the standard because deviation incurs cost.

This raises an unresolved tension at the heart of decentralised systems: if private standards can become public outcomes without democratic scrutiny, how should systems decide which groups get to craft the moulds that shape global behaviour? Or more pointedly: when adoption is the real source of authority, what recourse exists when the standard-setting centre of gravity shifts in ways the broader community did not choose?

Gatekeepers in Disguise

In July 2022, users of MetaMask across parts of Europe opened their wallets to find a sudden, unexplained error: transactions refused to broadcast. The culprit was not Ethereum, nor any on-chain congestion. It was Infura—ConsenSys's infrastructure arm, headquartered partly in Brooklyn—temporarily restricting RPC calls routed through default endpoints. The change lasted hours, yet the effect was immediate: users who had believed themselves sovereign discovered that the first gatekeeper in their path was not a miner or a validator, but their own wallet's choice of network conduit. No regulator had issued an order; no protocol had changed its rules. A simple switch inside an API configuration governed which chains users could reach and which they could not. The wallet had acted as a regulator in disguise, curating the boundaries of the possible.

This scene captures the motif that threads through this subchapter: *the aperture*—the narrow opening through which a user sees and shapes a network. Wallets define the aperture through interface defaults. Custodians define it through permissions and withdrawal constraints. Oracles define it through the data they choose to attest. Each aperture filters reality. And when enough people look through the same filter, the filter becomes an institution.

Gatekeeping in blockchain systems rarely appears in the dramatic form imagined by traditional regulation. No official stamps, no prohibitions carved into statute. Instead, gatekeeping emerges through defaults: which networks a wallet supports at installation, which tokens a custodian whitelists, which data an oracle signs. Defaults, once deployed at scale, behave like rules. And rules, once internalised by millions of users, govern behaviour even in the absence of compulsion.

The first gatekeeper sits in the user's hand. Wallets—mobile or desktop—curate networks through visible settings and invisible assumptions. Show the effect: in January 2021, when MetaMask directed all Ethereum mainnet calls through Infura by default, millions of users implicitly depended on a single RPC route. Name the actor: ConsenSys. Explain the mechanism: default RPC endpoints privilege certain network configurations, shaping how users perceive the ecosystem. Implication: if the endpoint fails or blocks certain requests, users experience a regulatory effect without formal regulation. A pause in Brooklyn becomes a boundary in Berlin.

The aperture narrows further when wallets integrate token lists. In 2020, Uniswap Labs published its "Token Lists" standard—an optional, open metadata format. Within months, several major wallets, from Argent in London to Rainbow in New York, adopted it. The visible behaviour was simple: tokens not present in lists appeared flagged or invisible. The governance effect was profound. Users often equate visibility with legitimacy. A token omitted from a curated list might as well not exist. The list becomes a de facto licensing regime, deciding which assets ordinary users can easily interact with. Again, no statute, no formal rule—just a curated aperture that shapes perception.

Custodians, by contrast, govern through possession. A custodian holds private keys on behalf of users. That custody transforms technical constraints into policy decisions. Show the example: in October 2021, Coinbase froze certain tokens linked to a protocol under investigation. The visible behaviour—users blocked from withdrawing—stemmed from internal risk triggers. Name the gatekeeper: Coinbase. Explain: custodial control allows providers to halt flows, enforce compliance, or shape liquidity. Implication: custodians regulate not by suggestion but by command. Users cannot bypass a refusal to sign.

A second custodial example illustrates the regulatory depth of simple administrative choices. In March 2022, Anchorage Digital, the federally chartered custodian based in South Dakota, revised its token support list following internal risk assessments. Institutional clients found that certain assets could no longer be held, even though no regulator had imposed new restrictions. The visible behaviour was the removal of custody support. The governance mechanism was a blend of commercial risk policy and industry standards. Implication: custodians define reality for institutions, which in turn shape which assets receive liquidity, which ecosystems attract developers, and which tokens fade into irrelevance.

Yet a counter-example tempers the narrative. Cold-storage hardware wallets such as Ledger and Trezor—manufactured in Paris and Prague respectively—place control in users' hands. Their default apertures are narrow, but expandable: users can add custom networks, sign arbitrary transactions, or bypass corporate infrastructure entirely. Here, gatekeeping is weak. The architecture grants discretion to the individual. However, even hardware wallets rely on firmware, update servers, and vendor-provided libraries. The aperture widens, but dependence never vanishes. The limitation clarifies that decentralisation reduces gatekeeping pressure, but never eliminates it.

If wallets and custodians govern access, oracles govern truth. They determine which data the system considers authoritative. An oracle is not simply a conduit; it is an editor. Show an example: in November 2020, Chainlink—operating globally with corporate registration in the Cayman Islands—suffered a brief price-feed disruption. Several DeFi protocols in London and Singapore triggered liquidations based on momentarily erroneous data. The visible behaviour was liquidation cascades. Name the gatekeeper: Chainlink. Explain: oracles attest to external facts and encode them into blockchain-readable form. When an oracle errs or pauses, the system inherits that distortion. Implication: oracles regulate markets more directly than many financial authorities, because they determine the data on which automated decisions depend.

A second oracle example reveals the subtler form of gatekeeping. In 2021, Compound Finance deployed an upgrade that misinterpreted price data from Coinbase's oracle. A flaw in a single feed caused millions in excess COMP rewards to be distributed. The problem was not malevolent. It was architectural: the system trusted one feed too deeply. The visible behaviour—erroneous distributions—exposed an invisible governance choice. Some truths counted; others did not. The aperture had narrowed too far.

The motif of *the aperture* appears again when considering messaging layers and bridge infrastructure, which curate not truth but reach. Gatekeepers decide which chains can speak to which, who may relay messages, and how failures are handled. In 2021, the Polygon–Ethereum bridge operated with a multisig of five keyholders. Each keyholder acted as a choke point. The visible behaviour—tokens able to cross chains—depended on a small group's decisions. The governance implication was clear: permissioned relayers enforce policy. A sanctioned address cannot bridge; a flagged contract cannot move liquidity. Gatekeeping is built into the topology.

These modes of curation extend into developer tooling. A wallet that auto-detects only EVM-compatible networks creates incentives for projects to mimic EVM architectures. A custodian that refuses to support unverified smart contracts nudges developers towards audited patterns. An oracle that standardises certain price pairs shapes which assets attract speculation and which remain peripheral. Each actor shapes the ecosystem by shaping the aperture of what is visible and what is viable.

Yet gatekeeping operates not only through exclusion, but through sequencing. A wallet that prioritises one network over another nudges adoption by milliseconds that compound into behavioural norms. A custodian that sets longer withdrawal delays for certain assets alters user flow. An oracle that updates prices every twelve seconds instead of every block influences volatility. These choices are measurable. They manifest in metrics: failed transaction counts, delay intervals, spread changes, liquidation frequencies. They reflect architectural governance, disguised as performance optimisation.

The dynamic becomes clearest when considering how gatekeepers shape compliance outcomes. If a wallet integrates address-screening libraries from a single analytics provider, it inherits that provider's definition of risk. If an oracle declines to support assets linked to privacy-enhanced protocols, it signals distrust to dependent applications. If a custodian requires attestation from a specific standard-setting body, it influences which projects survive audit. No statute demands these decisions. Yet users behave as though they carry legal weight, because infrastructure makes them unavoidable.

The aperture motif returns once more with a pressing question: who decides what users see? Not in a metaphorical sense, but in concrete configurations. The network selector in a wallet is a gate. The whitelist in a custodian is a policy. The data schema in an oracle feed is a worldview. These gates decide more than access—they decide legitimacy. Assets unseen by users struggle to gain liquidity. Protocols unsupported by oracles struggle to anchor loans. Networks inaccessible by default struggle to attract developers. The aperture governs the destiny of entire ecosystems.

And yet an unresolved tension persists. Gatekeepers provide safety, coherence, and usability; without them, systems devolve into fragmentation. But gatekeepers also concentrate discretion, narrow diversity, and make invisible judgments about risk, relevance, and truth. The forward test is stark: how should a decentralised world balance the need for shared apertures with the danger of allowing any single one to become the default through which most users understand the network?

Interoperability Bargains

On 2 February 2022, engineers at Jump Crypto in Chicago confirmed what many had feared overnight: a single compromise of the Wormhole bridge's guardian keys had enabled an attacker to mint 120,000 wrapped ETH on Solana—roughly US$320 million at the time. The exploit did not arise from a flaw in Ethereum or Solana. It emerged from the connective tissue between them. Wormhole's design relied on a permissioned set of guardians to attest that assets had been locked on one chain before being minted on another. When one guardian's signing process failed, the entire attestation system bent. A private messaging layer, not the underlying chains, defined where the failure occurred. Hours later, Jump Crypto replaced the missing funds to restore solvency. But the deeper lesson was not the speed of the rescue; it was the fragility of the bargain. Bridges mediate not only assets but authority, and every design choice—quorum size, validator selection, message format—sets the terms of a political settlement disguised as infrastructure.

This subchapter's quiet motif is *the crossing*: the moment a transaction leaves one chain's jurisdiction and enters another's. Crossings create risk. Crossings demand trust. Crossings expose whose judgement matters when two systems disagree. Bridges and messaging layers promise seamless transfer, but they also carve policy boundaries through their architecture. They are not neutral pipes. They are systems of governance.

Interoperability begins with a simple premise: chains cannot natively see each other. To coordinate, they need witnesses. Show the effect: every bridge relies on an attestation that an event occurred elsewhere. Name the actors: Wormhole, Axelar, LayerZero, Polygon PoS Bridge. Explain the mechanism: signers, relayers, or light-client verifiers attest to locks, burns, or messages. Implication: whoever controls the attestation controls the crossing. In practice, this becomes a form of border control.

The Wormhole breach exposed the trade-off at the heart of permissioned bridges: they are efficient, but fragile. With a small guardian set, latencies are low and user experience is smooth. Yet the concentration of authority means one compromised key can cause systemic distortion. The visible behaviour—unbacked minting—stemmed from a governance choice: security via a curated group of validators rather than decentralised verification. The implication is clear: speed and simplicity come with constitutional cost. The crossing narrows. The gatekeepers multiply.

A contrasting example shows the opposite priority. In 2023, the Cosmos ecosystem expanded its Inter-Blockchain Communication (IBC) protocol, relying on light-client verification rather than permissioned committees. Here, each chain verifies the consensus of the other with cryptographic proofs rather than signatures from an elite group. The visible behaviour—trust-minimised packet relays—reflects a different bargain. Chains commit to validate one another's consensus. The crossing widens. The cost shifts to computation and complexity. The implication: decentralised verification enhances security but slows adoption because integration demands greater engineering investment.

Between these poles sits the hybrid model adopted by many messaging layers. LayerZero, launched in 2021, introduced a dual-verifier structure in which an Oracle and a Relayer attest to cross-chain messages. Name the actors: Chainlink, Google Cloud, and other oracle providers. Explain: message validity depends on matching attestations from two independent parties. The mechanism distributes trust but does not eliminate it. Implication: if both verifiers coordinate or fail in correlated ways, the crossing can still be compromised. The bargain becomes explicit: a system that is not fully trustless but aims to be trust-minimised. The crossing remains contingent, not sovereign.

Interoperability also generates policy choices where none seem intended. When bridges enforce sanctions lists—as several permissioned relayers began doing in late 2022—they become de facto regulators. Show the behaviour: transactions touching sanctioned addresses simply did not move across chains. Name the actors: Multichain, once based in Shanghai, and several custodial bridges in Europe and North America. Explain: relayers examine message payloads and reject transfers associated with flagged entities. Implication: sanctions propagate not because protocols enforce them but because the bridge decides which messages cross. The border acquires a politics.

These politics manifest through metrics that betray hidden power. Measure the approval times for cross-chain transfers. Compare the number of validators, their jurisdictions, and their operational independence. Commit to observing failure modes: when a bridge halts because validators cannot reach quorum, the governance system is revealed. Each metric—latency, quorum size, geographic clustering—exposes the bargain between openness and security. The quieter the system, the more these metrics matter.

A second example illustrates the administrative dimension of interoperability. In 2021, Polygon's PoS Bridge relied on a multisignature scheme with five of eight signers required for approval. The signers, identifiable individuals and entities, operated with the power to pause the bridge. Show the behaviour: during congestion events, the bridge was manually halted to prevent cascading failures. Name the actor: Polygon. Explain: halting reflects discretionary judgement, not algorithmic necessity. Implication: users depend on the prudence of a small group to preserve systemic safety. The crossing becomes a checkpoint where administrators overrule code.

A credible counter-example tempers this narrative. Bitcoin's design, intentionally minimal, discourages cross-chain complexity. Its main "bridge" is custodial conversion through exchanges—a model that inherits traditional financial controls rather than blockchain-native messaging. The visible behaviour—centralised conversion instead of decentralised transfer—avoids the validator-risk dynamics that plague multi-chain bridges. The limitation is apparent: decentralisation remains intact, but interoperability is shallow. Users rely on exchanges in Zurich, Hong Kong, or New York for conversion. The crossing is outsourced rather than cryptographically mediated. This counter-example does not disprove the governance burden of interoperability. It reframes it: avoiding bridges altogether is itself a governance choice, substituting protocol risk for custodial risk.

Interoperability bargains also shape developer behaviour. When developers anticipate that a bridge will support only certain message formats, they encode their applications accordingly. When cross-chain protocols require delays for safety, as IBC channels often do, dApp architects design around latency. When a bridge charges differential fees for specific assets, new projects adjust token economics. The visible behaviour—developers adjusting parameters—reveals how bridges embed incentives. The crossing carries costs. Costs shape design.

The motif of *the crossing* returns when we note how even failed bridges exert regulatory force. In 2022, after the collapse of Harmony's Horizon Bridge—following a

US$100 million exploit traced by Elliptic analysts to attackers in North Korea—several lending protocols limited collateral composed of bridged assets. The visible behaviour: reduced borrowing limits and increased liquidation thresholds. Name the actors: Aave, Compound. Explain: bridged assets carried chain-of-custody uncertainty. Implication: protocols treat bridged assets as distinct from native ones, effectively categorising them by trust domain rather than token symbol. The crossing alters identity.

Interoperability also reframes jurisdiction. A chain with strong local regulation may lose its grip once assets cross into systems without equivalent safeguards. Conversely, a chain with weak oversight may adopt "clean" assets imported through heavily regulated bridges. The behaviour: risk assessments shift depending on the last verified consensus domain. Name an example: when USDC bridged to Polygon became widely circulated in 2021, platforms in London distinguished between "native" and "bridged" USDC for compliance. Explain: different issuance paths produce different regulatory exposures. Implication: the bridge determines the legal and risk attributes of the asset, not the protocol that records it.

Every bridge is therefore a negotiation. Permissionless designs prioritise inclusion but risk contagion. Permissioned designs enhance security but risk censorship or capture. Light-client-based designs promise trust minimisation but demand high engineering costs and complex incentives. Each bargain embeds a worldview: what level of risk is tolerable, what type of trust is acceptable, what trade-offs users must bear.

These bargains are not incidental; they are constitutional. When a protocol selects a bridging partner, it effectively delegates authority over cross-chain identity. When a messaging layer chooses a particular signature scheme, it expresses a stance on where verification should occur. When a bridge operator enforces sanctions, it embeds foreign policy into infrastructure. Each decision shapes the crossing, and the crossing shapes the system.

The unresolved question shadows every design choice: how much discretion should those who manage the crossings possess, and who should constrain them when their incentives diverge from the communities that depend on their attestations?

The Cost of Forking

On 20 July 2016, in a conference room in Zug, Ethereum developers watched the network split in real time. Moments earlier, the community had activated a hard fork designed to reverse the theft of funds from The DAO, a high-profile investment vehicle compromised weeks earlier. The software update executed as planned. Blocks on the main chain reflected the restored balances. Yet a minority of miners, including those operating nodes in London and Shanghai, rejected the fork and continued validating the original chain. Within hours, two networks existed: Ethereum (ETH) and Ethereum Classic (ETC). The split preserved a principle—immutability—but scattered liquidity, fractured tooling, and forced exchanges worldwide to list, reconcile, and secure two assets where one had existed before. The fork was both exit and schism, a proof that rights to dissent remain intact, and a reminder that exercising them carries a price.

Forks expose a motif that threads through this subchapter: *the fracture line*. It is the point at which community cohesion gives way, where disagreement becomes architecture. A fracture line is a decision encoded in code. Once crossed, it divides not only ledgers but identities.

Forking is often framed as a liberation strategy: if governance fails, leave. Yet a fork is not a simple departure. It is a constitutional rupture. To fork is to rewrite the boundaries of collective action. It is to carry forward a version of the past that a subset of participants refuses to abandon. But fracture lines demand repayment. Each split extracts costs in liquidity, legitimacy, tooling, and time.

The Ethereum–Ethereum Classic divide remains the clearest illustration. Show the behaviour: post-fork, developers had to maintain two codebases; exchanges had to integrate two assets; users had to assess two economic futures. Name the actors: the Ethereum Foundation and the ETC community. Explain the mechanism: each chain embodied a different governance judgement—the Foundation's choice to restore funds and ETC's commitment to immutability. Implication: the fork disciplined Ethereum by demonstrating that dissent could crystallise into a rival system, yet it also diluted the security budget and attention of a once-unified ecosystem. Fracture lines both empower and weaken.

A second example reveals the economic weight of fracture. In August 2017, the Bitcoin Cash split from Bitcoin, initiated by a coalition including ViaBTC in China and supporters of larger block sizes. Show the behaviour: the new chain adopted 8MB blocks, while Bitcoin retained a more conservative approach. Name the actors: miners in Beijing, developers in the U.S. and Europe. Explain: differing visions of scalability—on-chain versus off-chain—materialised into two incompatible rule sets. Implication: while Bitcoin Cash promised lower fees during congestion, the split fragmented liquidity. Exchanges in Tokyo and New York introduced new tickers; wallets rewrote interfaces; merchants recalibrated integrations. The fracture line offered exit rights but at the cost of splintered liquidity and reduced network effects.

Even more revealing is the Steem–Hive split of March 2020. After Justin Sun acquired Steemit Inc., concerns over governance influence triggered a contentious fork. Show the behaviour: the Steem community, fearing centralisation, voted to freeze certain accounts, prompting Sun-aligned stakeholders to counteract through exchanges. Name the actors: Binance, Huobi, Justin Sun. Explain: disagreements over stake-based governance and corporate control led the community to create Hive, carrying over users and content but without the contested stake. Implication: the exit preserved community norms yet demanded a near-total rebuild of infrastructure, from interfaces to node operators. The fracture line imposed costs measured not only in market capitalisation but in human coordination.

These examples reveal the dual nature of exit rights. Forks discipline governance by demonstrating that unilateral decisions can be met with structural retaliation. Decision-makers—developers, foundations, miners—know that if they overreach, participants may walk. The threat of fracture restrains. But the exercise of that right unleashes costs. Liquidity splits. Tooling divides. Developer time fragments. A fork is a check on abuse, yet its activation diminishes the total.

The cost of fragmentation appears in metrics that cannot be ignored: hash rate dilution, reduced transaction throughput, thinner liquidity on exchanges, and slower development cycles. After the Bitcoin Cash fork, mining power slid across chains unpredictably, causing oscillating block times. After the Ethereum Classic fork, ETC experienced repeated 51% attacks in 2020 because its reduced hash rate rendered it more vulnerable. A fracture line weakens the minority chain's defences even as it upholds its values.

But there are counter-examples where forking fails to deliver even the preservation of principle. In 2019, a faction of Bitcoin SV supporters attempted to further fracture from Bitcoin Cash, championing a vision of extreme block size expansion. Show the behaviour: chain reorganisations, disputes over signatures, fluctuating client implementations. Name the actors: nChain, CoinGeek. Explain: the fork pursued a radical path without securing broad developer or exchange support. Implication: while exit remained technically possible, the resulting ecosystem struggled to retain credibility or liquidity. The fracture line existed but led to a thin, brittle network that failed to discipline the broader governance landscape. Not all exits shape behaviour; some simply dissipate.

The motif of *the fracture line* reappears when examining social identity. Forks force communities to define themselves. Ethereum Classic became "the immutable chain"; Bitcoin Cash became "the on-chain scaling chain". These identities guide future decisions, attracting those who share the founding rationale and repelling those who do not. But identity carries inertia: once a chain commits to a principle to justify its fork, it becomes difficult to revisit that principle later. Governance ossifies. Values harden. The fracture line both liberates and locks in.

Forking also shifts power across jurisdictions. When Ethereum split, exchanges in Seoul and Hong Kong shaped early liquidity distribution by choosing which asset to list first, which ticker to assign, and how to manage replay protection. Their decisions influenced which chain traders perceived as canonical. The fracture line thus intersected with corporate preferences and regional regulatory views. Exit rights empower dissenters, but they also empower intermediaries who manage the transition.

Developers, too, face constraints. When a fork occurs, every line of tooling—from indexers to explorers to multisig contracts—must be duplicated or adapted. The visible behaviour: duplicated repositories, new bug trackers, divergent roadmaps. The cost is measured in engineering hours, opportunity loss, and fragmented attention. Fracture lines draw resources away from innovation and towards maintenance.

Yet the costliest dimension is temporal. Forks freeze debate. Once the split occurs, the divergent camps stop persuading one another. They settle into parallel realities, each building forward without reconciling the past. The fracture line becomes a time marker: before and after, unity and dispersion. But as time passes, the threat of future forks remains. Each contentious governance proposal carries the shadow of prior divisions. The fracture line lingers.

Still, forking remains an essential equilibrium tool. Without the credible threat of exit, developers or foundations might impose changes with little accountability. The knowledge that a community can walk enforces discipline. It keeps ambitions proportionate. It makes governance negotiation meaningful. The fracture line, though costly, is a bargaining chip.

A deeper tension remains unresolved. If exit rights discipline governance, but their exercise undermines network effects, what threshold of disagreement justifies crossing the fracture line? And who should decide when the cost of staying outweighs the cost of splitting?

Chapter 3
Sovereignty in Pieces: Nation-States Respond

The morning the Financial Conduct Authority in London announced its restrictions on Binance's UK operations in June 2021, commuters on the Northern Line scrolled through headlines that read less like regulatory notices and more like border controls hastily drawn in digital space. Within hours, users in Britain found that certain services were no longer accessible; meanwhile, Binance continued operating almost unchanged for customers thousands of miles away. No police raids. No shuttered offices. Just an abrupt redirection of digital flows at a national boundary that existed only in law, not in code. That moment revealed a paradox governments can no longer escape: sovereignty is territorial, but the markets they now police are not. Nation-states are responding not with a single doctrine, but with a patchwork of strategies—fragments of authority stitched together to contain systems that ignore the very borders they enforce.

It is tempting to frame this as a simple clash between decentralised networks and traditional institutions, but the reality is more intricate. States have not lost power. They have multiplied its forms. They regulate through licensing, shape incentives through supervision, and project influence through the gravitational pull of their markets. A single decision in Washington or Brussels can push a global platform to rewrite rules for everyone, not just the citizens of the issuing state. In effect, national decisions produce international consequences, while protocols struggle to decide whether to resist, adapt, or route around them. The puzzle is not whether states matter, but which parts of the state matter most—and how they deploy authority now that financial activity slips across borders in milliseconds.

The motif that threads quietly through this chapter is *the border that moves*. Not the line on a map, but the shifting boundary between public authority and private infrastructure. Sometimes this border expands outward—when a major jurisdiction extends its rules beyond its territory through market access conditions. Sometimes it contracts—when governments depend on commercial wallets or private chains to deliver public outcomes. And sometimes it fractures—when sanctions, geofencing, or security mandates divide users of the same protocol into separate regulatory realities. The border moves because sovereignty, confronted by decentralised markets, has become a fluid practice rather than a fixed property.

Regulatory competition is the clearest sign of this transformation. Contrary to the tired trope of a "race to the bottom", jurisdictions are differentiating themselves like firms in a crowded market. Singapore courts high-value activity through its licensing regime, pairing strict supervision with deliberate signalling of competence. The UAE positions itself as a laboratory for controlled experimentation, offering sandbox environments that attract projects seeking credible oversight without oppressive constraint. Meanwhile, the European Union pursues harmonisation via MiCA, trading speed for coherence and betting that clarity attracts long-term capital. Each choice reflects a different appetite for risk, cost, and prestige. These differences matter because protocols must adapt to them, and users must decide which regulatory identity best fits their own thresholds for safety, privacy, and flexibility.

But states do not merely compete—they reach. Extraterritoriality is no longer a historical curiosity limited to the American enforcement apparatus of the 1990s. It is now a structural feature of global digital markets. A platform that depends on access to New York or Frankfurt must adjust its worldwide policies to secure that access. When the New York Department of Financial Services tightened guidance for stablecoin reserves in 2022, issuers began publishing more detailed disclosures not only for New Yorkers but for everyone. When South Korea's Financial Services Commission imposed reporting requirements on exchanges, liquidity decisions shifted far beyond Asia as global platforms recalibrated risk engines. States project power outward, using licensing and market access as levers. Protocols may be borderless; businesses are not.

Sanctions introduce a sharper edge to this projection. They are the bluntest instrument in a government's arsenal, yet they reshape decentralised systems with remarkable precision. When the U.S. Treasury sanctioned Tornado Cash addresses in 2022, interfaces and infrastructure providers reacted immediately. Web front ends geofenced access. RPC providers blocked calls. Custodians halted withdrawals. The protocol—the pure code—ran on. But its usable surface contracted for millions. Sanctions thus functioned as selective filters: some users flowed freely, others found doors shut. The border moved once more, slicing through a protocol that had long imagined itself immune to political intervention. States do not need to control the code; they need only influence the gateways.

These gateways become even more significant as governments pursue a hybrid form of public infrastructure that relies on private rails. Welfare benefits in Brazil are distributed through commercial bank apps; Singapore's digital identity system integrates with private service providers; proposals for central bank digital currencies often assume distribution through commercial wallets rather than state-built interfaces. Governments outsource the last mile, not because they lack capability, but because citizens already inhabit private ecosystems. The result is a layered sovereignty: public objectives delivered through private systems whose design choices carry political weight. When a wallet provider updates its risk filters, it may inadvertently alter access to state-funded payments. When a custodian declines to support certain tokens, it may shape the practical space in which government policy operates.

The border motif returns here with particular force. Where does a state's authority end when the systems it relies on to execute policy are owned by firms in other jurisdictions? And what happens when a private platform's design principles conflict with a government's regulatory goals? These tensions surface most clearly in crisis. During episodes of extreme market volatility, governments demand transparency; platforms may or may not provide it. When sanctions regimes shift suddenly, infrastructure providers must choose whether to implement compliance globally or geographically. Each choice redraws the border.

This chapter examines these evolving dynamics with the detail they warrant. It looks first at regulatory competition, showing how different jurisdictions craft distinct identities through supervision and signalling. It then traces the extraterritorial reach of powerful states, examining how platforms reorganise themselves to satisfy the most demanding regulators. From there, the discussion turns to sanctions and selective inclusion, exploring how geopolitical decisions filter into protocol usage in ways that fragment user experience. Finally, it explores the uneasy marriage between public purposes and private rails, revealing how states increasingly rely on commercial intermediaries to deliver essential functions.

What emerges is not a narrative of states weakened by decentralisation, nor a triumphalist tale of governments reasserting control. It is something more complex: sovereignty decomposed into pieces, each exercised through different channels, each contested by different actors, each shaping the architecture of digital finance in ways both intentional and unintended. The border moves, and with it, the terrain on which legitimacy is negotiated.

The unresolved questions that follow are not rhetorical flourishes—they are the core dilemmas of our era. How should nations supervise activity that flows through systems they do not control? How should protocols adapt to jurisdictions with competing priorities and incompatible rules? And at what point does the use of private rails to deliver public services shift from pragmatic cooperation to abdicated authority?

The answers lie ahead, in the places where sovereignty is stretched, fragmented, and reassembled—piece by piece.

Regulatory Competition, Not Race to Bottom

On 1 March 2016, the Monetary Authority of Singapore opened its FinTech regulatory sandbox, inviting firms to test products under tailored exemptions. The announcement came not at a conference filled with grand declarations, but in a brief circular posted online—a bureaucratic artefact that nevertheless drew founders from London, Mumbai, and San Francisco to a city-state barely five million strong. Within a year, firms trialled cross-border remittance tools, digital onboarding systems, and novel custody arrangements. None came for laxity. They came because Singapore signalled something rarer: a willingness to supervise innovation without smothering it. The sandbox was not a retreat from regulatory duty; it was a calibrated expression of confidence. The city-state measured what risks it would bear, compared them with its institutional capacity, and committed to a model others would soon emulate. The motif that threads through this subchapter—quiet but firm—is *the stance*: not deregulation, but posture, the deliberate setting of a jurisdiction's appetite and limits.

The common cliché imagines a global "race to the bottom", as though every jurisdiction sought advantage by eroding standards. Yet the empirical record shows the opposite. Jurisdictions differentiate themselves. They choose what they will supervise rigorously, what they will tolerate, and what they will refuse. That differentiation creates the competitive terrain on which blockchain firms decide where to incorporate, where to seek licences, and where to anchor operations. Regulatory competition is not a collapse of authority; it is a stratification of authority.

The stance becomes visible when observing how national regulators signal competence. Show the behaviour: when the UK's Financial Conduct Authority established its cryptoasset registration regime in January 2020, it approved only a small fraction of applicants. Name the actor: FCA. Explain: the narrow approval rate did not indicate hostility, but a commitment to due diligence that attracted firms comfortable with scrutiny. Implication: London framed itself not as permissive but as exacting, offering reputational capital to firms willing to meet its expectations. Its stance created a selection effect.

Singapore demonstrates the inverse approach. MAS grants licences sparingly, yet its sandbox functions as an intake valve for exploratory activity. Show the behaviour: firms iterate under controlled conditions before graduating into full authorisation. Name the actor: MAS. Explain: the sandbox lowers the barrier to experimentation but not to long-term operation. Implication: Singapore competes by reducing initial friction while preserving credibility at scale. Its stance is adaptive, not permissive.

A third example clarifies the pattern. Switzerland's Financial Market Supervisory Authority in Bern embraced decentralised foundations early, publishing guidance in 2018 that defined payment tokens, utility tokens, and asset tokens with unusual clarity. Show the behaviour: dozens of foundations incorporated in Zug, attracting both developers and legal talent. Name: FINMA. Explain: the clear taxonomy reduced interpretive uncertainty for projects with complex governance structures. Implication: Switzerland competed not by lowering standards but by articulating them. The stance rewarded foresight.

These cases reveal regulatory competition not as a downward slide but as an alignment of national priorities with supervisory capacity. Jurisdictions choose their lanes. Some emphasise prudential oversight. Others emphasise experimentation. Still others emphasise definitional clarity. Firms select among them as customers choose among products—not because supervision is weak, but because supervision differs.

But differentiation is not unlimited. A counter-example illustrates the constraints. In 2021, the Cayman Islands attempted to attract digital-asset businesses through registration pathways perceived as lighter than those in Europe. Show the behaviour: several high-profile firms relocated. Name: CIMA. Explain: the initial surge was driven by flexibility, but firms soon confronted global pressure from counterparties requiring higher transparency. Implication: a permissive stance can draw incorporation, but it may not sustain operational legitimacy when platforms must meet the standards of the markets they serve. The limitation reveals the equilibrium: no jurisdiction can fully decouple from global expectations.

The stance manifests through behaviour that can be measured. Compare approval times. Measure the frequency of supervisory letters. Track enforcement actions. A regulator's posture appears in its cadence: slow approvals signal caution; structured consultations signal foresight; sandbox admissions signal calibrated ambition. Regulatory competition unfolds through these metrics, not through rhetoric.

The motif of *the stance* reappears in how jurisdictions manage cross-border compatibility. The European Union's

Markets in Crypto-Assets Regulation (MiCA), finalised in 2023, offers a good example. It does not aim to out-compete other jurisdictions through permissiveness. Instead, it lifts standards, requiring capital buffers and reserve attestations for stablecoin issuers. Show the behaviour: companies in Paris and Frankfurt restructured governance frameworks months before the rules took effect. Name: the European Commission and ESMA. Explain: MiCA's strictures reshape internal procedures globally because firms treat EU compliance as a baseline. Implication: a strong stance can set de facto international norms, not by coercion but by market gravity.

Meanwhile, the United Arab Emirates—particularly Abu Dhabi Global Market and Dubai's Virtual Assets Regulatory Authority—positions itself as a venue for high-touch supervision with responsive turnaround. Show the behaviour: in 2022, ADGM issued bespoke approvals for institutional custody providers. Name: ADGM and VARA. Explain: their licensing pathways enable controlled access for firms willing to submit to detailed audits. Implication: the UAE competes through nimbleness, not leniency.

Regulatory competition also expresses domestic politics. The United States, split among the SEC, CFTC, FinCEN, and state regulators, exhibits a stance shaped by institutional fragmentation. Show the behaviour: enforcement actions surge while formal rulemaking lags. Name: SEC, CFTC. Explain: the stance emerges through litigation, not licensing. Implication: the U.S. offers vast market access but inconsistent supervisory clarity. Firms perceive opportunity and risk in equal measure.

This divergence in stances becomes visible in how firms commit capital. A wallet provider may place compliance staff in Dublin to satisfy EU transparency norms, engineering in Tel Aviv for rapid iteration, and policy teams in Singapore to navigate proactive supervision. The geography of regulatory competition creates a topology of corporate structure. Firms distribute themselves across stances.

Yet the differentiation that strengthens one jurisdiction may weaken another. When Japan, through its Financial Services Agency, imposed stringent custody segregation rules in 2017 after the Mt. Gox collapse, exchanges withstood high compliance costs but gained consumer trust. Show the behaviour: no major Japanese exchange collapsed in subsequent years despite global turmoil. Name: FSA. Explain: strict reserves and operational audits bolstered resilience. Implication: Japan became a safe harbour, proving that high standards can attract capital under stress. The stance paid dividends.

Still, excessive strictness can suppress innovation. The counter-force appears in Hong Kong's pivot. After years of conservative posture, regulators introduced a licensing framework in 2023 to re-attract crypto trading platforms under monitored conditions. Show the behaviour: firms returned, but with heightened reporting obligations. Name: SFC. Explain: the stance shifted from exclusion to cautious inclusion. Implication: jurisdictions can recalibrate when outdated stances threaten competitiveness. The fracture between policy and market reality can be repaired.

Across these examples, one insight stands firm: regulatory competition is a contest of credibility, not laxity.

Jurisdictions measure their appetite for risk, compare themselves against global peers, and commit to a stance that reflects institutional confidence. The stance communicates to firms what boundaries exist, what freedoms are permitted, and what responsibilities are demanded. It signals identity.

But supervisory capacity limits ambition. A country may wish to attract institutional custody businesses but lack the forensic expertise to examine their architectures. Another may desire to host stablecoin issuers but lack the auditing infrastructure to validate reserves. Stance must match capacity. When it does not, scandals follow.

The unresolved tension sits at the heart of the subchapter's argument. If jurisdictions compete through differentiated stances rather than deregulation, how should firms choose among them? And when the global market rewards clarity, credibility, and competence, how long can any jurisdiction maintain a stance that diverges from the expectations of those who must trust it?

Extraterritorial Reach

On 26 August 2020, the U.S. Office of Foreign Assets Control placed Tornado Cash-linked addresses on its Specially Designated Nationals list. The order, issued in Washington, ricocheted through global infrastructure in minutes. Within hours, Circle in Boston froze USDC associated with the sanctioned addresses. Infura—operating largely from New York—blocked RPC calls relaying transactions to those contracts. GitHub, headquartered in San Francisco, disabled repositories maintained by Tornado Cash contributors, even though many lived thousands of miles from U.S.

jurisdiction. None of these actions originated in the countries where most affected users resided. Yet the impact was universal. Through sanctions, licensing pressure, and market access rules, a decision taken in one capital constrained behaviour across dozens of networks, exchanges, and wallets worldwide. The border had moved.

This is the motif that threads through the subchapter: *the border that moves*. With every enforcement action, guidance note, or licensing condition, states push their regulatory boundaries outward—not by extending territory, but by reshaping incentives in the digital infrastructure that firms rely upon. The border shifts wherever a government can compel an actor whose services others cannot easily avoid. And because decentralised markets depend on highly centralised chokepoints—cloud providers, fiat gateways, custodians, analytics firms—the reach of a single jurisdiction often exceeds anything suggested by its size.

To understand extraterritoriality in this domain, start from what is visible: platforms changing global policies for the sake of a single market. Show the behaviour: when the New York Department of Financial Services issued detailed reserve requirements for stablecoins in June 2022, global issuers such as Circle updated disclosures and attestation cadences for all users, not merely New Yorkers. Name the actor: NYDFS. Explain: access to New York's financial system, with its institutional capital and correspondent banking ties, is indispensable. Implication: compliance for one state becomes compliance for many. The border moves outward.

A second example sharpens the picture. In early 2023, the European Banking Authority clarified that certain cryptoasset service providers needed to comply with its "travel rule" interpretations months before MiCA's full enforcement window. Major platforms in Paris, Amsterdam, and Dublin responded by altering global onboarding flows, adding data fields and risk checks that applied identically to customers in Nairobi, Seoul, and Toronto. The rule was European, but the implementation was global. The border moved again, not through coercion, but through the irresistible pull of a market block of 450 million consumers. Firms committed code as they committed compliance.

The pattern is not new. U.S. securities law has influenced global capital markets since at least the 1930s, when the SEC forged disclosure norms that foreign issuers eventually adopted to reach American exchanges. But what distinguishes the blockchain ecosystem is the speed at which extraterritorial force propagates. A wallet geofencing a region. A custodian refusing service to certain addresses. A mining pool blocking transaction propagation. These shifts can be observed in seconds. Metrics—the number of error messages, the volume of halted withdrawals, the percentage of transactions relayed through compliant RPC endpoints—become real-time indicators of where regulatory reach lands.

Yet extraterritoriality is not absolute. A credible counter-example reveals its limits. After the 2022 Tornado Cash sanctions, developers in Amsterdam and elsewhere continued to operate local Ethereum nodes that processed the same transactions U.S.-aligned infrastructure blocked. The protocol did not comply. The interfaces did. Name the actors: open-source node operators. Explain: decentralised systems allow users to route around national chokepoints, at least in principle. Implication: extraterritorial reach governs access, not existence. The border moves, but some paths slip beneath it.

Still, these evasions have boundaries. Most users do not run full nodes. They rely on custodians in Frankfurt or exchanges in Singapore or wallets whose RPC endpoints live in New York. The border meets them where they conduct their daily transactions. This is why market access remains the central instrument of extraterritoriality. Jurisdictions weaponise desirability. A listing on a regulated exchange in London or Tokyo requires a standard of disclosure that projects must meet whether or not they target British or Japanese users. A licence in Abu Dhabi Global Market demands risk frameworks that inevitably shape global practice for firms aiming to appear trustworthy. National rules become international templates because firms cannot afford to fragment their compliance logic endlessly.

Secondary liability extends this reach even further. When a regulator imposes obligations on intermediaries—analytics companies, custodians, fiat gateways—those intermediaries push obligations downstream. Show the behaviour: blockchain analytics firms in London and New York classify addresses based on proprietary risk scores. Custodians then block transfers linked to high-risk clusters to avoid supervisory scrutiny. Users worldwide experience these restrictions, even though the regulatory pressure originates in only a few capitals. Name the actor: a compliance vendor such as Chainalysis or Elliptic. Explain: by shaping the definition of risk, these firms indirectly determine which activities fall within regulatory tolerance. Implication: the border is redrawn not only by states but by the intermediaries they deputise.

The motif of *the border that moves* reappears in the way platforms harmonise global policies around the most stringent rule set they face. When Apple enforced App Store requirements regarding blockchain functionality, developers globally revised mobile features to comply with rules framed in Cupertino but felt everywhere. Similarly, when Binance agreed to strengthen its customer verification procedures in response to pressure from the UK and Japan, the upgraded KYC regime rolled out across Nigeria, Brazil, and Turkey. Geographically targeted rules became global defaults because maintaining regional differences raised operational risk.

Yet the movement of the border cuts both ways. Jurisdictions can push outward, but they can also pull inward. For example, after the collapse of FTX in November 2022, several regulators—including those in Australia and the Bahamas—tightened their domestic requirements in response to failures elsewhere. Show the behaviour: mandatory segregation of customer assets and strengthened audit obligations. Name the actors: ASIC, the Securities Commission of The Bahamas. Explain: the shock of a global failure triggered local recalibration. Implication: extraterritorial failures generate domestic reforms, which then propagate outward through market access controls. The border is a feedback loop.

The tension is most visible when states attempt to shape protocol-level behaviour. When the U.S. Treasury sanctioned specific smart contracts, some miners and validators hesitated to include transactions interacting with them. Yet miners in other jurisdictions continued unhindered. The behaviour fractured: a handful of U.S.-aligned validators produced OFAC-compliant blocks, while others did not. The border split the ledger into compliance zones. The implication: extraterritorial reach can fragment operational norms even when it cannot rewrite code.

This generates a deeper question about sovereignty in digital markets. States assert authority not through territorial control but through their ability to enforce consequences at vital chokepoints: custody, fiat convertibility, corporate presence, infrastructure dependencies. The strength of extraterritoriality flows from concentration. If wallets diversify RPC providers, if bridges decentralise relayers, if exchanges distribute custody across jurisdictions, the reach of any one state diminishes. But as long as global access depends on a handful of intermediaries, the border will continue to move with the decisions of those who regulate them.

The unresolved tension emerges here with clarity: if states extend their reach through the infrastructure on which decentralised systems rely, what responsibility falls on the designers of that infrastructure to decide whether they amplify or resist that reach? And when a single jurisdiction can, by shaping one gateway, shape behaviour everywhere, how should the global community measure the legitimacy of a border that no longer sits on a map but inside the interfaces we use each day?

Sanctions and Selective Inclusion

On 8 August 2022, the press office of the U.S. Department of the Treasury published a short notice adding Tornado

Cash-linked addresses to the Specially Designated Nationals list. Within hours, users in Berlin, Buenos Aires, and Nairobi found that common interfaces returned the same silent refusal: *"This service is unavailable in your region."* The code on Ethereum continued to function, but anyone relying on Infura's RPC endpoints or the default front ends maintained in Amsterdam and San Francisco found themselves abruptly partitioned. A sanction decision taken in Washington altered the practical experience of users far beyond American borders. A border had appeared where none existed the day before.

That sudden border—the quiet motif throughout this section—was not drawn on a blockchain. It was drawn across interfaces, infrastructure, and behaviour. The sanctions did not rewrite smart contracts; they reconfigured the social and technical scaffolding through which most people engage with them. Circle froze sanctioned USDC. GitHub removed repositories maintained by Tornado Cash developers. Protocol usage fractured not because cryptography changed, but because access changed. The core insight follows from that first scene: sanctions operate as tools of *selective inclusion*, dividing users into those whose actions remain compatible with the regulated substrate of global infrastructure and those pushed to its edges.

Sanctions impose policy not through statements but through measurable behaviour. Show the behaviour: front ends used by millions began rejecting sanctioned addresses or abstaining from relaying their transactions. Name the actor: OFAC. Explain: because major infrastructure providers fear penalties, they commit to enforcement even when the affected code resides abroad. Implication: sanctions reshape usage patterns not by altering protocol logic but by narrowing the channels through which most users interact with it.

A clearer example emerges from the aftermath of OFAC's decision. By October 2022, more than 50 per cent of Ethereum blocks were produced by validators filtering transactions deemed non-compliant with OFAC guidance, according to data aggregated by MEV Watch (Flashbots, 2022). The behaviour was concentrated among validators relying on U.S.-based MEV-relay providers. Name the actors: Flashbots, Coinbase. Explain: validators delegated transaction ordering to relays that excluded sanctioned interactions, thereby shifting the effective censorship boundary upstream. Implication: sanctions, though formally aimed at specific addresses, created a ripple that reached the consensus layer, differentiating the experience of users connected to compliant validators and those connected to non-compliant ones. The border shifted deeper into the infrastructure.

Selective inclusion, however, is not uniform. A credible counter-example illustrates its limits. In the Netherlands, where Tornado Cash developers Alexey Pertsev and others had contributed code long before the sanctions, users running local Ethereum nodes continued interacting with the censored contracts without interruption. Their transactions propagated through non-U.S. relays and non-filtering validators. Name the place: Amsterdam. Explain: independent node operation allowed users to bypass infrastructure chokepoints influenced by sanctions. Implication: selective inclusion impacts *access* more than *permission*. The border is porous for those willing and able to route around commercial intermediaries, though most users are not.

Sanctions also generate geographic asymmetry. Platforms that maintain unified global policies often amplify extraterritorial effects. Show the behaviour: when Uniswap Labs in New York updated its interface filters in 2022 to block sanctioned addresses, every user of that interface—whether in Lagos or Lisbon—experienced the ban identically. Name the actor: Uniswap Labs. Explain: to reduce legal risk, firms apply filters universally rather than regionally. Implication: one jurisdiction's sanction decision becomes a global rule through default implementation choices. The border expands.

The quiet motif—the border—reemerges in stablecoin infrastructure. In August 2022, Circle froze roughly USD 75,000 of sanctioned USDC (Circle, 2022). The number was small, but the message was unmistakable: the issuer could immobilise specific assets at will. Show the behaviour: balances remained visible on-chain but were marked as non-transferable. Name the actor: Circle. Explain: compliance was coded into token logic, enabling targeted enforcement. Implication: sanctions introduced a form of programmable exclusion, carving out prohibited pockets within a global asset. The border appeared not around the protocol but inside the token itself.

If sanctions segment access through intermediaries, analytics firms intensify selective inclusion through classification. Risk scoring by London- and New York–based companies such as Chainalysis and Elliptic becomes an indirect instrument of enforcement. Show the behaviour: exchanges in Seoul and Nairobi block withdrawals associated with flagged clusters even when local law does not require it. Name the actors: Chainalysis, Elliptic. Explain: these firms interpret sanctions expansively to protect themselves and their clients. Implication: sanctions propagate through *risk logic* rather than statute, creating de facto global compliance norms that exceed the written rule.

The border's movement becomes more visible in metrics: reduced liquidity around flagged addresses, increased transaction fees for those using non-compliant routes, and a surge in local node operation among technically sophisticated communities. After Tornado Cash's designation, daily usage fell sharply from around 3,000 transactions to under 300 by November 2022, according to public Ethereum data. Behaviour changed. Inclusion narrowed. Sanctions worked not through coercion, but through infrastructure alignment.

Yet selective inclusion carries costs. A counterpoint emerges from the decentralised finance platforms that refused to hard-code OFAC compliance. Show the behaviour: some front ends maintained by DAOs allowed interactions without geofencing, and some validators outside the United States committed to block neutrality. Name the place: non-U.S. validator clusters in Germany and Singapore. Explain: they asserted political independence by maintaining technical neutrality. Implication: resistance reduced global consistency, risking fragmentation of user experience. The border's movements created multiple regimes of usability.

This tension—between sanctions as instruments of public order and sanctions as catalysts of fragmentation—defines the policy landscape. States treat sanctions as tools of national strategy. Protocols treat them as stress tests of decentralisation. Infrastructure providers treat them as compliance hazards. Users experience them as sudden restrictions, often without explanation. Each group perceives a different border.

But the border does more than move; it multiplies. Consider RPC infrastructure. When Infura restricted calls associated with sanctioned addresses in August 2022, alternatives such as Alchemy or Pocket Network saw increased activity. Show the behaviour: traffic rerouted within hours. Name: Infura. Explain: the decision created demand for less restrictive endpoints. Implication: sanctions incentivise diversification of infrastructure, strengthening resilience for some while deepening exclusion for others.

Similarly, decentralised front-end hosting—via IPFS or ENS—grew incrementally after interface-level censorship intensified. Users who sought unfettered access turned to decentralised alternatives. Yet these alternatives introduced new frictions: slower load times, occasional broken dependencies, higher cognitive costs. The border was navigable, but not effortlessly. Inclusion became a spectrum, not a binary.

The asymmetry becomes stark in humanitarian contexts. Show the behaviour: during sanctions involving Afghanistan in 2021, aid organisations struggled to move funds through banking rails, but crypto interfaces applying global filters inadvertently restricted wallets flagged by analytics firms—even when used for legitimate purposes. Name: humanitarian NGOs attempting disbursements. Explain: sanctions filtered activity through algorithms unable to distinguish lawful survival from illicit finance. Implication: selective inclusion can unintentionally penalise those already on the margins, revealing the humanitarian stakes embedded in protocol access.

Across these examples, the border—our motif—demands repeated attention. It changes shape according to which intermediaries react, which users adapt, and which jurisdictions define compliance. The border is not a wall. It is a gradient of constraints imposed through wallets, oracles, relayers, custody policies, and the interpretive choices of compliance departments far removed from the chain itself.

The unresolved tension sits squarely at the centre of this landscape: if sanctions increasingly govern protocol access through private infrastructure rather than public law, how should societies judge the legitimacy of borders drawn by firms instead of legislatures? And when selective inclusion fragments users into those who remain inside the sanctioned perimeter and those forced outside it, what test should we apply to decide where that border ought to fall?

Public Infrastructure, Private Rails

On 7 April 2020, the Brazilian government launched its Auxílio Emergencial programme, distributing pandemic relief payments to millions through the Caixa Tem mobile app. The intention was clear: deliver public funds quickly, at scale, to households whose incomes had collapsed. Yet the infrastructure chosen to deliver that support was almost entirely private—telecom providers routing traffic, cloud platforms hosting servers, app marketplaces mediating updates, and commercial banks acting as the operational chassis beneath a state-branded interface. Within days, Caixa Tem became one of the most downloaded apps in Brazil, but it also revealed an uncomfortable truth: when states seek to act swiftly, they climb onto private rails because those rails already reach the citizen. The moment exposed the central motif running through this subchapter—the *junction,* where public purpose meets private architecture, where the line between state power and corporate design blurs into a shared but contested responsibility.

The same motif surfaced fifteen months later in San Salvador. When El Salvador's government declared Bitcoin legal tender in September 2021, the Chivo wallet—developed with private contractors and hosted on commercial cloud infrastructure—became the default mechanism for receiving state incentives. Tens of thousands queued in plazas and shopping centres to sign up. The experiment promised national transformation, yet the implementation depended on private stacks that carried their own contractual limitations and security assumptions. The junction was visible again: a sovereign legal act executed on infrastructure not wholly under sovereign control. One five-word sentence captures the tension: *The rails were not theirs.*

Public infrastructure increasingly rides on systems states neither own nor fully direct. This is especially visible in payment systems, where the ambition to modernise collides with the practical need to rely on commercial intermediaries. Governments may build the policy logic—eligibility criteria, fraud checks, supervisory rules—but the execution flows across private networks. Cards route through Visa or Mastercard. Bank transfers settle over rails operated by private clearing houses. Digital wallets rely on app store policies and cloud servers. Even central bank digital currency pilots in jurisdictions like Sweden and the Bahamas reveal the same pattern: public money delivered through private distribution channels.

The junction becomes more visible through specific behaviours. Show the behaviour: welfare payments in São Paulo reached users only after the Caixa Tem app synchronised with commercial authentication systems, which periodically failed under load. Name the actor: Caixa Econômica Federal. Explain: the state needed reach and reliability that only existing private mobile infrastructure could provide. Implication: the state absorbed political responsibility, but private actors determined uptime and user experience.

Another example sharpens the dynamic. In Singapore, where digital identity is deeply integrated with financial services, commercial banks distribute government payouts under schemes such as the GST Voucher. Show the behaviour: citizens receive funds through bank-linked wallets participating in Singapore's PayNow network. Name the actor: Monetary Authority of Singapore. Explain: MAS coordinates standards, but the transfer mechanisms are private. Implication: public disbursement becomes entangled with the operational practices of commercial institutions, from KYC thresholds to outage handling.

These examples illuminate the core tension: states target payment systems as national infrastructure, yet the rails that carry transactions remain privately operated, heterogeneous, and subject to corporate policies. For blockchain systems, this entanglement intensifies. A government may design a voucher scheme on-chain, but users reach it through wallets maintained by private teams, transmitted across RPC endpoints operated by companies in foreign jurisdictions, indexed by explorers that implement their own filtering logic. The junction expands in complexity, not clarity.

This dependence is not merely technical; it is political. When governments distribute funds via private wallets, they implicitly delegate questions of access, inclusion, and security to corporate governance processes. Show the behaviour: commercial wallets can freeze accounts, throttle throughput, or impose new identity checks overnight. Name the actor: any major wallet provider—whether Coinbase Wallet in the United States or Mercado Pago in Latin America. Explain: the provider's risk appetite influences the availability of public money. Implication: the boundary of the welfare state becomes partially defined by private compliance departments.

Yet the arrangement also carries advantages. States benefit from private sector scale, speed, and operational expertise. Brazil reached more than 100 million users within months during the Auxílio rollout. Singapore's PayNow network processes payments in seconds. These systems function because private actors have sunk the capital into infrastructure that governments can then appropriate for public tasks. Public infrastructure gains reach through commercial architecture.

A counter-example reveals the limits of this model. India's Unified Payments Interface (UPI), launched in 2016, is often described as a public digital rail. Show the behaviour: transactions settle almost instantly via a system overseen by the National Payments Corporation of India. Name the actor: NPCI. Explain: UPI reduces reliance on private payment processors by creating a state-adjacent standard. Implication: the junction narrows—public logic flows over quasi-public rails, creating less dependence on private actors for mission-critical functions.

Yet even UPI depends on private gateways for distribution. Banks deploy the applications. Telecom firms carry the data. App stores mediate access. And when NPCI approved WhatsApp Pay in 2020, although initially with transaction caps, it signalled willingness to allow Big Tech to participate in a system that still ultimately relies on commercial software stacks. The model is hybrid, not purely public.

Blockchain-related initiatives amplify these tensions. Consider Ukraine's rapid adoption of crypto donations in early 2022 to support defence and humanitarian efforts. Show the behaviour: funds flowed into addresses controlled by the Ukrainian government, but the usable rails were exchanges such as Binance and wallets such as Kuna. Name the actor: Ministry of Digital Transformation of Ukraine. Explain: the state leveraged crypto rails but relied on private infrastructure to convert tokens into real-world procurement. Implication: state capability existed, but execution required corporate cooperation, which could not be mandated across borders.

Another case: the Bahamas' Sand Dollar, launched nationally in 2020. Show the behaviour: citizens access the CBDC through regulated financial institutions and wallet providers. Name: Central Bank of The Bahamas. Explain: distribution hinges on private intermediaries that implement identity checks, run customer support, and harden security. Implication: even a sovereign digital currency depends on private rails, raising questions about consistency, resilience, and accountability.

The motif of the junction returns in the context of sanctions and compliance. When states rely on private actors for distribution, those actors import external regulatory obligations. Show the behaviour: a U.S.-based wallet geofencing Venezuelan users, preventing them from receiving funds routed through that wallet even if the funds originate from a non-U.S. government. Name: a major U.S. wallet provider. Explain: the wallet implements sanctions rules universally. Implication: geopolitical boundaries infiltrate public payment schemes just because they rest on corporate infrastructure.

The political implications deepen further. Private actors control interface design, data retention, user verification workflows, and transaction risk scoring. These elements determine who can access state benefits, how they authenticate, and how their activity is recorded. When a glitch prevents logins, citizens blame the state, not the cloud provider whose servers failed or the software vendor whose patch introduced an error. Responsibility diffuses while accountability concentrates.

Yet private rails also introduce fragility. The outage of a major cloud provider can disrupt welfare payments, tax disbursements, and even emergency aid. Behaviour reveals the risk: in December 2021, an AWS outage in the United States temporarily affected services used by several government-linked applications. Name: Amazon Web Services. Explain: a single point of failure interrupted multiple public services. Implication: states relying heavily on private rails inherit private-sector fragilities as public-sector liabilities.

There is another dimension: competition between private providers can distort public policy. A government contract for payment distribution can funnel millions of users toward a particular wallet or bank, shaping market structure for years. Show the behaviour: when El Salvador tied Bitcoin incentives to the Chivo wallet, commercial wallet competitors struggled to gain traction. Name: Government of El Salvador. Explain: the state's choice created a default provider. Implication: public policy acts as market-maker—intentionally or otherwise.

Still, the junction offers possibilities. Private rails may accelerate innovation, improve user experience, and reduce cost. Governments cannot match the pace of private engineering teams nor the capital budgets of multinational firms. But the junction must be governed, not assumed. It requires clear rules on data retention, liability allocation, service continuity, and contingency planning. Without these safeguards, states risk ceding more than distribution—they risk ceding sovereignty by fragmenting the control logic over essential public functions.

And that leads back to the motif. Every payment touches the junction: public intent flowing across private rails. The contact point shifts depending on architecture, governance, and political pressure.

The unresolved question is therefore unavoidable: if states increasingly depend on private rails to execute public missions, how far can they stretch that reliance before the rails—not the state—define the boundaries of public inclusion?

Chapter 4
Corporate Consortia: Governance by Enterprise Stack

The first warning arrived not from a regulator, but from a supermarket. In late 2018, Carrefour announced that its new traceability system—built on a permissioned blockchain operated by a consortium of food suppliers—would determine which farms could supply chicken to its French stores. The press release read like a celebration of transparency. Yet producers soon realised that access to the retailer's network had become a gatekeeper in itself: a farm was not "verified" unless the consortium admitted it, and its data was not "trustworthy" unless formatted precisely to the standard the network owners defined. For customers buying chicken breast in Lyon or Marseille, the packaging now carried a QR code pointing to a glossy interface promising safety and integrity. But behind that simple scan lay a governance structure in which private firms set the rules, implemented the rules, and judged compliance with the rules. Sovereignty, in this quiet domain of barcodes and supply chains, had migrated from public authority to corporate architecture.

That migration is neither accidental nor marginal. Across industries—logistics, finance, pharmaceuticals, digital identity—corporate consortia increasingly operate the systems that determine who may participate in essential transactions and on what terms. Their networks are labelled "enterprise chains", yet their effects spill into public life. A supply-chain ledger determines not just how a retailer manages stock, but which farmers stay in business. A digital identity system built for contractors influences how citizens access public services. A permissioned trade-finance platform shapes the costs borne by importers and exporters, which in turn shape prices borne by families far removed from boardrooms. The public feels the consequences even when the governance remains private.

A subtle motif runs through this chapter: *the boundary that is drawn but not declared*. Corporate consortia draw boundaries through technical standards, contractual obligations, integration requirements, intellectual property rights, accreditation rules, and exit fees. Yet they rarely call these boundaries what they are—forms of governance. Instead, the language of enterprise software softens their political character. What looks like a protocol parameter is, in practice, a policy choice. What reads like a service-level agreement is, in effect, a substitute for a public guarantee. And what appears to be a branding requirement often functions as a regulatory gate.

The first arena where these boundaries materialise is permissioned networks. Public blockchains declare openness as a design principle; enterprise networks declare control. Yet the distinction between private and public consequences is far from clean. When Walmart and IBM piloted food traceability on Hyperledger Fabric, the move was framed as a business optimisation. But as farmers in Arkansas discovered, participating in the system was no longer optional once the retailer adopted it at scale. The network became an infrastructure, and infrastructure demands conformity. Even when the nodes are run by corporations, the impact is felt by communities, producers, and consumers who never consented to the arrangement. Permissioned networks are portrayed as neutral tools, but they impose rules that resemble administrative orders delivered by technical means rather than statutes.

The second arena concerns ownership of standards. The phrase evokes engineering committees, but in corporate blockchains it often refers to intellectual property portfolios, trademark control, and open-source licences that define who may implement a protocol without fear of infringement. If a consortium controls the branding for "compliant" implementations, it controls the market. If it owns a reference design, it can dictate which integrations are recognised as valid. The power is subtle but pervasive. A company might publish its code under an open-source licence while retaining trademarks that restrict use of the consensus algorithm's name. Others might grant patent licences only to consortium members, transforming IP into a fence disguised as collaboration. The boundary drawn here is not only legal; it is commercial. Firms decide not only how a standard works, but who counts as compliant, credible, or admissible.

Risk and assurance form the third arena. When enterprise networks govern essential processes, participants seek guarantees normally provided by public law: predictability, reliability, recourse. In consortia, these guarantees appear as attestations, audits, and service-level agreements. A platform might promise 99.99 per cent uptime, binding itself to financial penalties if it fails. Another might establish a dispute mechanism that resembles arbitration. Yet these mechanisms derive their legitimacy not from democratic authority but from negotiation power. The promise of uptime on a blockchain run by ten corporations is not a public right; it is a private contract. The assurance is only as strong as the consortium's willingness to honour it and the participants' willingness to litigate when it fails. Corporate governance fills the vacuum where public oversight cannot reach.

Exit completes the picture. Enterprise chains love to proclaim interoperability, but in practice, the cost of leaving a consortium can be prohibitive. Data portability clauses often require members to export years of historical records in highly specific formats. Identity systems lock institutions into credentialing pathways that cannot be migrated without breaking trust assurances. Some consortia impose interchange fees for moving data off-network, citing operational costs that conveniently discourage migration. The boundaries drawn here are economic. Firms stay not because the consortium is irreplaceable, but because leaving is too costly, operationally or politically. The lock-in is a feature dressed as a technical constraint.

What links these arenas—permissioned networks, standards, assurance, exit—is not the technology itself but the model of governance they embody. Corporate consortia operate at the junction where private incentives meet public consequences. They construct infrastructures in which accountability is contractual rather than constitutional. They design rules whose legitimacy is measured by market adoption rather than civic consent. And they bind participants into ecosystems whose logic may diverge from national priorities or public expectations.

The stakes are high. As governments explore central bank digital currencies, as supply chains digitise compliance reporting, as identity systems integrate with healthcare and education, the frontier between public infrastructure and private governance will sharpen. Corporate consortia will increasingly operate the systems on which states depend. Their decisions—about compatibility, liability, data retention, and access—will shape societies even when their meetings take place in quiet conference rooms far from public view.

But if the boundaries drawn by consortia are political, not merely technical, who holds them accountable? How should society evaluate the legitimacy of a governance model where rules are set by firms, enforced by code, and rubber-stamped by contracts? And when exit becomes so costly that participants cannot leave without impairing their operations, is the consortium still a collaboration, or has it become a jurisdiction?

These questions shape the path ahead. They matter not only for engineers and executives, but for policymakers, citizens, and communities whose daily lives will be shaped by decisions they did not witness, and perhaps do not understand. The chapter that follows invites the reader to examine those decisions with clarity and scepticism, tracing how the enterprise stack has become a new site of governance—and how its quiet boundaries define the world beyond the boardroom.

Permissioned Networks with Public Consequences

In November 2018, Carrefour began placing QR codes on poultry products in its Lyon stores, directing customers to a blockchain-based traceability system built with IBM Food Trust. The move was marketed as a triumph of transparency. Yet beneath the polished interface lay a permissioned consortium network in which access, data formats, and validation rights were controlled not by farmers or regulators, but by a small circle of corporate participants. A producer unable to meet the consortium's data requirements risked losing its place on Carrefour's shelves. A technical decision by a retailer—implemented through an enterprise ledger rather than public law—changed the economic fate of farms across France. A quiet motif emerges here and threads through the analysis that follows: *the gate with no statute*. No public vote created that gate; no regulator oversaw it. Yet it shaped livelihoods with the force of an administrative decree.

The same motif surfaced earlier in 2017, when Maersk and IBM launched TradeLens, a permissioned blockchain intended to streamline global shipping documentation. The launch was heralded in Copenhagen as a step toward paperless trade. But participation required alignment with a technical standard and governance structure established by the consortium. By the time the platform ceased operations in late 2022, firms in Mumbai, Rotterdam, and Singapore had integrated internal systems around rules they did not set. Even though the project ultimately collapsed, the experiment illuminated a crucial shift: enterprise chains often act as de facto public infrastructure in sectors where public agencies have limited digital reach. And because these networks govern how records are stored, verified, and exchanged, their influence extends far beyond the corporate members that maintain them.

Permissioned networks present themselves as operational tools, yet they govern through engineering. Their design choices—permissions, node roles, data schemas, update mechanisms—function as policies. Show the behaviour: a retailer requires suppliers to upload origin data in a fixed format for a product to be "verified" on the chain. Name the actor: Carrefour, IBM Food Trust. Explain: the rules are enforced by membership criteria, APIs, and workflow dashboards. Implication: conformity becomes a condition for economic participation, even when no public authority mandates it. The gate with no statute tightens.

A second arena reveals the same dynamic: digital identity. In 2020, the Canadian provinces of British Columbia and Ontario piloted the Verifiable Organisations Network (VON), enabling businesses to share credentials with government agencies. While the initiative grew from public institutions, its backbone relied on Hyperledger Indy and corporate operators like the Sovrin Foundation before its restructuring. Show the behaviour: service providers had to issue and accept credentials using formats prescribed by the consortium. Name the actor: Sovrin Foundation. Explain: public services required interaction with a technical layer governed by private actors. Implication: identity, a core instrument of citizenship, became entangled with governance structures outside democratic oversight.

Permissioned networks create consequences not only through participation requirements but through *non-participation*. When Walmart mandated in 2018 that leafy-greens suppliers join its blockchain traceability programme within one year, small farms lacking technical capacity faced a stark choice: integrate or exit. Show the behaviour: suppliers in California and Arizona invested in new systems solely to meet Walmart's specification. Name the actor: Walmart. Explain: technical compliance became a market access requirement. Implication: the boundary between corporate procurement and public regulation blurred; the consortium's rules shaped agricultural practice as forcefully as statutory food-safety regimes.

A credible counter-example demonstrates nuance. Estonia's public X-Road infrastructure—while permissioned—remains state-governed and uses private firms only as service providers, not rule-setters. Show the behaviour: hospitals, banks, and government agencies interact through a standard controlled by the state's Information System Authority. Name the actor: Estonian Information System Authority. Explain: although vendors implement software, sovereign oversight defines access conditions. Implication: permissioned infrastructure need not cede governance to corporations; institutional design determines where authority sits. The counter-example reveals that corporate dominance is not inevitable, but a choice—often made by default.

Yet most consortia do not operate under such sovereign guardrails. Their governance bodies, usually structured as steering committees or technical councils, often comprise large firms whose incentives skew toward operational control, not public value. For the participants subject to their decisions, legitimacy is contractual, not civic. Show the behaviour: TradeLens required onboarding validation by Maersk-affiliated entities. Name the actor: Maersk. Explain: competitors feared asymmetrical influence and hesitated to join. Implication: the network's governance logic inhibited its growth, revealing that private rule-making can fragment rather than unify markets.

The motif of *the gate with no statute* reappears when considering dispute resolution. Public registries anchor conflicts in legal process. Permissioned ledgers resolve disputes through operational mandates: a node operator decides whether to accept late data, overwrite an entry, or revoke a credential. Show the behaviour: an enterprise identity network may suspend a credential based on internal policy, instantly restricting access to services. Name a case: the Sovrin Foundation's governance stack prior to 2021 allowed stewards to revoke misissued credentials. Explain: power was operational rather than judicial. Implication: revocation outcomes shape individual opportunities, yet appeal rights are undefined or non-existent.

Another feature of permissioned networks—immutability with exceptions—further complicates their public consequences. Public chains enshrine immutable records by design. Enterprise chains provide a simulation: data is "immutable" except when privileged roles amend it through governance votes or administrative patches. Show the behaviour: in supply-chain systems built on Fabric, privileged nodes may issue "corrections" to rectify errors. Name the actor: IBM Food Trust. Explain: rules for amendments exist but lack external oversight. Implication: immutability becomes a marketing term rather than a public assurance, yet consumers presume the latter. The boundary between auditability and authority remains opaque.

The effects extend to data protection. When a permissioned network processes identity or credential data, its operators define retention periods, access rights, and deletion processes. Show the behaviour: VON-style identity networks store metadata in ledgers governed by consortium rules rather than statutory data trustees. Name:

Hyperledger Indy's Sovrin-era deployment. Explain: governance determines who sees what, and for how long. Implication: privacy becomes dependent on private rule-making, not democratic procedure.

The limitations of private-led governance appear when such networks fail or collapse. When TradeLens shut down in November 2022, ports and logistics firms had to migrate years of integrated workflows. Show the behaviour: participants scrambled to retrieve and reconstruct data using proprietary export tools. Name: TradeLens. Explain: permissioned networks provide data portability only as far as their operators define export pathways. Implication: public consequences persist even when the private governance structure dissolves, highlighting the fragility of entrusting systemic functions to corporates without redundancy.

Against this backdrop, efficiency gains—often cited as justification for enterprise chains—must be evaluated against the governance costs they impose. Speed in locating contaminated produce, reduction in paperwork delays, faster authentication: these benefits are real. But they come bundled with silent forms of control. The decision to encode a compliance rule as a smart contract is also a decision to remove that rule from negotiation. The choice to require membership for ledger write-access is also a choice to exclude those without the resources to join. The presentation of chain-validated records as objective truth masks the institutional politics embedded in who controls write permissions.

The unresolved tension grows sharper: when private consortia operate infrastructure whose consequences reach farmers, small businesses, contractors, and citizens, where should the boundary of their authority lie? And if a retailer, shipping giant, or technology firm can impose de facto rules on entire sectors through a permissioned ledger, what test should society apply to determine when such power deserves oversight, restraint, or democratic visibility?

Who Owns the Standard?

In June 2019, a legal team at a European bank sat with two documents open side by side. On one screen, R3's Corda open-source licence; on the other, R3's trademark and compatibility guidelines. The engineers wanted to fork Corda to build a bespoke network for trade-finance workflows that would not connect to the public Corda Network. The lawyers saw something subtler. The Apache 2.0 licence allowed them to copy and modify the code. The trademark policy did not. They could run the software, but they could not call it "Corda", nor claim compatibility with "Corda Network" without passing R3's tests and accepting its governance. In effect, R3 owned not just a brand but a standard. The code was free. The name was not. And for counterparties deciding whether to join, the name was what mattered. The badge opened doors.

This is the quiet motif of this subchapter: *the seal*. A standard is only as powerful as the seal that certifies compliance. That seal might be a trademark, a logo, a certification mark, an "official" library, or an "EIP-compatible" label. Whoever controls the seal controls what "standard" means in practice. And in corporate consortia, the seal is often guarded more jealously than the code.

Blockchains arrived wrapped in the rhetoric of openness, yet the industrial layer surrounding them looks very familiar to any competition lawyer: portfolios of patents, carefully managed trademarks, "business source" licences that delay forking, and compatibility programmes that certify some implementations and exclude others. Intellectual property no longer concerns only revenue. It concerns architectural power. It decides who may implement a standard on equal footing, who must seek permission, and who will forever sit at the periphery.

The first dimension of this power lies in the split between code licences and trademark control. Corda is illustrative because it makes the distinction explicit. The core ledger is open-sourced under Apache 2.0, but the Corda name and logo are registered marks. Use of those marks requires adherence to R3's network and compatibility criteria. Show the behaviour: banks in London, Frankfurt, and Zurich describe their projects as "Corda-based" or "Corda-certified" only after contracting with R3. Name the actor: R3. Explain: the firm separates implementation freedom (you can run the code) from naming freedom (you cannot market as Corda without approval). Implication: the standard's economic value flows through the seal, not the repository. The seal becomes a gate.

Hyperledger Fabric, under the Linux Foundation, uses a softer version of the same pattern. The Fabric source code is permissively licensed and broadly forked, but the "Hyperledger" brand and logo sit under the Foundation's stewardship. Show the behaviour: only projects accepted into the Foundation's greenhouse may use the "Hyperledger X" naming convention. Name the actor: The Linux Foundation. Explain: trademark policy enforces coherence across frameworks and prevents confusing derivatives. Implication: control over the seal allows the Foundation to decide which codebases count as part of the standard-setting family and which remain external, even if they share ancestry.

Open-source licences themselves operate as tools of control, especially when combined with branding strategies. Uniswap v3's code, for instance, was released under a Business Source Licence in 2021, delaying permissionless commercial use of its core algorithm for several years. Show the behaviour: competing decentralised exchanges could inspect the code, but could not legally deploy it for profit until the licence converted. Name the actor: Uniswap Labs. Explain: the firm balanced openness with a statutory moat, using licensing to slow direct competition while the "Uniswap" name and interface consolidated network effects. Implication: in practice, the Uniswap team steered the standard for concentrated-liquidity AMMs, not by owning the idea but by owning the most legitimate implementation and its brand.

The Uniswap–SushiSwap history illustrates how seals direct legitimacy. SushiSwap forked Uniswap v2's code in 2020 under a permissive licence. The behaviour was clear: the protocol duplicated functions and interface patterns while redirecting fees. Yet it could not call itself "Uniswap". Name the actor: Uniswap Labs. Explain: the trademark lock meant that, in public perception, Uniswap remained the canonical pool model even as Sushi claimed innovation. Implication: the standard is anchored not only in code but in the association between name, logo, and interface. Forks may function identically yet sit outside the perceived standard because they lack the seal.

A second dimension lies in who drafts and controls the written specification. ERC-20 and ERC-721, for example, emerged from Ethereum Improvement Proposals owned in a collective sense by the Ethereum community rather than a single vendor. The EIP process is open; anyone may submit, comment, or implement. Show the behaviour: wallets and exchanges worldwide treat "ERC-20" as a basic requirement for fungible tokens. Name the actor: Ethereum community, curated via the EIP editors. Explain: because no single corporate entity holds a trademark over "ERC-20" as a compatibility label, the standard retains a genuinely open quality—forks can still claim ERC-20 semantics if they adhere to the function signatures. Implication: here, the seal is dispersed. No single gatekeeper can say "you may not call your implementation ERC-20" if it conforms. Control exists, but it is rooted in social consensus rather than IP rights.

Contrast that with corporate consortia defining proprietary variants of "compliance". A supply-chain consortium might run a "Trusted Farm" programme where the phrase itself is a registered mark. Only participants meeting technical and contractual requirements may put that logo on packaging. Show the behaviour: Carrefour's blockchain-enabled labels or Walmart's "Blockchain-verified" pilots. Name the actors: Carrefour, Walmart and their tech partners. Explain: the term "trusted" here is not a generic descriptor; it is a branded certification. Implication: the standard for what counts as "traceable" or "safe" lives in a private mark. Regulators may mandate food-safety baselines, but the higher commercial standard is owned.

Patents add a third, sharper edge. While many blockchain consortia pledge royalty-free licensing for core components, several maintain patent portfolios designed to deter rival structures. Ripple, for instance, has filed patents around aspects of distributed payment networks; IBM and Mastercard have done likewise for various blockchain and digital identity techniques. Show the behaviour: participation agreements in some consortia include cross-licensing commitments or defensive covenants. Name the actors: IBM, Mastercard, R3, and others. Explain: these provisions both reassure members that they will not be sued for using the standard and fence out outsiders who refuse to sign the pact. Implication: ownership of patents becomes a bargaining chip in defining who can implement the standard without legal risk. Again, the seal sits in legal paperwork, not in code.

The counter-example that clarifies what is at stake comes from the early internet. TCP/IP, the backbone of global networking, emerged under the stewardship of the IETF's "rough consensus and running code" process. No single entity owned a trademark over "TCP/IP-compatible". No firm held exclusive patents over its core handshake. Show the behaviour: any operating system implementing the RFCs could claim compatibility without asking permission. Name the actor: IETF. Explain: the absence of tight IP control allowed diverse implementations—BSD, Linux, Windows—to flourish while remaining interoperable. Implication: here, the standard's seal was cultural rather than legal. If the code passed interop tests, it was "TCP/IP". No gate with paperwork stood in the way.

Blockchain consortia often invoke that lineage while quietly pulling in the other direction. They host open working groups, publish whitepapers, and talk of "ecosystems", yet they reserve key levers: the right to certify nodes, the right to approve client software, the right to veto usage of a brand. The seal is centralised even when the rhetoric is not.

Open-source licences, too, can encode governance. Copyleft licences like the GPL ensure that derivatives must share the same freedoms, constraining corporate appropriation. Permissive licences like MIT or Apache grant broad freedoms, but when combined with tight trademark control, they create a curious hybrid: anyone can run the code, but only some can stand under the standard's banner. Business-source licences delay that freedom temporally, setting a date after which the code becomes open. Each legal choice reflects a stance on who should own the standard's evolution.

These legal structures produce visible behaviours in markets. Projects seeking legitimacy gravitate toward standards whose seals are recognised by key intermediaries. A stablecoin aspiring to institutional adoption might pursue an ISO registration and adopt particular messaging standards defined by SWIFT, even if a more efficient alternative exists, because the seal "ISO-compliant" opens doors with banks. A consortium ledger might target a "Hyperledger" affiliation because that mark reassures procurement teams. The seal reduces due-diligence costs, but at the price of concentrating agenda-setting power in the hands of whoever grants it.

At the same time, communities sometimes reclaim standards from corporate originators. The "OpenChain" project, initially trademarked by a single firm, moved under the Linux Foundation to widen participation and neutralise control concerns. Show the behaviour: contributors in Tokyo, Berlin, and San Francisco adopted the standard more readily once it sat in a vendor-neutral home. Name the actor: Linux Foundation. Explain: institutional relocation shifted the perception of ownership. Implication: who holds the seal can be renegotiated, but only through deliberate institutional design.

Behind the legalities lies a political question: when standards govern essential economic functions—payments, identity, trade reporting—should their seals live in private hands? Code alone does not answer this. A protocol can be flawlessly open-sourced yet effectively closed through trademarks. A license can promise freedom while a certification scheme narrows entry. The gate with no statute reappears, this time as a logo at the bottom of a PDF, or as a compatibility badge in a marketing deck.

For professionals navigating this landscape, the diagnostic questions are deceptively simple. Who can decide that an implementation is "compliant"? Who can revoke that judgment? Who can fork the code and still use the name? And crucially, what remedies exist when the owner of the standard uses the seal not to maintain interoperability, but to exclude rivals or bend an ecosystem to its strategic aims?

Risk, Assurance, and Audit

On 28 February 2017, a mistyped command in an Amazon Web Services maintenance operation took down the S3 storage service in the us-east-1 region. For several hours, major websites, mobile apps, and internal tools across North America simply failed. Status pages blinked red. Dashboards froze. Engineers in banks, retailers, and logistics firms watched core systems stall because a single cloud region was unavailable. When the dust settled, disputes did not centre on public regulators or statutory obligations. They centred on contracts. Lawyers reached for AWS's service-level agreement. What did the uptime commitment say? How would credits be calculated? Could any party plausibly argue breach? The outage was a vivid reminder that, in much of the digital economy, the closest thing to public law is a PDF buried in a vendor portal promising "four nines" of availability. The paper guarantee was everything.

Permissioned blockchain consortia inhabit the same world. Their participants—banks, retailers, identity providers, logistics firms—depend on networks that lack clear statutory regimes. If a shared ledger fails at a critical moment, there is no regulator ready with a bespoke compensation framework. There is no long-settled case law on "consensus failures" or "node misbehaviour". What there is, instead, are attestations, audits, and SLAs: third-party reports asserting the system's robustness; contractual uptime promises; operational covenants that define incident response. In practice, these artefacts substitute for public law. They define risk, allocate blame, and determine who pays when something goes wrong.

The motif threading through this subchapter is *the promise on paper*. It might be a SOC 2 report, an external smart-contract audit, a service-level schedule, or an attestation about reserves and controls. Whatever its form, the promise shapes behaviour. Participants connect to a consortium network, commit data, or route trades not because a statute compels them, but because a bundle of documented assurances persuades them that the residual risk is tolerable.

The first layer of this substitute law is the audit report. Large custodians and infrastructure providers in the blockchain space have embraced the language of SOC 1 and SOC 2, the assurance frameworks originally defined by the American Institute of Certified Public Accountants. When Coinbase, for example, advertises SOC 1 Type II or SOC 2 Type II attestation for certain services, it is offering more than marketing. It is offering a quasi-legal artefact: an independent auditor's opinion that internal controls operated effectively over a defined period. Participants do not read these reports for pleasure. They read them to answer questions that, in a public system, would fall to a prudential supervisor: how is access controlled? How are changes deployed? How is data retained? The report becomes a proxy for ongoing oversight.

In enterprise consortia, similar dynamics play out. When IBM Food Trust touts its compliance with ISO information-security standards, or when a trade-finance network publishes an external penetration-testing certificate, these documents do not merely reassure procurement departments. They become bargaining chips in risk committees, substituting for the regulator's comfort letter that does not yet exist. Show the behaviour: a European supermarket chain agrees to route supply-chain data through a permissioned ledger only after its security team has reviewed external audit opinions. Name the actors: IBM, Carrefour. Explain: the company relies on private assurance to justify moving critical data from in-house systems to shared infrastructure. Implication: the threshold for adoption is not a statute but a comfort level set by attestations.

Service-level agreements sit alongside audits as the operational expression of that comfort. In a public utilities regime, lawmakers might specify minimum service obligations. In enterprise blockchain consortia, those obligations are calculated in percentages: 99.95 per cent uptime, maximum four-hour recovery time, defined maintenance windows agreed months in advance. These numbers shape what counts as acceptable harm. If a permissioned settlement network goes offline for three hours during a trading day, and its SLA allows such downtime with limited credits, participants must absorb the cost. Their recourse is not to a court enforcing a public standard of resilience, but to a contractual clause specifying the value of a lost basis point.

TradeLens again offers a useful lens. During its operational life, shipping companies and port authorities integrated their documentation flows into the platform. For a port in Rotterdam or an exporter in Shanghai, the decision to rely on TradeLens rested on comfort that the network would be available when needed. That comfort came from SLAs and IBM's reputation, not from a maritime regulator decreeing minimum blockchain uptime. When the consortium wound down in 2022, participants looked not to public law for continuity, but to their contracts: What did the exit clauses say? How would data be archived and accessed? The promise on paper governed the disentanglement.

Attestations also extend into the on-chain world, especially where enterprise stacks intersect with public networks. Stablecoin issuers such as Tether and Circle have long faced scrutiny over their reserves. In response, they commission attestations from accounting firms, offering snapshots of assets held and their composition. These are not full audits, as securities regulators would understand them. They are, nonetheless, the primary documents many institutional users rely upon when deciding whether to hold or accept a given token. Show the behaviour: an exchange in Zurich lists USDC because it trusts Grant Thornton's or Deloitte's recurring attestations of reserves. Name the actors: Circle, its attestation providers. Explain: in the absence of tailored stablecoin law, the market treats private assurance as sufficient grounds to treat a token as cash-equivalent. Implication: the attestation becomes a private statute, setting expectations about redemption and solvency.

The counter-example that reveals the limits of this model comes from public payment systems. The UK's Faster Payments Service or the EU's TARGET2 operate under explicit statutory and regulatory frameworks. If they fail, central banks and banking supervisors step in. There is clear legal doctrine about liability, consumer protection, and systemic risk. Participants do not rely on SLAs alone; they rely on the state's commitment to financial stability, backed by lender-of-last-resort powers. In those systems, the promise on paper is embedded in law, not merely in contracts.

Blockchain consortia lack that scaffolding. When an enterprise identity network fails to issue credentials for a day, students might miss exam registration, lorry drivers might be unable to access secure terminals, contractors might lose pay. Yet the remedy sits in the fine print of an SLA: perhaps a fee rebate, perhaps nothing. There is no doctrine of "right to be issued a credential" comparable to a right of access to courts or registers. The network's governance board decides whether the failure warrants compensation. Risk is managed by committee rather than by statute.

This is not inherently malign. Private assurance has strengths. It is faster to adapt than law. It can tailor obligations to particular technical architectures. Audit frameworks can evolve as threat models change. A consortium can adjust its incident-response metrics after a major outage without waiting for parliamentary cycles. The agility is real.

But agility without public anchor introduces asymmetries. Who commissions the audit? Who pays the auditor? Who drafts the SLA? In many consortia, the largest participants drive these processes. Their risk tolerances dominate. A small logistics firm joining a permissioned trade-finance ledger has little leverage to negotiate bespoke uptime terms. It must accept the base SLA, even if its own customers hold it to higher standards. If a dispute later arises—say, a missed customs clearance due to network outage—the small firm may find that its contractual remedies against the consortium fall far short of the penalties its own clients now demand. The chain of private promises does not align.

The motif of *the promise on paper* appears again in the way consortia handle audits of smart contracts and protocol code. Many enterprise networks now commission code reviews from firms like Trail of Bits, Quantstamp, or NCC Group, publishing reports that detail vulnerabilities and fixes. These audits are vital. They catch design flaws before they become exploits. However, they are rarely accompanied by binding guarantees. The auditor's contract almost always disclaims liability for missed vulnerabilities. Participants see "audited" and infer safety, but the legal weight of that label is thin. If a bug later causes loss, the audit report serves more as an artefact for insurance underwriting than as a basis for legal redress.

And yet, these assurances matter deeply. They structure trust among institutions that would otherwise refuse to bet their reputations on untested code. A bank joining a consortium ledger may require evidence that all critical contracts have undergone formal verification or independent review. A government agency using a blockchain-backed land registry pilot may demand penetration tests and operational insurance. Each artefact is a negotiation between risk and action: how much evidence is enough to proceed?

There is a further, subtler function of assurance: it shapes governance outcomes in disputes. Imagine a consortium where one node operator alleges that another has failed to meet performance obligations, causing settlement delays. The SLA and associated monitoring reports will define who is at fault. If the monitoring infrastructure is itself part of the service, the operator effectively judges its own case. Audit and assurance frameworks can concentrate power by giving one actor privileged epistemic authority: its logs become the truth. Its measurements determine whether penalties trigger. The promise on paper decides which narrative prevails.

A credible counter-pattern exists in some public blockchains that rely on transparent, community-run monitoring. Here, anyone can inspect uptime statistics, block-production histories, or slashing events. Disputes play out in public forums, and although there is still no formal court, social consensus can impose reputational sanctions. But even these systems are beginning to absorb private assurance, as institutional validators tout ISO certifications and SOC reports to attract delegations. Public and private logics interweave.

As corporate consortia assume roles once reserved for public registries and critical infrastructure, their reliance on attestations, SLAs, and audits will deepen. Participants will continue to ask the same questions: Who measured this? Under what assumptions? What happens if the guarantee fails? The answers will determine whether these networks can credibly underpin trade, identity, and payments at scale.

The unresolved question is simple to state and hard to answer: when the promise on paper becomes the primary source of assurance in systems with public consequences, who should define its minimum content—and what recourse should exist when that promise proves inadequate at the moment it is needed most?

Exit and Interchange Fees

In July 2021, Maersk announced that TradeLens—the global shipping consortium it co-developed with IBM—had reached over 300 participants, including ports in Rotterdam, Singapore, and Los Angeles. The network promised a unified flow of customs documents, container status updates, and bills of lading. Yet behind the press releases, several regional freight forwarders complained privately that leaving the platform, or even migrating part of their workflow elsewhere, had proved harder than joining. The challenge was not contractual; it was technical. Extracting historical data required custom scripts. Rebuilding integrations demanded weeks of engineering time. Even identifying which documents had been referenced across interlinked ledgers involved combing through proprietary APIs. One logistics manager in Rotterdam summed up the dynamic with weary precision: "We could exit, but we can't unwind." The bill for departure was not a penalty; it was the architecture itself.

This tension—ostensible freedom of exit paired with opaque, costly disentanglement—defines the power of exit and interchange fees in corporate consortia. Public law imagines markets as spaces where dissatisfied participants vote with their feet. But in consortium-led digital infrastructure, exit is not a gesture. It is a system migration, a rewiring of dependencies, and often a reconstruction of institutional memory. Lock-in is not merely an economic strategy. It is a governance instrument, shaping who can challenge rules, who must tolerate them, and who bears the cost of dissent.

The motif that recurs here is *the weight of accumulated history*. Every interaction, document, credential, or settlement that passes through a consortium network becomes sediment. The deeper the sediment, the harder it is to lift oneself out.

The first layer of lock-in is the data model itself. When the GSMA introduced the Mobile Connect identity framework in 2014, telecom operators in countries such as India, Spain, and South Korea integrated customer authentication flows into a shared standard. By 2018, operators participating in the scheme had generated millions of identity assertions. The catch was structural: even though Mobile Connect followed open standards, each operator extended its implementation to fit local authentication policies and KYC obligations. A bank that relied on an operator's Mobile Connect integration often depended on custom attributes defined by that operator alone. Should the bank later want to migrate to a different consortium or identity provider, those attributes had to be remapped or abandoned. Show the behaviour: banks in Madrid retained legacy Mobile Connect fields because rewriting their onboarding systems cost more than the benefits of switching. Name the actors: Telefónica, GSMA. Explain: the technical standard created a dependency that persisted beyond its strategic relevance. Implication: the cost of exit silently cemented the consortium's influence.

Blockchain-based enterprise consortia amplify this effect. Data written to a permissioned ledger—whether trade documents on Marco Polo (launched 2017), customs declarations on TradeLens (2018), or supply-chain attestations on Food Trust (2017)—is not merely stored. It is referenced, hashed, cross-linked, and anchored into workflows. These relationships create an implicit web: removing one party requires touching every thread that references their contributions. It is not simply a matter of downloading a CSV. It is a matter of reconstructing meaning.

Participants often discover this when renegotiating fees. A bank connected to a trade-finance consortium may wish to switch node operators or move its workload to a cheaper hosting partner. Technically, it has the right to operate its own node. Yet the consortium's operational manuals might require certification by an approved vendor. The vendor list is short. The interchange fees—costs paid to change providers—are high. The effect is not coercive in form, but coercive in outcome. Participants remain because departure is arduous.

A credible counter-example exists in traditional markets: the SWIFT network. Despite its vast influence, SWIFT historically maintained a principle of provider neutrality. Banks could choose among many interface vendors, and message formats, while complex, were well-documented and widely supported. Migrating gateways was costly but tractable. The limitation, however, reveals itself in the 2020 migration to ISO 20022 standards. Banks worldwide have invested billions updating systems. Many now rely on specific middleware vendors because local adaptations increased complexity. Even SWIFT's openness could not prevent technical lock-in when the data model evolved. Reconcile the difference: while SWIFT's governance sought neutrality, the complexity of modern messaging standards created lock-in outcomes despite open design intentions.

The blockchain analogue is instructive. Consider the decision by the Australian Securities Exchange (ASX) to cancel its planned CHESS replacement using Digital Asset's DAML-based distributed ledger (announced 2016, cancelled 2022). Participants had spent years preparing migrations, updating interfaces, and training teams. Despite the project's halt, both ASX and market participants bore lasting technical debt: partial implementations, specialised integrations, data mappings. Even abandoning a network can impose burdens equal to staying. The cost of exit is not theoretical; it is quantifiable in engineering hours, delayed releases, and sunk investment.

The second layer of lock-in lies in *shared operational logic*. Corporate consortia rarely standardise solely on data formats. They standardise on flows: the order in which events occur, the states a transaction must pass through, the validation rules applied at each step. These flows often shape internal processes in participating firms. For example, when a consortium requires digital signatures following a specific sequencing rule, a participant's internal approval system must adapt to match it. Over months, the internal logic reorganises itself around the consortium's expectations. Leaving the network then requires unpicking not just integrations, but habits.

Hyperledger Fabric consortia illustrate this well. Each consortium defines endorsement policies specifying which members must sign a transaction. These policies become embedded in participants' compliance workflows: which teams approve which documents, how exceptions are escalated, which individuals hold signing keys. Show the behaviour: a food distributor in Lyon restructures its quality-control process so that the same role responsible for verifying batch numbers also approves blockchain attestations. Name the actors: Carrefour, IBM Food Trust. Explain: the organisation aligns its internal responsibilities with the consortium's endorsement logic. Implication: leaving the consortium or switching to a different platform requires reorganising both technical integrations and human roles.

The third layer is financial. Consortia often charge membership fees, transaction fees, or data-access fees. These costs are defensible—they fund shared infrastructure—but they also shape behaviour. If a consortium charges high exit fees, participants hesitate to challenge governance decisions for fear of triggering a departure they cannot afford. Even without formal exit charges, the opportunity cost of migration creates a similar dynamic: a bank weighing whether to contest a governance change must consider whether the cost of dissent exceeds the cost of compliance. Interchange fees—the costs of switching operators or service providers—reinforce this gravity.

A pointed example lies in identity consortia built atop verifiable credentials. When the UK's digital identity trust framework pilot began in 2021, several private providers adopted proprietary schemas for credentials. Organisations that onboarded early found that their staff, customer, or contractor credentials were valid only within that provider's trust network. Should they choose to migrate to a different identity provider, they would need to reissue all credentials—tens of thousands in some cases. The vendor did not impose an exit fee. The architecture did. The weight of accumulated history kept clients local.

Yet a limitation to this pattern deserves attention. Some technical communities have attempted to design for portability explicitly. The W3C's Decentralized Identifiers (DIDs) specification, finalised in 2022, sought to ensure that identity artefacts could move across networks. Projects such as Europe's ESSIF initiative aim to enable cross-provider interoperability. These efforts show that lock-in is not inevitable. However, even here, practical barriers persist. A DID method tied to a specific consortium ledger remains effectively immobile unless the consortium supports exports and reissuance. The open standard reduces friction but cannot eliminate the web of relationships built on top of any given implementation.

The most consequential implication of lock-in economics is governance inertia. When exit is costly, governance boards face less pressure to justify decisions. A consortium might introduce new data-sharing rules, adjust membership tiers, or modify dispute-resolution processes knowing that the majority of participants lack credible outside options. This dynamic mirrors telecommunications markets of the early 2000s, when number portability was limited. Users stayed with suboptimal providers because switching was painful. Only when regulators mandated portability did competition accelerate. In blockchain consortia, there is no regulator to mandate portability. Participants must bear the cost.

This inertia can serve stability. A consortium processing customs declarations across Europe, for instance, may need to enforce uniform standards and cannot easily accommodate forks. High switching costs deter fragmentation. But stability can shade into complacency. If a consortium handles identity for millions of citizens indirectly—as some municipal digital identity pilots already do—the cost of exit means that bugs, delays, or governance failures propagate through dependent institutions with little recourse.

The motif *the weight of accumulated history* returns in the question of data portability clauses. Many consortium agreements contain clauses stating that a participant may retrieve its data "in a mutually agreed format". This language appears neutral. In practice, it often conceals asymmetry. A logistics firm leaving a supply-chain network might require a full export of document hashes, metadata, and cross-references. Generating this export may require engineering effort not covered by baseline fees. The network operator holds de facto discretion. The cost is measurable: weeks of work, thousands of euros in staff time, missed shipping deadlines. The clause becomes a promise on paper without operational teeth.

Some consortia attempt to mitigate this through escrow arrangements or independent operators. The Swiss-based Global Legal Entity Identifier Foundation (GLEIF), while not a blockchain consortium, offers an instructive design: it accredits multiple issuers and allows entities to port LEIs across providers. Yet even here, portability requires re-validation processes. The principle is sound; the practice remains burdensome.

What emerges is a policy landscape shaped not by statutory authority but by technical friction. Exit rights exist, but their exercise is rare because the cost is prohibitive. Participants learn to negotiate within the consortium rather than against it. They adapt their systems, staff roles, and expectations to the consortium's rhythm. Governance becomes centripetal: power accumulates at the centre because leaving the circle is painful.

The unresolved tension sits at the intersection of design and power. If exit is the ultimate safeguard in decentralised governance theory, what happens when the practical cost of departure strips the safeguard of meaning? And if interchange fees quietly determine which actors can credibly dissent, how should consortia design their architectures to ensure that lock-in reflects genuine value rather than accidental entrapment?

Chapter 5
Decentralised Communities: Voice, Vote, and Veneer

The moment that fractured the illusion arrived quietly. In March 2022, during a routine governance vote for a major DeFi protocol, fewer than two hundred wallet addresses determined a parameter change that altered the borrowing costs for hundreds of thousands of users worldwide. The proposal itself was not extraordinary. What startled observers was the arithmetic: a community that spoke the language of collective ownership had, in practice, handed its fate to a voting pool no larger than the audience of a village hall meeting. A handful of well-capitalised delegates carried the motion. Most token holders stayed silent. The governance forum, filled with sharp analysis and earnest debate, seemed suddenly like theatre—important, symbolically charged, but ultimately peripheral to where real power pooled. The episode crystallised a paradox: decentralisation promised voice for all, yet its mechanisms often amplified the loudest few.

The roots of that contradiction stretch further back, to August 2016, when The DAO collapsed after a vulnerability allowed a draining of funds that sent shockwaves across the cryptocurrency world. Its aftermath produced a schism. One chain, Ethereum, reversed the exploit. Another, Ethereum Classic, refused on principle. Identity, authority, and legitimacy were contested not through parliaments or courts, but through hashes, miners, and community forums.

It was a constitutional crisis without a constitution, adjudicated not by judges but by the choice of which codebase to run. The fault line exposed a deeper truth: decentralised communities inhabit a political landscape every bit as complex as the states they claim to transcend, yet they must navigate it without the centuries-old scaffolding of civic institutions, legal doctrine, and democratic compromise. They improvise, and improvisation breeds fragility.

Yet out of that fragility comes experimentation unmatched elsewhere. Decentralised communities have become laboratories of governance—messy, aspirational, occasionally naive, but persistently inventive. Their voting systems stretch from one-token-one-vote plutocracies to quadratic schemes that try to temper wealth with voice. Their charters range from elaborate constitutional drafts to minimalistic statements of intent. Their crisis-response mechanisms include emergency multisigs staffed by pseudonymous guardians scattered across continents. And, above all, their legitimacy is tested not in courtrooms but in the quiet, persistent decision of users to stay, to build, to transact, or to walk away. *Staying* becomes the ultimate vote.

What gives these communities their political charge is the mismatch between surface appearance and operational reality. The veneer is powerful: talk of "the community", "the collective", "the chain", "the will of token holders". Yet beneath this narrative lie hard constraints. Token voting embeds the biases of wealth concentration. Delegation markets privilege the articulate, the visible, and the well-networked. Voter apathy creates power vacuums that sophisticated actors can occupy. A governance proposal might present itself as an expression of broad consensus, yet the turnout figures quietly reveal a democratic deficit. The rhetoric of decentralisation is compelling; the practice is uneven.

This chapter explores the consequences of that unevenness. It begins with the inner mechanics of token voting—what it enables, what it obscures, and why communities repeatedly return to it despite its limitations. Voters who hold governance tokens can, in theory, shape protocol direction. Yet governance tokens themselves often concentrate in the hands of early investors, core contributors, and large treasuries. This concentration creates a structural tilt toward plutocracy. When turnout is low, that tilt becomes decisive. Communities then turn to delegation, hoping representation will broaden participation. Delegates emerge as informal legislators, drafting proposals, engaging in public debate, and accumulating reputational capital. But delegation introduces its own puzzles: how accountable is a delegate with no formal constituency? How durable is a mandate that depends on voluntary renewal rather than explicit elections? These tensions are not incidental. They determine whether a decentralised system can claim any meaningful democratic legitimacy.

Beyond voting lies the push towards *constitutional design*. Several prominent networks have attempted to draft on-chain constitutions—documents that codify rights, limits, and processes. They enumerate the conditions under which a fork becomes legitimate, the powers of emergency councils, the obligations of contributors, the sanctity of treasuries. These texts echo centuries of political thought, yet they are written for a domain where enforcement cannot rely on courts or police. Their authority depends on adoption, on clarity, and on whether they embed enough social legitimacy to survive a moment of crisis. The ambition is admirable: to write a ruleset that offers predictability where none existed, and to bind powerful actors to constraints they cannot unilaterally amend. But ambition encounters implementation. When a crisis hits, communities often revert to expediency. The rules bend. Multisigs intervene. Forums erupt with debate over whether the constitution was meant to be absolute or aspirational. The gap between political theory and protocol reality widens.

That gap is most evident in emergency governance. Multisigs—those wallets controlled by multiple signers—are treated as neutral guardians of last resort. They can pause contracts, redirect funds, or apply patches. They operate under the banner of "safety". Yet they also concentrate enormous power. A multisig with five signers located, intentionally or not, in the same legal jurisdiction is one subpoena away from being forced to act. Emergency powers, originally framed as temporary scaffolding, become standing fixtures. Over time, their discretionary authority expands. The guardians become, in effect, administrators. They may be diligent, transparent, and well-intentioned, but their existence contradicts the decentralised ethos. What happens when a guardian refuses to act? What happens when they act too readily? What happens when legal pressure collides with technical neutrality? These are not abstract questions. They have emerged repeatedly in high-stakes moments across protocols managing billions.

And yet, despite the frictions, decentralised communities persist. They adapt. Some grow into formidable ecosystems with thousands of active contributors and functioning governance pipelines. Others fragment, ossify, or fade. The distinction often traces back not to their charters or their voting systems, but to something far harder to quantify: *whether users continue to show up*. Legitimacy in decentralised systems is not conferred; it is accumulated, block by block, transaction by transaction. A front-end interface that survives controversy because its users refuse to leave becomes, in practice, more authoritative than any constitution. A protocol whose governance forums fall silent loses authority even if tokens remain widely held. Habit becomes law. Momentum becomes mandate.

Through these dynamics, decentralised communities reveal a core truth about power without institutions: it flows toward those who act, those who persist, and those who can weather apathy. They also expose something timeless: democracy, whether on-chain or off, depends not on the architecture of voting, but on the willingness of people to participate consistently and conscientiously. And participation is fragile. It competes with time, incentives, and the subtle fatigue of governance overload.

A deeper question sits beneath all of this: to what extent can decentralised systems escape the gravitational pull of centralisation when the tools they rely on—tokens, delegates, guardians, front ends—create their own centres of power? The previous chapters explored how states, corporations, and standards exert authority. Here, within communities that claim to resist those forces, we find new power structures emerging with equal force. Their legitimacy rests not on statute, nor market share, nor international consensus, but on a delicate blend of belief, habit, coordination, and code.

This chapter invites the reader into the political interior of decentralised systems—not the marketing slogans, not the ideological manifestos, but the lived governance. It examines what people do when they disagree, when they are apathetic, when they must choose between principle and convenience. It traces how communities justify authority, how they distribute it, and how they obscure it. It shows the beauty of experimentation and the fragility of legitimacy. Above all, it asks how these communities can claim democratic intent when their structures, incentives, and behaviours often edge toward centralisation despite themselves.

The unresolved tension driving the chapter is simple: can a system built on voluntary participation, global coordination, and cryptographic guarantees sustain a meaningful notion of collective voice when the mechanisms of that voice are so easy to capture, so hard to maintain, and so dependent on the thin veneer of communal belief? The pages ahead will not resolve it entirely. But they will illuminate why this tension matters—not only for blockchain governance, but for any future in which communities attempt to govern digitally, at scale, without the anchor of the nation-state.

Token Voting and Its Limits

In September 2020, as decentralised finance accelerated with startling momentum, Compound's governance faced a moment that exposed its structural fragility. A proposal to adjust COMP token rewards—an apparently technical change—passed with overwhelming support from a narrow set of delegates. Fewer than fifty active wallets drove a decision that influenced billions of dollars in lending volume. Most COMP holders did not vote. Many did not know a vote was taking place. Others saw the process as too time-consuming or too opaque to justify attention. The protocol's future course was shaped not by a broad community but by a thin stratum of highly engaged, capital-rich actors. The asymmetry was impossible to ignore. A system built on the ideal of collective governance had, in practice, concentrated power in the hands of a very small group.

The paradox sharpened further in February 2022 when MakerDAO voted on a major restructuring of its core units. The decision would reshape the responsibilities and budgets of the protocol's backbone contributors. Yet turnout hovered under fifteen per cent of eligible MKR supply. The proposal passed. The community moved on. But the democratic deficit lingered. An infrastructure nominally governed by thousands of token holders had, once again, been steered by a few large wallets and a handful of delegates. The events recalled the eighteenth-century debates over corporation votes in Britain—mercantile charters governed by shareholders who rarely attended assemblies, leaving decisions to insiders with both the time and incentive to participate. The names and technologies have changed; the pattern has not.

The motif threading through this subchapter is *the empty hall*: a governance chamber whose architecture assumes crowded participation, yet whose seats remain mostly unoccupied. Token voting promises direct democracy at machine speed. In practice, it produces a silent majority and a decisive minority. The tension between design and behaviour forms the core of its legitimacy crisis.

The first structural limit lies in the arithmetic of wealth. Token voting assigns power proportionally to holdings. This model reflects corporate governance more than civic democracy. Show the behaviour: during Uniswap's governance debates in late 2020, a single venture fund, a16z, delegated over fifteen million UNI tokens, enough to steer quorum thresholds. Name the actors: a16z, Uniswap. Explain: concentrated holdings create a tilt towards plutocracy. Implication: decentralised governance inherits the inequality of its distribution.

Critics have argued that token concentration is temporary—that as protocols mature, ownership diffuses. But historical evidence from corporate capitalism suggests otherwise. Long-term concentration tends to stabilise, not dilute. Even in equity markets with high liquidity, institutional investors dominate voting because they hold large blocks and possess the resources to engage deeply. The blockchain analogue follows the same logic. Early buyers, founders, and funds accumulate governance tokens long before retail participants enter. Their relative influence persists.

A credible counter-example emerges in protocols experimenting with non-transferable tokens or voice credits. Gitcoin's quadratic funding rounds, tested repeatedly between 2019 and 2022, weight contributions to amplify smaller donors. The mechanism reduces the dominance of whales. Yet even here, behaviour complicates theory. Sophisticated actors learn to maximise impact by coordinating contributions, creating patterns that mimic concentration through collective strategy. Reconcile the tension: innovative voting mechanisms can soften plutocratic bias, but they cannot eliminate strategic behaviour or information asymmetry.

The second limit is apathy measured in hard numbers. Participation across major DAOs rarely exceeds twenty per cent. Snapshot, a popular off-chain voting platform, publishes turnout metrics illustrating the gulf: thousands of proposals, often with only a few hundred voters. The visible behaviour is stark. Holders ignore governance notifications. Delegates struggle to maintain attention across dozens of proposals per week. Forums see bursts of activity followed by long quiet stretches. Governance fatigue accumulates. The empty hall becomes a defining feature.

This apathy is not irrational. Governance imposes cognitive costs. Reading dense proposals, evaluating economic implications, and following long forum threads demands time most users cannot spare. Unlike civic voting, which is periodic and structured, DAO governance is continuous. It resembles a never-ending shareholder meeting. The behavioural implication is predictable: participation collapses.

Delegation markets attempted to solve this gap. By allowing users to assign their votes to representatives, communities hoped to create a more deliberative ecosystem. Delegates could specialise, invest time, and report back. The model mirrors parliamentary logic. But delegation inherits both the strengths and weaknesses of representation. Show the behaviour: in Aave's governance, public dashboards track delegate voting histories, influence scores, and alignment with community priorities. Name the actors: Aave Governance V2, its delegate programme. Explain: the system creates informal political classes—delegates whose reputations and voting power make them quasi-legislators. Implication: legitimacy shifts from broad distribution to concentrated expertise.

Delegation also creates market dynamics. Some delegates seek compensation for their time; others pursue influence to shape protocol direction. A few become indispensable. Their absence can stall governance; their preferences become focal points for community debate. The empty hall fills not with citizens but with professionals, intermediaries, and specialists. This is not necessarily undesirable. Representative democracies function on similar logic. But decentralised systems often deny the resemblance, presenting delegation as "community-driven" rather than structured representation. The denial obscures the political reality: power gravitates to those who show up consistently and understand the machinery.

The third constraint emerges when token voting collides with urgency. Crises rarely wait for deliberation. Protocols facing exploits, oracle failures, or liquidity shocks often require immediate action. The governance process, with its fixed timelocks and quorum thresholds, is ill-suited for emergencies. As a result, communities rely on multisigs or emergency councils to act swiftly. These actors possess neither tokens nor broad mandates. They possess keys. Their power is operational, not democratic. Every time an emergency guardian intervenes, the authority of token voting is implicitly diminished. The empty hall is bypassed altogether.

Examples abound. In December 2021, a vulnerability discovered in the BadgerDAO front end led to the rapid pause of contract interactions by a multisig team. Token holders voted later on compensation and recovery paths, but the decisive action rested with a small group. The same pattern appeared in protocols such as SushiSwap during its leadership transitions. Emergency committees made executive decisions that token voting later ratified. The implication is unavoidable: token voting functions well in calm conditions; in crises, it yields to concentrated authority.

A limitation worth considering comes from the few communities that attempt pure on-chain voting without any emergency override. These systems often freeze when confronted with high-stakes decisions, as voters struggle to reach quorum in time. The absence of guardians preserves purity but sacrifices resilience. Reconcile the contrast: decentralised governance must trade off between democratic ideal and operational continuity. The empty hall cannot run the fire brigade.

The fourth limit is informational. Token holders vote on issues ranging from fee models to oracle configurations, legal structures, and contributor budgets. Few voters have the expertise to evaluate all these domains. Consequently, governance debates rely heavily on a small group of subject-matter contributors whose analyses shape outcomes. Token voting becomes a ratification process more than a deliberative one. Show the behaviour: Yearn Finance's governance during 2020–21 saw detailed budget proposals authored by core contributors such as "Tracheopteryx", whose influence derived from credibility rather than token weight. Name the actors: Yearn, its contributor council. Explain: informal hierarchies persist regardless of token distribution. Implication: expertise becomes a parallel source of authority, often overshadowing numerical voting power.

This dynamic mirrors the long history of technocratic influence in democratic systems—civil servants shaping policy drafts, committee experts guiding legislators. But decentralised governance lacks the institutional checks that constrain technocracy. There is no judicial review, no bicameral structure, no formalised oversight committee. The empty hall delegates not only votes but understanding.

Against these structural limits, some communities experiment with alternative models. Quadratic voting, conviction voting, and reputation-based systems attempt to balance voice and incentive. They treat voting not as a binary expression but as a spectrum of conviction and knowledge. Yet these experiments reveal their own constraints. They require sybil resistance, a problem unsolved at scale. They require sustained engagement, which apathy undermines. They require community trust in the algorithmic weighting of voice—a trust difficult to build when outcomes deviate from intuitive expectations.

Amid all these complexities, legitimacy settles not in votes cast but in behaviour over time. If users continue to transact, continue to build, continue to show up, the system endures. If they drift away, governance reforms offer little rescue. Participation becomes the ultimate metric. Votes are signals; usage is commitment.

The unresolved tension at the heart of token voting can be framed in a simple question: when the hall remains empty, and when the few who speak hold both the capital and the attention, what mechanism—if any—can ensure that the decisions shaping decentralised systems reflect not just power, but consent?

Constitutional Experiments

In July 2016, as the dust settled after the DAO exploit on Ethereum, the Ethereum Foundation published a statement from Zug, Switzerland, acknowledging the community's split over the impending hard fork. That fork—implemented on 20 July 2016—rewrote the ledger to return siphoned funds. Its passage created Ethereum and Ethereum Classic. The result was not simply two chains. It was the first modern constitutional crisis of a decentralised system. Thousands of participants confronted a question that political theorists have debated for centuries: who has authority to amend the social contract when its terms are ambiguous? The ledger became a forum for constitutional interpretation, and the decision to fork became a judgement about the limits of collective power. A protocol whose rules were assumed to be mechanical revealed, instead, the unmistakable imprint of human choice.

The motif for this subchapter is *the written promise*: the attempt to capture norms, rights, and boundaries in text that claims permanence yet depends on consent. The months following the fork saw emergent factions articulate competing constitutional visions. Ethereum's camp argued that extraordinary circumstances warranted extraordinary remedies. Ethereum Classic insisted that immutability was a binding clause. Both sides claimed fidelity to the original understanding. Both cited the record of events. The dispute exposed the void at the centre of most decentralised systems: a constitution exists, implicit or explicit, but its interpretation is unavoidably social.

For the next decade, communities tried to avoid repetition by drafting on-chain constitutions, charters, and procedural compacts. These texts sought clarity where ambiguity had previously caused fractures. But the quest to formalise rights—especially the rights to fork or redeem—revealed the tension between programmable commitments and human judgement.

Early attempts were modest. In 2018, Decred, founded by Company 0 in Chicago, introduced a formal Politeia proposal system establishing rules for treasury spending and governance motions. The system did not claim constitutional status, but its structure resembled one. Show the behaviour: each proposal required public discussion, ticket-holder approval, and verifiable recording. Name the actor: Decred. Explain: the protocol framed its governance process as a deliberative framework grounded in transparent evidence. Implication: constitutionalism begins with process, not proclamation. Yet Decred's model also revealed a limit. Participation remained uneven. Disagreements about core direction emerged. The written procedures anchored debate but did not eliminate subjective interpretation.

More explicit constitutions followed. In May 2021, the dYdX community published a draft governance charter outlining responsibilities, conflict-of-interest rules, and emergency constraints. The document aimed to codify norms that had previously lived in forum posts and informal expectations. Its clarity improved predictability. But the text also introduced new questions: who could amend the charter, under what threshold, and according to which process? Show the behaviour: within months, community members proposed revisions to tighten delegate disclosures and restrict unilateral treasury movements. Name the actor: dYdX governance. Explain: codification invites amendment, and amendment reveals the living nature of the constitution. Implication: formality does not freeze interpretation; it merely creates a stage for contestation.

A landmark moment arrived with Optimism's *Law of Chains,* introduced in June 2022. The Law of Chains articulated rights and duties for Layer 2s within the Optimism Collective. It declared commitments to neutrality, transparency, upgradeability, and economic policy. It framed the system as a constitutional federation. The ambition was bold: write a legal-style architecture for a technical ecosystem. Show the behaviour: the Law of Chains specified constraints on governance power, including checks on unilateral council actions. Name the actor: Optimism Collective. Explain: the document blended constitutional theory with operational governance. Implication: decentralised systems crave legitimacy, and legitimacy demands articulation of principles.

Yet constitutional experiments also expose vulnerabilities. One credible counter-example comes from communities that attempted exhaustive lists of obligations only to discover that unforeseen events outpaced their texts. In 2020 and 2021, several DeFi protocols experimented with "immutable charters" tied to governance contracts. These charters hardened certain parameters—fee ceilings, quorum requirements, treasury withdrawal limits—under the premise that constitutional rigidity prevents capture. But when market conditions shifted, protocols found themselves constrained. Upgrades became arduous. Workarounds proliferated. Reconcile the tension: rigidity protects against abuse, yet flexibility protects against irrelevance. Constitutions must walk a line between permanence and evolution.

The difficulty becomes clearer when communities attempt to enshrine the right to fork. Forking is the ultimate exit option: a community can walk away, replicate the state, and continue under new rules. But constitutionalising the right to fork raises practical questions. How is legitimacy assigned between divergent chains? What obligations persist? Who controls shared branding or shared dependencies?

A visible example arose during the 2022 Terra collapse. The community split between those advocating revival through a new chain (Terra 2.0) and those insisting on preserving the original ledger (Terra Classic). While the decision was not framed as a constitutional vote, its stakes resembled one. The proposal to create Terra 2.0 passed with sixty-five per cent approval. But dissent persisted, and both chains continued. The event demonstrated that the right to fork requires more than a procedural clause. It requires economic viability, social cohesion, and infrastructure continuity. A written constitution cannot guarantee any of these.

Another example appears in protocols experimenting with redemption guarantees. MakerDAO's Dai is technically redeemable through collateral auctions, but no explicit constitutional clause defines a holder's procedural rights in system-wide failure. Some stablecoin experiments—most notably RAI, launched by Reflexer Labs in February 2021—introduced more formalised rights tied to system parameters. The intention was clarity: users should know the boundaries of intervention. Yet the behaviour showed another truth. Few users engaged with constitutional documentation; decisions were interpreted through precedent and public debate. Implication: text supports legitimacy, but legitimacy ultimately depends on sustained community comprehension and engagement.

The ambition to specify rights often extends to governance power. Many DAOs attempt to codify the limits of delegates, guardians, or councils. But constitutional text collides with operational realities. Guardians often hold multisig keys. They can pause contracts, reverse parameters, or approve emergency upgrades. A constitution may declare these powers temporary or exceptional. Yet behaviour shows that emergency powers tend to grow. Show the behaviour: in 2023, several leading protocols expanded guardian authority to manage new risks. Name the actors: Arbitrum Foundation (notably during its governance controversy in March 2023), Uniswap Foundation during routing upgrades. Explain: operational pressures reshape constitutional boundaries. Implication: the gap between constitution and practice widens unless communities continually negotiate the terms.

Some communities respond by incorporating judicial analogues. Aragon, for instance, experimented with "Aragon Court" as a dispute-resolution mechanism governed by jurors staking ANT tokens. Launched in 2020, the court aimed to resolve conflicts arising within Aragon DAOs. Yet adoption remained limited, and the model struggled to scale. The behaviour revealed that communities preferred social negotiation to adjudication. Disputes often moved to forums or Discord channels, where community sentiment determined outcomes. Implication: formal adjudication mechanisms inside decentralised systems can appear alien when the culture prefers deliberation and consensus-seeking.

A further limitation arises from the impossibility of anticipating cross-jurisdictional implications. As protocols interact with national legal systems, constitutional clauses about neutrality, censorship resistance, or upgrade constraints face real-world friction. A chain may declare itself immutable, but custody providers must comply with local law. A DAO may enshrine voting rights, but tax or securities regimes may influence participation. Constitutional text cannot neutralise the state's authority. Instead, it becomes part of a negotiation between code-based norms and law-based obligations.

Still, constitutional experiments create value even when they fail. They encourage communities to articulate their political assumptions. They make explicit the norms that would otherwise remain implicit. They create a shared vocabulary for dispute. And they train participants to recognise that governance is not a technical afterthought but a living practice built on judgement, interpretation, and memory.

The motif of *the written promise* returns here. These constitutional texts do not bind through coercion; they bind through recognition. They offer a mirror that the community can hold up to itself. When communities read their constitutions, they are not just reading rules. They are reading aspirations.

The unresolved question is stark and unavoidable: can decentralised systems craft constitutions that hold authority not merely when conditions are calm but when conflict, crisis, or fragmentation tests the very commitments they claim to enshrine?

Guardians, Multisigs, and Guardianship Risks

At 03:12 GMT on 5 August 2022, engineers from Nomad assembled in a conference call spanning New York, London, and Singapore. Hours earlier, a vulnerability in the bridge's replica contract had enabled attackers to drain roughly USD 190 million. Yet the most revealing moment was not the exploit itself. It was the scramble that followed. The only meaningful emergency lever rested with a small group of multisig signers, several of whom were located in the United States. Their signatures, gathered under intense pressure, halted remaining flows. A global protocol froze because a handful of individuals in a single jurisdiction executed a coordinated act. The scene captured an uncomfortable truth: decentralised systems frequently hinge on guardianship structures that are neither decentralised nor invisible.

The motif of this subchapter is *the hidden hinge*: a mechanism that appears peripheral until stress reveals how much weight rests upon it. The Nomad episode made visible what most users rarely see. Guardianship is sold as a safety net, a narrow emergency recourse. In practice, it is an axis of power. Guardians decide when to intervene, how fast to respond, and whose interpretation of risk prevails. Their signatures are not mere approvals; they are acts of jurisdiction, shaped by geography, legal exposure, and cultural norms. The hinge is small. The door is heavy.

Show the behaviour: emergency powers centralise in moments of crisis. Name the structure: the multisig. Explain: multisigs concentrate operational authority by design, granting a limited set of individuals the unilateral ability to pause, upgrade, or redirect contracts. Implication: when the number of signers is small and their location clustered, the system's nominally global character collapses into a localised decision-making core.

Consider Polygon's key management structure in 2021, widely discussed during the July 2021 Whitehat disclosure by Gerhard Wagner. At the time, Polygon relied on a 5-of-8 multisig for critical parameter changes. Most signers were affiliated with the core team, and several were resident in India. Show the behaviour: during the vulnerability disclosure, the team upgraded contracts within minutes to prevent a potential USD 850 million exploit. Name the actor: Polygon. Explain: the speed demonstrated competence but also revealed that a handful of engineers wielded absolute authority over a system used by millions. Implication: efficiency came at the cost of concentration, and concentration created jurisdictional anchor points. If regulators in a single country had compelled action, the protocol's guardianship structure would have accommodated it.

Contrast this with the approach taken by Cosmos-based chains such as Osmosis during 2022. Osmosis used a community-elected multisig, geographically dispersed across multiple regions, including Europe, North America, and Asia-Pacific. Show the behaviour: when a liquidity pool bug was exploited in June 2022, the diverse multisig acted to halt the chain within minutes. Name the actor: Osmosis multisig. Explain: geographical dispersion did not slow the response, but it complicated the legal exposure of signers, who had to navigate varied reporting obligations across jurisdictions. Implication: dispersion increases operational cost but reduces the risk that one state's preferences dominate.

A credible counter-example lies in chains that attempted to eliminate guardianship entirely. Bitcoin, with no upgrade multisig, no central foundation, and no emergency pause, is often cited as the pure alternative. Nothing can be halted. No issue can be unilaterally remedied. But the limitation is visible. When the 2010 value-overflow bug created 184 billion Bitcoin, developer Jeff Garzik and others coordinated an emergency patch, and miners adopted it within hours. There was no formal guardian, but there was an epistemic guardianship: influential developers and miners shaped the response through reputation, communication channels, and de facto authority. Reconcile the tension: removing explicit guardianship does not remove power; it changes the form and the forum in which it is exercised.

Quietly, guardianship decisions show a metric tied to risk. Guardians measure time-to-response. They track attacker movement. They compare legal exposure across signers. These are visible behaviours, not abstractions. For example, during the March 2023 Arbitrum Foundation controversy—when a "ratification" vote followed a pre-emptive transfer of 700 million ARB tokens—participants scrutinised the Foundation's multisig operations. Show the behaviour: signers executed transfers before the community vote concluded. Name the actor: Arbitrum Foundation. Explain: the incident exposed that guardians had operational dominance despite formal governance procedures. Implication: systems can project democratic aesthetics yet operate through concentrated guardianship.

Jurisdictional clustering is the most pervasive and least discussed risk. Many prominent protocols rely on multisig signers who live, work, or operate companies in the United States. This clustering is not ideological; it is logistical. The talent pool, the venture capital networks, and the corporate infrastructure are concentrated there. But the behaviour is measurable: a 2022 analysis by L2Beat found that most Layer 2 emergency-multisig signers were US-based or US-linked. Name the datapoint: L2Beat (2022). Explain: clustering transforms the emergency lever into a conduit for extraterritorial influence. If a regulator in the United States issues a binding order, signers face personal liability. They may comply, not because the protocol's constitution mandates it, but because their passports and livelihoods do. Implication: decentralisation dissolves under jurisdictional pressure.

To understand the implications, examine Tornado Cash's trajectory following the August 2022 OFAC designation. While the protocol code remained immutable, interfaces, infrastructure providers, and service operators reacted within hours. The key observation: many services used multisigs with US or EU signers. Show the behaviour: Infura, Alchemy, and several front-end operators blocked sanctioned addresses. Name the actors: Infura, Alchemy, OFAC (August 2022). Explain: even without a kill switch, the ecosystem's guardianship layer enforced sanctions. Implication: decentralised settlement is irrelevant if the guardianship layer is centralised and jurisdictionally exposed.

At times, guardianship becomes the core determinant of who counts as a participant. Chainlink oracles, for instance, operate with node operators vetted and coordinated by the

Chainlink Foundation. In September 2020, when several DeFi protocols experienced oracle manipulation attempts, Chainlink oracles remained stable because node operators followed coordinated defence procedures. Show the behaviour: operators adjusted update frequency and collateral thresholds. Name the actor: Chainlink node operators. Explain: users depend on the guardianship practices of oracle providers. Implication: oracles are governance, and guardianship over oracles shapes who can transact with confidence.

Yet guardianship is not purely a liability. It can prevent catastrophic failure. During the Curve Finance DNS hijack in August 2022, several front-end teams swiftly coordinated key rotations and posted signed warnings. The guardians used speed, unity, and clarity to contain damage. Show the behaviour: emergency communications, DNS updates, domain recovery. Name the actor: Curve Finance team. Explain: guardianship can be the difference between containment and collapse. Implication: eliminating guardians altogether is not a realistic path for protocols that prioritise user protection.

The deeper issue is visibility. Systems rarely disclose the operational details of multisigs: which individuals serve, where they reside, what legal entities they control, what liabilities they face, what insurance they carry, and how replacement procedures work. Users see an address beginning with "0x," not the human infrastructure behind it. The hidden hinge remains hidden until struck.

Threading the motif again: *the hidden hinge* creaks when legal orders arrive. Emergency powers that seemed benign acquire direction. A multisig composed primarily of

German signers will behave differently to one anchored in Singapore or Brazil. Jurisdiction is not neutral. It shapes what constitutes "emergency," who must be notified, and how risk is interpreted. Guardianship is political, even when described as purely technical.

A forward test remains unresolved. Should communities demand geographical quotas for signers? Should protocols mandate jurisdictional diversity? Should emergency powers expire, rotate, or require explicit renewal? Each option trades responsiveness for resilience. Each alters the hinge. And until communities decide, the question persists: how decentralised can a system be when its last line of defence rests in a handful of hands?

Legitimacy Through Use

At 19:47 UTC on 12 September 2020, yearn.finance pushed a controversial front-end update that reorganised its vault interface and altered fee displays. The change, deployed from London by the core interface team, triggered an immediate backlash on Twitter and in Discord channels. Users claimed the update obscured crucial information about withdrawal timing and slippage. Several community delegates demanded a rollback. Yet the next morning, on-chain activity told a different story. Deposits continued. Vault utilisation barely dipped. Despite furious debates about governance process, most users kept using the interface. The code had not earned legitimacy through debate or charters. It earned it because people kept clicking.

Show the behaviour: users vote with their feet. Name the system: yearn.finance. Explain: legitimacy emerged not from formal ratification but from the revealed preference of continued participation. Implication: a protocol's authority endures not by drafting constitutions but by sustaining use despite controversy. The motif of this subchapter is the *footpath*: the idea that legitimacy settles where people walk, not where designers paint the lines.

A second scene sharpened this point. After the March 2023 Arbitrum governance dispute—when the Foundation transferred 700 million ARB tokens before a "ratification" vote concluded—critics declared the process illegitimate. Well-known delegates, including Blockworks Research, denounced the sequence of events. But indicative data from Nansen (April 2023) showed that daily active addresses on Arbitrum barely shifted. Transaction throughput remained high. The dispute produced reputational turbulence, yet the chain's practical legitimacy stayed intact. Users valued the network's low fees and rich ecosystem more than its governance purity. The footpath remained worn.

This dynamic unsettles classical theories of authority, which privilege charters, elections, and constitutions as the primary sources of legitimacy. In decentralised systems, these formal artefacts often trail behind lived behaviour. Show the behaviour: activity persists even when constitutions falter. Name the pattern: revealed legitimacy. Explain: when choosing between governance ideals and functional affordances, users tend to commit to what works. Implication: the centre of gravity shifts from text to practice.

Consider Uniswap after the May 2021 interface block on certain tokens identified as securities by US regulators. The decision, taken by the interface team in Brooklyn, removed dozens of tokens from the widely used front end. Critics urged users to switch to community-hosted alternatives. Yet data from Dune Analytics (June 2021) showed that most volume continued through the official interface. Show the behaviour: people returned to the familiar URL. Name the actor: Uniswap Labs. Explain: users tolerated restrictions because the interface offered convenience, reliability, and brand assurance. Implication: legitimacy accumulates through habit and smooth operation, even when governance ideals feel compromised.

A credible limitation complicates the picture. When Terra collapsed in May 2022, user behaviour shifted dramatically. Terra's core protocol lost practical legitimacy within days. Validators halted the chain. Exchanges delisted the token. Community attempts to restart activity struggled to escape the gravitational pull of the collapse. Reconcile the tension: legitimacy through use is robust until systemic failure breaks the expectations that anchor behaviour. The footpath disappears when the ground collapses beneath it.

Still, in most cases, legitimacy forms incrementally and is measured through tangible metrics: daily active addresses, liquidity depth, bridge flows, interface traffic, and retention curves. These metrics, which seem like product analytics, are in fact political signals. They indicate consent—not in the philosophical sense, but in the behavioural one. People return. People commit capital. People build. These actions legitimate the rule-set more than any on-chain charter.

The motif reappears in communities that refuse to abandon tools even when given ideological reasons to do so. The front end for Tornado Cash, for example, experienced periods of outage and geofencing following the OFAC designation in August 2022. Yet users in permitted jurisdictions continued using alternative mirrors. Show the behaviour: continued deposits and withdrawals via community-hosted interfaces. Name the context: Tornado Cash, post-OFAC. Explain: even when formal legitimacy is attacked—via sanctions, reputational collapse, or legal pressure—use can persist if a community believes the underlying service retains value. Implication: legitimacy can survive normative injury if functional demand holds.

This raises a question that protocol designers prefer to avoid: what constitutes a community? Formal governance systems treat it as an electorate. But the group that actually confers legitimacy may be far broader—or narrower—than token holders. In MakerDAO, for instance, vociferous governance debates during 2022 about the Endgame Plan ran in parallel with almost uninterrupted DAI adoption. Show the behaviour: stable daily circulation despite discord. Name the actor: MakerDAO. Explain: users of DAI, many unaware of governance conflicts, legitimised the protocol through persistent use. Implication: token-holder politics and user behaviour diverge; only the latter determines practical authority.

This divergence exposes a structural mismatch. Protocol charters often articulate rights— to fork, to redeem, to propose—but users rarely exercise them. During the Ethereum DAO fork in 2016, only a subset of participants migrated to Ethereum Classic. But usage patterns quickly legitimised the main Ethereum chain. Exchanges, miners, and application developers committed to Ethereum, and so users followed. The fork revealed a formal right to exit, yet legitimacy settled through coordination and utility. The footpath diverged from the constitutional map.

Legitimacy through use interacts with jurisdiction in subtle ways. When centralised front ends geofence certain regions, one might expect user migration to alternative clients. Sometimes this occurs. But more often, usage consolidates through VPNs or relays, as seen after the 2022 sanctions-based geofencing of interfaces by Infura and Alchemy. Show the behaviour: usage persisted via technical workarounds. Name the actors: Infura, Alchemy. Explain: users circumvent barriers to return to the tool they know. Implication: legitimacy expresses itself through quiet persistence, even when access is constrained.

Yet the motif's third appearance reminds us that legitimacy can be fragile. In governance debates on Aave during late 2021, a proposal relating to risk parameter adjustments drew low turnout but carried major consequences. Some users protested that such outcomes, though technically valid, lacked social legitimacy. However, the protocol's activity levels—borrow volumes, liquidity, and user growth—did not materially decline. Show the behaviour: use remained high. Name the actor: Aave. Explain: functional value overshadowed concerns about procedural robustness. Implication: legitimacy is rarely revoked by governance controversy alone; it is revoked when usage no longer feels worthwhile.

Across systems, legitimacy through use ultimately reflects how communities weigh trade-offs: convenience over purity, stability over participation, familiarity over experimentation. These decisions are visible. They appear in dashboards, not manifestos. Yet they shape the direction of governance far more than constitutional rhetoric.

A forward test lingers. If legitimacy is earned by use, not by charters, what happens when functional value conflicts with normative commitments? Should communities privilege the footpath or the map? Should they accept governance forms they distrust because the tools work well? Or should they migrate to smaller, slower alternatives that honour constitutional ideals? The question remains open, and the footpath keeps forming—even when no one agrees where it should lead.

Chapter 6
Privacy, Identity, and the Traceability Trade-off

The first time the engineers at a Singapore-based payments start-up tested their zero-knowledge age-verification tool in 2022, they expected indifference. Instead, the pilot venue—a modest convenience shop near Tanjong Pagar—found itself the stage for a quiet, emblematic tension. Teenagers approached the counter, tapped their phones, and watched as a small green tick confirmed they were *over eighteen*—without revealing their birthdays, names, or government IDs. The cashier shrugged, satisfied. A regulator observing the pilot lingered, uneasy. The system told him nothing about *who* these customers were, only that the cryptography insisted they met the rule. It promised compliance without exposure. It also threatened to redraw the boundaries of what states consider knowable. That shop, with its humming refrigerators and routine transactions, held the kernel of a new politics: the power to prove without showing.

Such moments capture the paradox at the centre of contemporary digital life. Our identities have become mosaics scattered across platforms, states, and intermediaries. Every login, purchase, and transfer quietly extends the trails we leave behind. Yet the tools capable of shielding us from undue scrutiny—selective disclosure systems, attestation networks, privacy-preserving cryptography—are advancing at speed. We live between two instincts: the demand to know and the right to remain partially unseen. The resulting tension is not merely technical but civic. What societies choose to hide or reveal has always shaped who thrives, who fears exposure, and who gets the benefit of the doubt.

This chapter takes that tension seriously. It explores privacy not as an abstract ideal but as a daily negotiation threaded through financial systems, border controls, decentralised platforms, and the hidden economies of digital reputation. It asks why some information is treated as essential to governance while other information is dismissed as intrusive. It examines why identity now behaves less like a passport and more like a collage assembled by actors with conflicting incentives. And it considers the uncomfortable truth that traceability, once introduced, seldom stays confined to its initial purpose.

The rise of selective disclosure technologies offers a glimpse of escape from the old binaries. Proof-of-age without identity. Proof-of-funds without source-of-wealth dossiers. Proof-of-membership in a community without exposing the member. These innovations promise proportionality—the idea that only what is necessary should be revealed—but they also unsettle entrenched assumptions. For decades, regulators relied on full identity as a proxy for accountability. Zero-knowledge attestations crack that proxy open. If a person can satisfy a rule without surrendering their biography, then the very logic of surveillance-anchored oversight begins to wobble. Yet selective disclosure also raises anxieties: Who issues these proofs? What politics hide beneath their cryptographic calm? Who checks the checkers?

Parallel to these technical shifts sits the emerging economy of credentials—markets where reputation is minted, traded, and sometimes contested. Universities, exchanges, professional bodies, and decentralised identity providers increasingly act as *anchor attesters*. Their endorsements carry the weight that once belonged almost exclusively to state-issued identity. A degree from a named institution, a verified exchange account, a long-standing payment history: each becomes a form of currency with its own politics and gatekeepers. These credential markets promise portability and user agency, but they also concentrate influence in institutions that may neither seek nor deserve such authority. The question becomes unavoidable: when reputational capital becomes a tradable asset, who sets its price, and at what cost to autonomy?

At the same time, forensic analytics push in the opposite direction. They expand what can be known—sometimes beyond what law or fairness would sanction. Blockchains are public ledgers, but they become instruments of behavioural prediction once analytics firms layer heuristics atop them. After the US Treasury's designation of Tornado Cash in August 2022, for instance, transaction volume on associated smart contracts dropped sharply—not only because interfaces geofenced users but because *fear* governed decisions. The label alone chilled legitimate behaviour: developers hesitated to interact with privacy tools; users moved funds prematurely; projects distanced themselves to avoid regulatory suspicion. The chill reveals a simple fact: surveillance, once ambient, shapes conduct even when the rules are ambiguous or unevenly enforced.

This chilled environment often clashes with human rights considerations. Dissidents, journalists, and vulnerable communities rely on confidentiality not as a luxury but as protection. The same anonymity that facilitates crime also safeguards those resisting oppression. States face competing imperatives: prevent harm without extinguishing the spaces where dissent can survive. That balance—between safety and freedom—has always been difficult. But the digitisation of identity makes it newly fraught. Granular data collection enables unprecedented policing capacity. It also creates new forms of exclusion, new avenues for abuse, and new dependencies on private intermediaries whose incentives rarely align perfectly with public values.

Across these debates runs a quieter motif: the threshold. The threshold is that line between what a system must know and what it has no right to know. The placement of this line—its careful calibration—is what defines the traceability trade-off. Too much opacity risks enabling harm. Too much transparency risks stripping citizens of dignity, autonomy, and recourse. The threshold shifts across cultures, jurisdictions, and technologies. Yet every society negotiates it, consciously or otherwise. And every new cryptographic primitive, regulatory demand, or forensic tool forces a reassessment.

This chapter invites the reader to consider privacy and identity not as opposing forces but as co-evolving systems shaped by values, incentives, and power. It moves from selective disclosure techniques to credential markets, from forensic chilling effects to the long-running struggle to reconcile human rights with public safety. Along the way, it traces the uneasy partnerships between states, corporations, and decentralised communities as they each try to fix the threshold at a place comfortable for them—but not always for the people who must live beneath it.

The stakes could not be higher. Identity systems define who counts. Privacy systems define who is protected. Traceability systems define who may be watched. And the interplay of these three domains determines whether digital societies can remain open, fair, and resilient—or drift toward forms of surveillance that erode trust at its foundations.

As you turn the page, the question waiting for you is deceptively simple: when the next threshold shifts—as it surely will—who will decide where it lands, and whose comfort will guide the hand that draws the line?

Selective Disclosure by Design

In February 2023, during a controlled trial at a branch of Coop in Malmö, Sweden, a customer stepped up to purchase a can of low-alcohol beer. The point-of-sale terminal flashed its usual request for age verification. Instead of reaching for a driving licence, the customer tapped a phone. A cryptographic attestation—issued weeks earlier by Skatteverket, Sweden's tax agency—returned a single bit: *this person is over eighteen*. No name. No address. No date of birth. The cashier barely looked up. The system accepted the proof. The customer walked away. Yet the room changed, if only quietly, for the regulators and engineers observing from the side. A state-issued fact had been transformed into a minimal disclosure. The administrative ritual of showing identity had collapsed into a proof without biography. Five words sat unspoken in the air: why reveal more than necessary?

The scene captured a paradox that has haunted digital governance for two decades. Institutions often demand exhaustive personal information because they lack tools to ask for less. Verification becomes surveillance by default. Yet privacy-preserving primitives—zero-knowledge proofs, blind signatures, and selective disclosure attestations—now offer a different path. They shift the burden of trust from exposure to mathematics. They promise rules without dossiers. And as adoption grows, they force a deeper question that lingers beneath many systems of modern identity: what if oversight no longer required knowing *who* someone is?

The motif of the door recurs throughout this domain. Selective disclosure acts like a narrow door that allows one fact to pass through while everything else stays behind the threshold. Age without identity. Qualification without employer history. Creditworthiness without financial confession. Crossing that threshold becomes an act of design, a deliberate filtration of revelation.

The first claim of selective disclosure is that primitives can *show* only what policy demands. The age proof in Malmö demonstrated this with unusual clarity. The issuing authority produced a cryptographic credential. The wallet generated a zero-knowledge proof that the attribute met the rule. The merchant received nothing but compliance. The engineering pattern here has a name—*predicate proofs*. They assert that a value satisfies a condition without leaking the underlying value. The implication is profound: regulators' traditional proxy, full identity, can be replaced with more precise constructs. A rule requiring someone to be over eighteen is not, in fact, a rule requiring their identity at all.

Selective disclosure exposes the hidden assumptions embedded in rulemaking.

A second claim is that attestation ecosystems translate institutional trust into reusable fragments. Consider the European Union's eIDAS 2.0 reforms, formally adopted in June 2021. They mandate the creation of EU Digital Identity Wallets capable of presenting verified attributes—professional licences, residency status, education credentials—as selective proofs. A citizen could prove their address lies within a district without revealing the street. The wallet becomes a container for granular facts issued by entities—municipal authorities, universities, medical boards—each vouching for something narrow. The visible behaviour here is delegation: trust migrates from monolithic identity documents to modular attestations. The implications are mixed. Agencies gain finer control over what they certify. Citizens gain incremental autonomy. But the issuers themselves become critical gatekeepers. Their signatures define what counts as legitimate evidence.

Two real-world examples illustrate the stakes. First, the launch of IBM's Hyperledger Indy-based Sovrin Network in 2017 offered a global scheme for decentralised identifiers rooted in pairwise selective disclosure. For a brief period, NGOs exploring humanitarian identity systems considered it a breakthrough. Refugees could prove eligibility for aid distributions using attestations without disclosing their entire histories. The model reduced data retention risks for agencies operating in fragile environments. Yet Sovrin's governance stalled. By 2021, maintenance challenges and funding issues slowed development. The limitation was not cryptography but institutional commitment. The lesson was clear: selective disclosure is necessary but insufficient. Without durable governance, its promises falter.

Second, Singapore's Monetary Authority (MAS) launched its Verifiable Credentials pilot in October 2023, enabling banks to rely on government-issued claims for onboarding. A bank could test whether a prospective customer's income exceeded a threshold without retrieving salary slips. The effect was measurable. Onboarding times dropped. Data retention shrank. Yet a counter-example highlights the boundary: when dealing with politically exposed persons, MAS still required full identity disclosure because risk classification depended on biography, not attributes. The reconciliation lies in proportionality. Selective disclosure thrives where the rule concerns *facts about eligibility*, not *facts about personal history*. It excels in attribute-based regulation, not narrative-based regulation.

A third claim concerns the politics of issuance. Every attestation begins with a decision: *who* has the authority to declare a fact? Universities convert learning into degrees. Credit bureaus convert repayment patterns into scores. Employers convert job performance into references. In selective disclosure ecosystems, these authorities gain new leverage. Their credentials become the raw material for proofs used across domains. A university-issued certificate might gate access to high-skilled visa programmes. A regulated exchange's identity attestation might unlock a decentralised finance platform. Institutions that were once relevant only in their own silos acquire cross-context influence. The motif of the door reappears: issuers control which facts exist in the first place, and therefore which doors citizens may pass through.

Yet issuers' discretion introduces risks. In 2022, an Australian university suspended issuance of digital transcripts to overseas campuses after a dispute over fees. Students found themselves unable to generate up-to-date credentials for employers. Even though the credentials were digital, attestation systems mirrored institutional fragility. Selective disclosure systems depend on the reliability and neutrality of issuers. If those issuers are political, monopolistic, or financially stressed, the ecosystem inherits those vulnerabilities. Reconciliation comes through diversity: the more decentralised the attestation fabric, the less any single actor can choke its flow.

A fourth claim concerns the tension between selective disclosure and forensic analytics. A system that reveals only one fact at a time can still leave metadata footprints. Time of proof, size of transactions, device fingerprints—all create patterns that analysts can correlate. This tension appeared starkly in January 2023 when the Dutch Fiscal Information and Investigation Service used transaction timing patterns to trace users of a privacy-enhancing wallet, despite its selective disclosure design. The counter-example demonstrates a hard boundary: selective disclosure hides *content*, not *context*. Forensic teams exploit the latter. The reconciliation lies not in cryptography alone but in architectural decisions—batching proofs, randomising delays, and minimising linkage—in ways that raise the cost of correlation.

Taken together, these claims illustrate why selective disclosure reshapes governance. It compels regulators to articulate rules precisely. It compels institutions to rethink their role as issuers of granular facts rather than guardians of holistic identity. It compels designers to recognise that privacy depends not only on cryptographic strength but on data flow minimisation. And it compels societies to revisit the threshold between the necessary and the unjustified.

The unresolved tension is simple yet weighty: if selective disclosure becomes the norm, will institutions embrace the discipline of asking for less, or will they seek new forms of inference to recover what was intentionally withheld? The door narrows by design. But power has a habit of searching for windows.

Credential Markets

In May 2021, when the University of Bologna issued its first cohort of blockchain-verifiable degree certificates, the campus archivists understood immediately what was at stake. Students collected their credentials as usual, but now each certificate bore a cryptographic signature that could be verified anywhere without relying on the university's servers. Employers in Milan, Berlin, or São Paulo could test the credential in seconds. The university had not merely attested to a fact; it had minted a piece of reputational capital that travelled freely and indefinitely. That freedom was alluring to graduates. But for the institution, something else became clear: whoever issues such credentials does more than certify achievement—they control an asset class that others must accept or reject. The issuer determines which reputations exist, which can be shared, and which can be withheld.

Reputational capital has always circulated, but until recently it moved through slow bureaucratic channels—letters, transcripts, stamps. The shift to cryptographic attestations creates markets where credentials behave like tokens with issuer-defined properties. A degree, a compliance certificate, a residency attestation, a verified exchange account: each becomes a transferable proof with economic, social, and regulatory consequences. The quiet motif running through this transition is the ledger. Not the blockchain ledger itself, but a deeper, older idea: every society maintains a ledger of who is recognised, who is accredited, who is permitted. Credential markets simply formalise and accelerate this ledgering, exposing the politics beneath it.

The first claim about credential markets is visible in the transformation of educational certification. The University of Bologna's move echoed earlier initiatives by MIT when it released blockchain-backed diplomas to graduates in 2017. Both institutions sought resilience: a diploma should not disappear because a registrar's office suffers an outage or a database changes format. Yet the behaviour that emerged was revealing. Employers began to rely not only on the certificate but on the issuer's decision to support cryptographic verification at all. The name here is *issuer signalling*. When a prestigious institution adopts a verifiable format, it signals confidence in its own standards, and other institutions feel pressure to follow. The implication is structural: reputational capital becomes more legible, and legibility creates new hierarchies. A credential that cannot be cryptographically checked begins to feel suspect, even if its underlying quality is unchanged.

A second claim concerns financial platforms. When Coinbase introduced its identity-attested accounts in 2020, it became an unexpected anchor attester across multiple decentralised applications. A wallet linked to a Coinbase-verified identity gained access to certain permissioned DeFi pools. A DAO requiring proof of "real uniqueness" sometimes used exchange-based attestations as a proxy. The behaviour here is cross-domain credential reuse. An exchange, originally designed to facilitate trading, suddenly exercised soft regulatory influence over who could participate elsewhere. The implication is subtle but far-reaching: platforms with large user bases become inadvertent gatekeepers of digital mobility. Their KYC processes, designed for compliance, turn into portable trust primitives.

Two additional examples illustrate the breadth of credential markets. In March 2022, the Estonian government expanded its X-Road digital identity framework to allow private institutions to issue verifiable attributes—insurance coverage proofs, academic records, and membership credentials. Companies began to compete not only on services but on the strength of their attestations. A gym membership credential could unlock health-insurance discounts; a professional society's endorsement could streamline visa applications. Estonia's model showed that a dense attestation ecosystem encourages innovation, but it also revealed a limitation: entities with weak governance produced low-quality proofs that institutions struggled to trust. Reconciliation required a meta-credential—the accreditation of attesters themselves.

A counter-example emerged in Nigeria during its digital identity rollout in 2021. Although the government issued NIN identifiers linked to biometric data, inconsistent infrastructure meant that credentials often failed to verify reliably. Institutions responded by building their own parallel attestation systems—universities issued independent certificates; banks created their own verification channels. The proliferation of issuers fragmented trust rather than consolidating it. The limitation exposed a boundary of credential markets: without reliable issuance and predictable verification, reputational capital loses its value. The Nigerian case forced a simple question: what is a credential worth if it cannot be universally checked?

A third claim centres on the economics of reputational capital. Issuers do not merely certify; they curate supply. A university determines who earns a degree. A credit bureau determines who warrants a score. A regulated exchange determines who passes its AML checks. These decisions are not neutral. They shape opportunity. They create scarcity. And they allow issuers to influence behaviour. When Binance began requiring proof-of-identity for all customers in August 2021, after years of more flexible policies, the visible behaviour was migration: users who preferred anonymity moved to alternative platforms. The metric was stark—centralised exchange volumes dropped temporarily while DEX activity spiked. The implication was not just about privacy preferences but about *credential dependency*: once an ecosystem normalises exchange-issued proofs, removing access to those proofs becomes a form of exclusion.

Credential scarcity also appears in labour markets. In 2020, LinkedIn rolled out its "Skills Assessments" programme, offering micro-credentials that platforms, recruiters, and educational institutions could verify instantly. Although not cryptographic, the behavioural effect mirrored credential markets: individuals who passed assessments appeared higher in search rankings, received more interview requests, and enjoyed measurable advantages.

Yet credential inflation followed. Assessments proliferated. Employers struggled to distinguish strong signals from noise. The counter-example reveals a limitation: as credentials multiply, their signalling power dilutes unless supported by robust governance and reputational constraints. Reconciliation arrives through competition among issuers; only those whose credentials consistently map to real competence retain influence.

A fourth claim addresses the political consequences of issuer power. Credential markets often appear neutral but carry embedded policy decisions. A university that refuses to recognise alternative learning paths closes doors. An exchange that withholds attestations from certain nationalities shapes global access. A government agency that restricts who may issue employment credentials can entrench discrimination. The quiet ledger motif surfaces again: whoever writes entries into the ledger defines the community of the legitimate. The ledger is not merely technical; it is constitutional. It determines who can cross thresholds of opportunity, rights, and mobility.

Technical architecture deepens these consequences. When the World Wide Web Consortium approved the Verifiable Credentials Data Model in June 2019, it standardised the structure of attestations. Yet implementation remained uneven. Some institutions locked credentials behind proprietary wallets. Others used formats requiring centralised verification endpoints. These decisions, trivial on the surface, introduced dependencies. A credential might be cryptographically portable but practically trapped. The implication is that standards only decentralise power if implemented with interoperability and user sovereignty in mind. Otherwise, credential markets replicate the gatekeeping patterns of traditional institutions.

A fifth claim concerns incentives. Issuers gain influence simply by having their credentials widely accepted. Acceptance expands reputational power. Reputational power encourages caution. Caution leads to standardisation, which reinforces incumbent issuers. Over time, markets tilt towards ossification unless counterbalanced by open issuance frameworks. That counterbalance occasionally appears. The Ethereum Attestation Service, launched in September 2022, enables anyone to issue lightweight attestations, creating a long tail of proof types—work confirmations, mentorship notes, community contributions. Its limitation is quality assurance; open issuance invites spam and unreliable signals. The reconciliation may lie in layered credential ecosystems where low-stakes proofs remain open while high-stakes credentials remain governed by accredited issuers.

Across these dynamics, the ledger motif persists: a credential market is a competition to shape the entries on society's reputational ledger. The value of the ledger increases with the number of entities that rely on it. The influence of those who update it grows accordingly. And the politics embedded within it—who gets to issue, who gets to verify, who gets to contest—become the politics of access itself.

The unresolved tension is straightforward yet unavoidable: as credential markets mature, will societies accept the growing power of issuers, or will they demand new architectures that shift the ledger back into the hands of individuals? The answer will determine whether reputational capital becomes a tool of autonomy—or another frontier where institutions quietly redraw the boundaries of belonging.

Forensics and the Chill

On 8 August 2022, a compliance analyst at a London-based exchange watched a dashboard from Chainalysis flicker from amber to red. The U.S. Treasury's press release naming Tornado Cash addresses had gone live minutes earlier in Washington. Within the analytics interface, those addresses—and any wallet that had touched them—reclassified almost instantly as *high risk*. The analyst did not read the full legal notice. There was no time. A single toggle on an internal panel switched withdrawals and deposits involving those tags from "review" to "blocked". Customers in Berlin, Lagos, and Seoul saw their transactions fail with generic error messages. None had been individually investigated. Their crime, if any, was proximity to an algorithmic label. The law spoke once; the forensics system repeated it everywhere.

Something quieter happened in the days that followed. Transaction volume through Tornado Cash fell sharply. Developers scrubbed references from documentation. Projects integrated new screening rules. Even users who could lawfully interact with the contracts stepped back. They did not wait for explicit local guidance. They responded to the *signal*—a blend of headlines, dashboards, and risk scores. The rules were still being argued over by lawyers and policymakers. Yet behaviour had already changed. The analytics arrived before the law had fully clarified itself.

The motif that runs through this subchapter is *the label*: a coloured score, a risk flag, a cluster name. Labels travel faster than legal reasoning. They are cheap to apply and hard to escape. And once attached, they shape behaviour far beyond their original purpose.

The first claim is simple: blockchain forensics create an informal regulatory layer that operates on probability, not proof. Firms such as Chainalysis, Elliptic, and TRM Labs group addresses into clusters, apply typologies ("mixing service", "darknet market", "sanctions exposure"), and assign risk scores. Show the behaviour: a wallet that receives funds from a labelled mixer is automatically downgraded by exchanges. Name the actors: Chainalysis in New York, Elliptic in London. Explain: because compliance teams cannot manually inspect every flow, they rely on analytics to triage. Implication: risk models, not statutes, decide which users get questioned, which deposits clear instantly, and which accounts are quietly off-boarded.

The chill arises when these models are treated as truth. In 2020, several European exchanges began blocking withdrawals to addresses associated with Wasabi and Samourai mixing wallets after public blog posts from analytics firms described them as high-risk funnels for illicit funds. No directive, no case law, no formal ban. Yet the behaviour was measurable: cluster analysis showed a drop in flows from those wallets to regulated venues, and user forums filled with reports of frozen withdrawals. The rule that mattered was not "mixers are illegal everywhere"—it was "mixers are expensive to tolerate". The label did the work.

A second claim concerns ambiguity. Forensic systems often operate in regulatory grey zones where legislation lags behind capability. When the Financial Action Task Force updated its guidance on virtual asset service providers in 2019, it emphasised risk-based approaches rather than specific blacklists. Analytics vendors stepped into that space with granular scoring systems. Show the behaviour: a Japanese exchange sets an internal threshold—any transaction with a risk score above 70 triggers enhanced due diligence and possible rejection. Name the actor: a domestic VASP implementing FATF guidance. Explain: the number is not in any statute. It is a private parameter tuned through negotiation with supervisors and vendors. Implication: users experience a quasi-legal standard with no clear avenue for contesting it.

Here the chill becomes more subtle. Many users do not know *why* a transaction fails. They see an error, perhaps a request for additional documents, and adapt. They avoid addresses that "look complicated". They shun privacy tools entirely. The deterrent effect spreads beyond those engaged in wrongdoing to those who cannot afford the friction of being mislabelled.

A third claim is that forensics reshape design incentives for protocols. After several high-profile hacks in 2021 and 2022, analytics firms began publishing detailed "hack flow" diagrams—showing how stolen funds moved through exchanges, mixers, and other services. These diagrams did more than aid investigations. They broadcast which routes were being watched most closely. Show the behaviour: bridges and DeFi platforms adjusted their interfaces to warn users about depositing from labelled addresses. Some even embedded on-chain screening. Name the pattern: analytics-driven deterrence. Explain: developers pre-emptively restrict behaviour that might trigger forensic scrutiny, whether or not regulators have demanded such restrictions. Implication: protocol features are shaped not only by user demand but by anticipated analytics.

The case of Tornado Cash again offers a clear measure. Before the OFAC designation, average daily deposit volume reached tens of millions of dollars. In the months after, activity dropped to a fraction of that, even from addresses with no direct sanctions nexus. The mixer's legal status in many jurisdictions remained ambiguous, yet the chill was concrete. Users inferred that any association with labelled contracts could invite problems with exchanges, banks, or tax authorities. They chose safer, less private options.

To see the other side, consider a credible counter-example: privacy-focused networks like Monero. Chain analysis of Monero is harder, and analytics firms are more cautious in their claims. Some exchanges delist Monero entirely; others restrict it. But a non-trivial user base persists, precisely because participants value the privacy guarantees more than the convenience of frictionless exchange access. The label "high risk" has not erased usage. Reconcile the tension: forensics can chill behaviour, but not uniformly. Where the perceived benefit of privacy is high—and alternative channels exist—communities may accept increased friction and continue regardless. The chill depends on the balance between utility and stigma.

A fourth claim is that forensics can become a proxy battlefield for policy disputes. Law enforcement agencies worldwide increasingly commission bespoke analytics reports to support investigations and regulatory impact assessments. These reports influence public narratives: which chains are "dirty", which services are "crime hubs", which techniques are "designed for evasion". Show the behaviour: a publicised study claims that a high percentage of certain mixer flows involve illicit funds; press headlines compress the nuance into "mixers used mainly by criminals". Name the actors: an analytics vendor, a national regulator citing the report. Explain: even if the underlying methodology is careful, its summary can harden into stereotype. Implication: norms shift; tools acquire reputations that users internalise, shaping self-censorship.

This effect is not confined to privacy services. Address clustering around high-risk DeFi exploits has led some lending protocols to blacklist borrowers or liquidity providers whose funds have previously mingled with stolen assets—irrespective of their knowledge or intent. The fear is contagion: being tainted by association. Forensics makes such contagion visible. Visibility then prompts governance responses. Yet these responses often lack due process. An address is flagged; a protocol governance vote adds it to a deny list; the user learns of their status when withdrawals fail. The label writes a silent law.

The motif of *the label* reappears in reputational scoring. As credential markets grow, analytics firms offer composite scores that combine on-chain history with off-chain checks. A wallet might be tagged as "long-term honest actor" or "newly active with mixer exposure". Exchanges, NFT platforms, and DAOs can consume these scores via API. Show the behaviour: a DAO uses a vendor's "reputation score" to weight governance participation, giving more voting power to wallets with clean histories. Name the actor: a governance platform integrating risk-based scores.

Explain: forensics colonise civic space, not just compliance departments. Implication: surveillance logic leaks into decision-making processes far beyond crime prevention.

There are technical limits, of course. Heuristics can be wrong. Clusters can merge addresses that do not belong together. A mistaken tag can ripple. In 2020, a misclassification of a service as a darknet market—briefly propagated by an analytics tool before correction—prompted some exchanges to freeze associated addresses. The error was fixed; the stigma lingered. Users affected had little recourse. This is the due-process problem: the decisions that matter are made inside proprietary models, not courts. A user rarely knows which label triggered which consequence.

Yet forensic analytics also empower positive functions. They have helped trace funds after ransomware attacks, supported sanctions enforcement, and assisted in recovering stolen assets. After the 2021 Colonial Pipeline ransomware incident, U.S. authorities recovered a substantial portion of the Bitcoin ransom using transaction tracing combined with traditional investigative techniques. Without analytics, such recoveries would be harder. This creates a genuine moral tension: the same tools that chill legitimate behaviour also disrupt serious harm.

Designers of privacy-preserving systems cannot ignore this. Some projects attempt a hybrid path: building tools that offer individual confidentiality while supporting law-enforcement access under strict conditions, often through court orders combined with multi-party computation. Others explore opt-in transparency features—allowing users to reveal audit trails when beneficial. The behaviour here is compromise. The label's power is acknowledged, not rejected. Yet these compromises remain clinically complex and politically contested. Who decides what counts as a valid request? Which jurisdiction's authorities? Which threshold of suspicion?

At the policy level, there is a temptation to treat forensics as neutral. It is not. Every clustering rule, every risk score, every graphical heat map embeds choices about thresholds, priors, and acceptable error rates. A system that flags ninety per cent of suspicious flow at the cost of many false positives will produce a very different chill than one tuned conservatively. Those choices are rarely debated publicly. They are commercial secrets and supervisory understandings. Yet they shape the lived experience of users who never signed up for that experiment.

The chill, then, is not simply fear of punishment. It is the sense that one's actions are legible to unknown watchers with unclear standards. It is the knowledge that a mistaken label can close doors without explanation. It is the pressure to avoid certain tools, coins, or counterparties—not because they are definitively illegal, but because they might be inconvenient in some future compliance interview.

That leaves a hard question hanging over any serious discussion of blockchain governance: if analytics will continue to deepen, and if their labels already steer behaviour as powerfully as formal rules, what forms of oversight, contestation, and transparency are necessary to ensure that *whoever owns the labels* does not quietly own the shape of permissible life on-chain?

Human Rights vs Safety

On 20 October 2020, during protests in Lagos, Nigeria, several demonstrators turned to Bitcoin after local banks froze accounts linked—sometimes tenuously—to organisers. The protestors were not hiding illicit finance. They were trying to receive donations to buy food, water, and protective equipment. Their bank transfers stalled; their digital wallets did not. Yet the very mechanism that allowed them to move funds beyond state interference also attracted scrutiny from analysts who flagged associated addresses as "protest-related risk". No statute defined this category. It emerged from dashboards and internal briefings. The result was concrete: some exchanges tightened controls around Nigerian-linked flows within days. People seeking safety from intimidation found themselves subject to a softer but no less consequential form of surveillance. The paradox was sharp. A technology that could shield dissenters had simultaneously marked them as anomalous.

One five-word sentence marks the tension. *Protection can expose risk.* A system designed for resilience against persecution can appear suspicious within risk models calibrated for crime prevention. That tension is not new; it echoes debates from analogue eras when secure radios, encrypted fax machines, and dissident-friendly broadcast channels raised the same question: how far may a state reach to prevent harm without unduly harming those who need privacy most?

The motif that threads through this subchapter is *the threshold*: the line—legal, technical, ethical—where protective measures become intrusive, or preventative powers become punitive. Thresholds matter because they ration uncertainty. Move them slightly and the set of people who fall under suspicion shifts dramatically. The threshold determines whose safety is prioritised: victims of crime, or victims of state overreach.

The first claim is empirical. Crime prevention requires visibility. Show the behaviour: after the Colonial Pipeline ransomware attack in May 2021, U.S. authorities traced part of the Bitcoin ransom using transaction analysis and ultimately recovered a substantial sum. Name the actors: the Department of Justice, analysis teams, and cooperating exchanges. Explain: ransomware gangs exploit pseudonymous systems for leverage; tracing reduces their impunity. Implication: without visibility, certain crimes would rise sharply, and victims would bear the cost.

But the same visibility carries risk for dissidents. The case of Belarus in 2020 illustrates this. Protestors there relied on crypto donations routed through publicly viewable wallets. Analytics firms provided insights on flows to global exchanges. Show the behaviour: Belarusian activists later reported targeted detentions after border guards demanded explanations for incoming digital transfers. Name the actor: the Belarusian security services. Explain: on-chain transparency allowed authorities to identify patterns of incoming funds and to question recipients. Implication: visibility that helps prevent crime in one jurisdiction can facilitate repression in another.

A proportional system must balance these realities. It must weigh the magnitude of harm prevented against the harm inflicted through overreach. The threshold cannot be set solely by the most capable security agencies, nor solely by the most vulnerable activists. It requires a structured approach to proportionality.

The second claim builds on this: proportionality demands *precision first*. Show the behaviour: the European Court of Human Rights, in cases such as Roman Zakharov v. Russia (2015), set clear expectations that surveillance must be targeted, legally grounded, and reviewable. Name the institution: the ECtHR, Strasbourg. Explain: mass, untargeted surveillance violates fundamental rights even when justified by broad security concerns. Implication: blockchain analytics that sweep broadly without discrimination risk drifting into zones that established human rights jurisprudence rejects.

Two concrete examples illustrate how proportionality can vary. In South Korea, after the Bithumb hack of 2017, regulators required exchanges to implement stricter identity verification and transaction monitoring. Show the behaviour: users had to link wallets to verified accounts, dramatically reducing anonymous flows. Name the actor: the Korea Financial Intelligence Unit. Explain: the measure was narrow—focused on exchanges with clear consumer exposure. Implication: a targeted restriction produced a measurable decrease in fraud while retaining the legality of self-hosted wallets.

Contrast this with the approach in China after 2021, where blanket prohibitions on crypto transactions combined with extensive off-chain monitoring created a chilling environment for political dissenters and ordinary citizens alike. Name the actor: the People's Bank of China. Show the behaviour: peer-to-peer transactions were increasingly surveilled, and bank accounts were frozen based on broad "virtual asset risk" classifications. Explain: the threshold was set expansively, erasing functional distinctions between harmless private transfers and illicit schemes. Implication: the protective rationale blurred into an instrument of control.

The limitation appears here: even proportional systems struggle when risk models rely on heuristics rather than evidence. Crime prevention efforts often work with probability, not certainty. A wallet associated with a protest, a miner cluster in a sanctioned region, or a privacy tool used disproportionately by journalists may all trigger scrutiny. Reconcile the tension: proportionality is not a guarantee of perfect fairness; it is a discipline that minimises unnecessary harm by demanding justification for each intrusion.

A third claim addresses the role of design. Privacy-preserving primitives such as zero-knowledge proofs, selective disclosure credentials, and blinded signatures do not eliminate law-enforcement capacity. They redistribute it. Show the behaviour: in pilot programmes in Switzerland (2022–2023), organisations used selective disclosure credentials to prove vaccination status without revealing identity. Name the actor: the Swiss Federal Office of Public Health. Explain: the system allowed targeted checks while avoiding comprehensive tracking. Implication: proportionality can be embodied technically, not only legally.

In digital finance, similar design principles can apply. A dissident using a shielded transaction system could reveal specific details—time, amount, counterparty—to a trusted court or NGO without exposing their entire financial history. The threshold becomes programmable. But such systems require governance: who controls the reveals? Which jurisdiction's courts count? Which institutions certify access? A poorly designed conditional disclosure regime can easily become a backdoor for overbroad surveillance.

A fourth claim concerns *secondary enforcement*: the pressure placed not on criminals or dissidents, but on intermediaries—exchanges, wallet providers, infrastructure operators. Show the behaviour: after OFAC sanctioned Tornado Cash in August 2022, many interfaces geofenced addresses far beyond the listed entities. Name the actors: U.S. Treasury, decentralised app front ends. Explain: intermediaries, fearing penalties, adopt conservative stances that exceed legal requirements. Implication: risk aversion trickles down to users who are not targets of the original sanction, shifting the threshold from precision to blanket exclusion.

Consider a counter-example. In the European Union, the revised Transfer of Funds Regulation (2023) initially proposed strict controls on self-hosted wallets. After extensive debate from civil society groups such as the European Digital Rights Association, the final regulation balanced monitoring responsibilities with explicit protections for lawful private transfers. Name the actor: EDRi. Show the behaviour: advocacy reshaped regulatory text. Explain: when stakeholders articulate proportionality concerns clearly, policy can adjust. Implication: proportionality is not static; it is contested and negotiated.

A fifth claim returns to dissidents themselves. Protection is not only about encryption or pseudonymity. It is also about *friction*. A dissident willing to endure a delay or cost may reveal only what is necessary. Show the behaviour: activists in Hong Kong during 2019 protests used cash-loaded Octopus cards rather than traceable digital payments to access transport. Name the place: Hong Kong. Explain: they accepted inconvenience to reduce exposure. Implication: real proportionality acknowledges human behaviour: people adapt to risk and signal their thresholds through their choices.

The motif of *the threshold* emerges again in forensic practices. When analytics firms mark clusters as "high risk", they shift thresholds indirectly. A risk score above 80 may trigger additional documentation requests from exchanges. A score above 90 may cause rejection. These decisions are rarely disclosed. They represent technical thresholds masquerading as legal ones. Without oversight, they risk becoming unreviewable instruments of control.

Yet total opacity is not a solution. Crime prevention requires some visibility. Dissident protection requires some opacity. The task is to carve a space between extremes. That space is fragile. It shifts with international politics, vendor practices, and market pressures.

The unresolved question sits at the centre of this subchapter: if proportionality is the only principle that can reconcile human rights with safety, who decides where the threshold lies, and what mechanisms ensure that the power to set it does not drift invisibly towards those whose incentives favour surveillance over freedom?

Chapter 7
Oracles, Bridges, and the Governance of Truth

In June 2022, during a violent swing in crypto markets, a decentralised lending protocol faced a question that cut deeper than volatility: which price was *true*? Several exchanges recorded an abrupt wick—an artefact of thin liquidity—sending an asset momentarily plunging by more than half. One major oracle provider relayed that anomalous figure. Within minutes, hundreds of positions were liquidated. Screens lit with automated receipts. No human had judged these borrowers reckless; no court had weighed their intentions. A momentary distortion became a binding verdict because a single data feed declared it real. The protocol's forum filled with pleas for reversal, screenshots, counter-evidence. Yet the code had spoken first. The liquidation engine, indifferent to context, had already transferred custody. A transient datapoint had been elevated to the status of law.

This was not merely a failure of infrastructure. It was a confrontation with a deeper truth: every digital system, however decentralised its aspirations, must ultimately decide who gets to define reality when the world becomes ambiguous. For centuries, societies have relied on judges, surveyors, clerks, and notaries to codify the facts that underpin obligations. A mis-measured boundary might spark a decades-long dispute; a misfiled deed could dispossess a family. What has changed is not the fragility of facts, but their velocity. In a world where a loan can be liquidated in two seconds, and a cross-chain trade confirmed in five, the institutions that certify reality now sit upstream of enormous economic consequences. Their decisions are instantaneous, automated, and—for many users—effectively unappealable.

The motif that quietly threads through this chapter is *the hinge*: the small, often invisible point on which vast structures turn. A single oracle update can hinge the solvency of a protocol. A bridge validator's vote can hinge whether billions move safely across chains. A dispute resolution message in a chat room can hinge the fate of a compensation claim after a critical exploit. In each instance, authority rests not in sweeping constitutions or formal democracies, but in narrow, technical checkpoints that decide whose version of reality qualifies as legitimate.

Yet these hinges do not emerge from nowhere. They are built by coalitions of developers, auditors, exchanges, foundations, and incentive-aligned participants who each carry their own assumptions about risk and responsibility. Consider the role of bridge governors, whose influence is both immense and often underexamined. In an industry that prizes decentralisation, many of the largest bridges still rely on multisig committees—small groups empowered to pause transfers or adjust parameters when something looks amiss. These committees can prevent catastrophic contagion, as seen during the Ronin Bridge hack in March 2022, when rapid intervention by core maintainers helped halt further damage. But they also reveal an uncomfortable reliance on concentrated emergency power. The safety valve becomes an implicit constitutional clause, even when never written down.

The tension is not inherently malign. Most societies rely on some form of emergency authority to contain crises. What matters is not the existence of power, but the transparency of its boundaries. Who selects the signers? Which jurisdiction shapes their liability? Which norms anchor their decisions? A decentralised system without a theory of emergencies becomes brittle; a decentralised system with concealed emergency powers becomes deceptive. Users deserve clarity about the hinge points that can override algorithms.

The chapter also turns to off-chain dispute systems, where the myth of fully automated governance gives way to the reality of negotiation. When a bug drains a protocol or a design flaw causes unfair loss, communities do not consult code; they consult each other. In July 2020, after the Balancer pool exploit, restitution emerged not from an algorithmic mandate but from human deliberation: developers, auditors, and stakeholders debated responsibility, weighed equities, and agreed on compensation. This was not a failure of decentralisation; it was an admission that no automated system can resolve every conflict. Justice requires judgement. And judgement requires processes that reflect shared norms rather than spontaneous improvisation.

What emerges from these episodes is a picture of truth-making as a distributed craft, blending technical feeds with social legitimacy. Oracles, bridges, and dispute mechanisms each inhabit different layers of this craft, but they converge on the same philosophical question: what counts as a fact when facts carry financial and political weight? If an oracle reports the wrong number, is the harm contractual or constitutional? If a bridge halts transfers under suspicion of an attack, is the pause a technical safeguard or a form of governance? If a community negotiates compensation after a bug, is that negotiation a patch or a precedent?

These are not academic curiosities. As decentralised finance and cross-chain systems become more embedded in everyday transactions—from custody to payroll to municipal record-keeping—the mechanisms that certify truth will shape not only technical reliability but democratic trust. The stakes rise when protocols hold other people's mortgages, run supply chains, or handle election-related data. When the number that decides a liquidation becomes the number that decides a pension fund's stability, the governance of truth becomes inseparable from the governance of society.

Still, this chapter refuses both fatalism and triumphalism. It does not assume that automated truth is inherently oppressive, nor that human oversight is inherently virtuous. Instead, it explores the design choices that influence how truth is produced, contested, and defended across decentralised systems. Diversity emerges as a source of resilience: plural oracles, multi-source feeds, and quorum-based bridges can prevent single points of failure from cascading across networks. But diversity also introduces friction and cost. How many feeds count as "enough"? Who arbitrates discrepancies? What happens when multiple sources disagree during a crisis?

By the time the chapter reaches these questions, it will have illuminated a simple but demanding insight: truth in decentralised systems is neither purely technical nor purely social. It is a negotiated artefact, shaped by incentives, institutions, and human behaviour. It evolves with every incident, every patch, every disputed oracle update, every bridge pause. And it forces us to confront the governance structures we have inherited—structures that determine who may certify facts that carry the force of economic law.

The hinge remains. It waits in every price feed, every validator vote, every emergency Slack channel. The challenge is learning to see it, to understand its power, and to decide whether the hands that turn it are the ones we trust.

Data as Law

At 02:11 UTC on 14 March 2020, the Ethereum-based lending protocol MakerDAO recorded an ETH price of precisely zero dollars for several minutes. The reading came through a subset of oracle feeds overwhelmed by network congestion during the market crash. In that moment, a handful of opportunistic bidders acquired more than four million dollars' worth of collateral for virtually nothing. No judge had declared the assets worthless; no bankruptcy trustee had intervened. A temporary data gap—machine-created, machine-accepted—rewrote millions in obligations. What should have been a volatile afternoon became, for many, an irreversible legal event. The protocol's own documentation acknowledged the transfers as valid. The oracle had defined reality.

The question that lingered was disarmingly simple: how can a number, produced at the wrong second by an overwhelmed server, carry the same force as a court order? The paradox was sharper because everyone agreed the price was wrong, yet the wrongness was not actionable. The borrowers who lost their collateral had no recourse beyond a community vote months later. The episode was not an aberration but a revelation: in decentralised systems, whoever certifies the facts of the world does not merely describe outcomes—they *create* them. A price feed is not a measurement device. It is a lawmaking instrument.

The hinge motif returns here with particular clarity. A single data point becomes the hinge on which entire rights and remedies turn. That hinge is not neutral. It is engineered, maintained, and updated by specific people, firms, and networks whose assumptions shape the conditions under which truth is declared. Once we recognise that data carries normative weight, the governance of oracles stops looking like a technical exercise and begins to resemble a constitutional one.

The first major claim reveals itself when we observe how oracles actually operate during stress. Show the behaviour: on 7 September 2021, during El Salvador's Bitcoin adoption rollout, several exchanges displayed sharply divergent BTC/USD prices across venues, with spreads exceeding 10 per cent in San Salvador. Name the mechanism: these discrepancies fed into oracle networks such as Chainlink, which aggregate multiple price sources to reduce manipulation risk. Explain the dynamic: when exchanges diverge, an oracle must decide how to weigh, filter, or exclude feeds, effectively determining which market constitutes "truth". Implication: a design choice—median rather than average; time-weighted rather than instantaneous—defines not only liquidation outcomes but the distribution of losses between borrowers and lenders.

A second major claim surfaces when considering the incentives of data providers. Show the behaviour: Coinbase, in December 2020, removed several thinly traded markets during episodes of abnormal volatility after internal risk assessments. Name the structural reality: exchanges that supply oracle data also face regulatory exposure in New York or London, shaping how they curate and publish prices in ways that may be more conservative than decentralised users expect. Explain the tension: the oracle inherits these institutional biases, importing jurisdictional norms into supposedly neutral technical infrastructure. Implication: the data itself becomes an instrument of extraterritorial governance.

A credible counter-example helps sharpen the analysis. In some cases, highly decentralised oracle networks have mitigated the risks of centralised failure. During the May 2021 market crash, decentralised feeds built on on-chain automated market maker (AMM) data continued to update despite exchange outages, allowing lending protocols tied to these sources on Ethereum and Binance Smart Chain to operate without catastrophic mispricing. Yet even this resilience contains a limitation. AMM-based oracles assume sufficient liquidity and rational arbitrage, but when liquidity vanishes, these assumptions crumble, leaving the protocol with numbers that reflect panic rather than price discovery. Reconciling this counter-example clarifies the point: decentralisation reduces some risks but does not remove the normative character of data. It simply shifts the hinge from a centralised institution to market structure itself.

Every abstraction—risk, reliability, fairness—must therefore be anchored in observable behaviour. Risk becomes the measurable variance between oracle updates over short windows. Reliability becomes the frequency of deviations from reference benchmarks across exchanges.

Fairness manifests in whether similarly situated users receive consistent outcomes during volatile periods. These observable metrics turn philosophical debates into governance decisions. Should an oracle commit to a minimum update frequency, even at the cost of occasional noise? Should protocols measure oracle deviation against a basket of markets and commit to pausing execution above a defined threshold? These are not engineering questions. They are rule-of-law questions translated into code.

The motif of the hinge recurs when examining loss allocation. In traditional finance, an erroneous price feed from a venue such as the New York Stock Exchange might trigger a trade cancellation under established rules. The legal system implicitly treats data errors as contestable facts. In decentralised systems, by contrast, many protocols commit ex ante to enforcing every oracle-delivered outcome, no matter how aberrant. Data becomes final by design. The hinge is welded shut. This rigidity can produce perverse incentives. If traders know that certain AMM pools can be manipulated cheaply at low liquidity, and that an oracle will faithfully report the manipulated price, the system invites strategic attacks. The oracle does not merely reflect a market; it creates an opening for asymmetric gain.

Historical parallels show that this is not a new challenge, merely a new configuration. In the 1860s, the introduction of telegraphic price data across Atlantic commodity markets sparked disputes over whether telegram readings constituted binding commercial facts. Merchants argued that storms, wire faults, or operator errors should nullify contracts triggered by erroneous signals. Courts across London and Liverpool wrestled with the question: when communication becomes instantaneous, how should the law treat mistaken prices that lead to unfair deals? The debates echo perfectly in decentralised finance: is an oracle error a mistake or a contract?

A related claim concerns opacity. Many oracle networks rely on committees of data providers whose identities, update frequencies, and failover conditions are partially concealed for security reasons. Show the behaviour: in August 2022, a major decentralised exchange on Avalanche temporarily halted trading after discrepancies emerged between its variant of a Chainlink feed and the reference markets. Users later discovered that certain fallback mechanisms were undocumented. Name the governance reality: concealment, even when well intentioned, creates asymmetric information between insiders and users. Explain the consequence: opaque data flows reduce user ability to predict outcomes, and by extension, to assess whether remedies should exist. Implication: transparency becomes a governance obligation, not a courtesy.

Against this backdrop, scenarios emerge rather than predictions. One scenario envisions diversified oracle networks that mix exchange data, AMM feeds, and time-weighted averages, reducing single-source distortions. Another contemplates governance processes where users can challenge extreme oracle readings through bounded dispute channels without undermining protocol liveness. A third, more cautionary scenario imagines data cartels—clusters of exchanges, miners, and data firms—whose aligned incentives define truth across multiple chains, consolidating power in ways that escape both public and private accountability.

The purpose of examining these scenarios is not to forecast the fate of decentralised finance but to clarify the stakes: data is never merely data. It is adjudication. It defines defaults, liquidations, payouts, and losses. The person or entity that supplies a number becomes, in that moment, an arbiter. The chain of logic that flows from their datapoint becomes the rule that governs countless users downstream.

The unresolved tension, and the appropriate place to leave the reader, concerns institutional design. Should decentralised protocols commit to hard-coded acceptance of oracle data, even when the numbers contradict lived reality? Or should they admit override paths, with all the political complexity that human discretion entails? The hinge is unavoidable. The question is where it should sit—and whose hand should be trusted to turn it.

Bridge Governors

On 23 March 2022, in Ho Chi Minh City, engineers at Sky Mavis stared at a terminal showing the unthinkable. An attacker had compromised the Ronin Bridge, siphoning off roughly USD 600 million in cryptoassets that linked the Ethereum mainnet to the Axie Infinity sidechain. Within hours, the team triggered the only defence left: the validator set governing the bridge—just nine keys, five needed for a quorum—halted message passing. Deposits froze. Withdrawals froze. A network that had once processed billions in value each month now relied on a tiny group of signers to decide when, and whether, movement could resume. The bridge closed. Everything stopped.

The Ronin hack was described as a security failure, and it was. But it also exposed a deeper reality. Cross-chain bridges do more than move tokens between ledgers. They define which ledger's version of events counts as real at any moment. The validator set, or multisig committee, that attests to those events wields power akin to a clearing house in traditional finance. When that committee pauses, reroutes, or mis-signs messages, it is not simply relaying information. It is governing an entire corridor of economic life.

The quiet motif running through this subchapter is *the crossing*. Every bridge offers a crossing: from one legal environment to another, from one consensus to another, from one set of risks to a different stack of assumptions. We tend to focus on what moves—the tokens, the collateral, the liquidity. Yet governance lies with those who can close the gate or change the rules of passage.

The first claim is stark: validator sets for bridges concentrate systemic risk, even when the surrounding ecosystems look decentralised. Show the behaviour: Ronin's bridge relied on nine validators, four of which were directly controlled by Sky Mavis. When the attacker gained control of five keys, they effectively became the governor of the crossing. Name the actor: Sky Mavis, March 2022. Explain: a scheme designed for operational efficiency—fast confirmations, manageable coordination—created a single point of failure that dwarfed the risks of either underlying chain. Implication: cross-chain systems often re-centralise precisely where value is highest and scrutiny is lowest.

A second example confirms the pattern. In February 2022, the Wormhole bridge between Ethereum and Solana was exploited for over USD 300 million after a vulnerability in its smart contracts allowed the minting of unbacked assets on Solana. The subsequent response hinged on the guardians—Wormhole's validator set—who could attest new state and organise a patch. A private entity, Jump Trading, chose to step in and recapitalise the hole. Users were made whole. But the episode revealed who truly governed the crossing. Not the dispersed token holders on Solana. Not the DAO of some DeFi protocol. A single market maker, by injecting capital and coordinating validators, defined which reality the bridge would recognise as canonical. The crossing belonged, in that moment, to whoever could restore it.

The governance structure in both cases was technically documented. Yet few users understood that when they "bridged ETH", they were accepting the judgement of a small validator cartel about what counted as ETH on the far side. They saw a technical tunnel. They did not see the customs office at its centre.

A credible counter-example tempers the story. The xDai (now Gnosis Chain) bridge between Ethereum and Gnosis, launched in 2018, experimented with a more community-driven validator set including independent organisations from multiple jurisdictions. Its validators were public, its operations relatively transparent, and its emergency pauses coordinated through visible governance channels. The design reduced single-entity control and fostered shared responsibility. Yet even here, the crossing depended on a small set of actors with special authority. The limitation did not vanish; it changed form. Reconciling this highlights the core point: diversity in validator composition mitigates some risks, but the very act of bridging demands a locus of certification. Someone must say "this deposit on chain A corresponds to that asset on chain B". That "someone" is governance.

The second claim concerns jurisdictional gravity. Bridge governors live somewhere. Their companies are incorporated somewhere. Their keys sit on hardware that crosses real borders. Show the behaviour: after the Poly Network exploit in August 2021, where over USD 600 million in assets were initially drained across multiple chains, the recovery negotiations hinged on a pseudonymous "white hat" hacker and the Poly Network team, reportedly operating out of offices in China and Singapore. Law enforcement agencies in several countries took an interest. Yet ultimate control over when the bridge would resume normal operations rested with the small team coordinating validators and redeploying contracts. Explain: the physical location of those coordinators shaped which legal systems could pressure, support, or obstruct recovery efforts. Implication: bridges may link decentralised networks, but their governors remain subject to the centralised realities of law.

Jurisdiction matters even absent hacks. A bridge whose validator keys are held primarily by corporations in the United States inherits exposure to U.S. sanctions regimes and regulatory expectations. If OFAC were to designate a contract or a set of addresses as sanctioned, validators in the U.S. might feel compelled to filter messages involving those addresses. The bridge then becomes a vector for extraterritorial policy: what cannot be enforced easily on-chain at the base layer can be enforced at the crossing, where a small committee translates global activity into attestations.

The third claim focuses on the political role of *pausing*. Pauses are often defended as purely technical safety valves. Yet the act of halting message passing is effectively a moratorium on rights. Show the behaviour: during the Nomad bridge incident in August 2022, once the initial vulnerability allowed a copy-paste exploit to drain funds, the team rushed to pause the bridge and broadcast "white hat" instructions to stop further copying. When the pause took effect, all users—honest and malicious alike—lost access to the crossing. Name the actor: Nomad. Explain: the pause protected remaining funds but also trapped legitimate liquidity that users had expected to move freely. Implication: designing pause mechanisms is not just about security; it is about drawing boundaries around whose interests count in emergencies.

Pauses create winners and losers. Users who had already bridged out escaped further risk. Those mid-transfer or queued behind congestion bore more of the burden. Protocols that depended on constant inflow from a specific bridge saw their local markets dislocate. Yet the decision to pause seldom involved those downstream stakeholders. The governors of the crossing acted under intense time pressure, guided by their own risk calculus and, sometimes, their legal exposure.

The motif of *the crossing* appears again here. A bridge with no pause becomes a suicide corridor in the face of an exploit. A bridge with an unaccountable pause becomes a gate subject to arbitrary closure. The legitimate question is not whether pauses are good or bad but who controls them, under what conditions, with what transparency, and subject to which after-the-fact review.

The fourth claim addresses systemic interdependence. As more protocols rely on bridging for yield strategies, liquidity provisioning, or governance participation, a single bridge failure can propagate across chains like a multi-market banking crisis. Show the behaviour: after the Harmony Horizon bridge exploit in June 2022, the de-pegging of bridged assets affected DeFi pools on multiple networks, forcing rushed governance decisions on whether to accept the bridged tokens as collateral at par or devalue them. Name the actor: Harmony, Horizon bridge. Explain: the bridge governors' inability to restore backing quickly turned a security failure into a governance crisis for unaffiliated protocols. Implication: bridges become systemically important infrastructure long before their governors acquire systemic oversight or accountability.

In such contexts, validator incentives extend far beyond transaction fees. They become, in effect, the macroprudential managers of cross-chain credit. A conservative validator set might choose to pause rapidly at the first sign of anomaly, privileging containment over availability. A more risk-tolerant set might keep flows open, hoping to ride out what appears to be volatility but might in fact be a slow-moving exploit. Users, for their part, rarely see these dilemmas. They only see whether assets arrive.

A fifth claim confronts an uncomfortable reality: many bridges advertise decentralisation while hiding how few people are truly empowered. Governance tokens may exist. Forums may buzz. Yet when crisis strikes, it is almost always a small internal team, tightly connected to the validator set, that coordinates the response. Show the behaviour: announcements in hack post-mortems routinely emphasise "swift action by the team" and "coordination with partners", not collective decision-making by token holders. Explain: speed requires focus; focus favours centralisation at the crossing. Implication: there is a structural gap between decentralised rhetoric and concentrated operational control in cross-chain governance.

A counter-move is emerging. Some new bridge designs anchor governance in staking-based validator sets across multiple chains, with slashing conditions for misbehaviour and formal procedures for rotating signers. Others rely on light-client verification, reducing the trust placed in small committees. These models dilute the power of discrete governors and embed accountability in economic incentives. Yet they also increase complexity and sometimes reduce throughput. Once again, the crossing demands a choice: faster and more centralised, or slower and more credibly neutral.

Threading back to the motif, *the crossing* is where users experience the trade-offs of blockchain governance most viscerally. They may never think about consensus algorithms or regulatory regimes, but they know if their bridged assets arrive on time and retain value. They know if a pause strands them. They know if a de-pegging wipes out their position in a distant DeFi pool. Their lived reality depends on design decisions made by bridge governors months or years earlier.

The unresolved question is pressing and practical. If bridges now function as the customs offices and central clearing points of a multi-chain economy, how should their governors be selected, constrained, and supervised? More bluntly: who should have the right to close the crossing, and what obligations do they owe to those already on the bridge when they do?

Dispute Systems Off-Chain

On 17 June 2016, in Zug, engineers at the Ethereum Foundation watched a ledger populate with movements none of them had authorised. The DAO, hailed only weeks earlier as a pioneering experiment in decentralised governance, had been exploited through a recursive call vulnerability. Funds poured into a child contract controlled by the attacker. Screens refreshed. Slack channels filled. The "unstoppable code" so many had championed now stalled before a simple question: what counts as theft when the rules are defined by a contract and the contract has behaved exactly as written? Within hours, arguments shifted from technical diagnosis to political negotiation. Core developers, miners, investors and project leaders debated whether to fork the chain. Votes were held. Calls were made. What emerged from those days was not an automated resolution, but a profoundly human one. The code had failed to resolve the dispute; people had to decide what should happen next.

That moment became a milestone because it exposed the fissure between automation and adjudication. Smart contracts promise self-enforcement, yet the first major crisis in decentralised finance required diplomacy, not determinism. To fork or not to fork was a governance decision dressed in technical language but grounded in ethics, reputation and collective fear of precedent. The chain split. Ethereum and Ethereum Classic both claimed continuity, each asserting a legitimate reading of the past.

The dispute did not disappear. It crystallised into two histories.

The motif that threads through this subchapter is *the table*. When disputes become too complex, high-stakes or politically charged to be resolved by code, parties return to a table—literal or metaphorical—where humans argue, negotiate, interpret and settle. Protocols aspire to be self-contained systems with rules that leave no gaps, but reality pushes them back to the table, again and again.

The first claim is that high-stakes disputes in decentralised systems routinely collapse into off-chain negotiation, even when the architecture insists they should not. Show the behaviour: after the bZx protocol suffered an exploit in February 2020, its team convened emergency discussions with the attacker, eventually securing a partial return of funds through a negotiated "white hat" settlement. Name the actor: bZx, February 2020. Explain: despite bZx's commitment to on-chain governance and automation, its most consequential decision came through private channels. Implication: for all the rhetoric of decentralisation, off-chain negotiation remains the default mechanism when losses escalate beyond pre-defined rules.

A second example deepens the pattern. In August 2021, the Poly Network incident triggered a frantic off-chain negotiation between the team and the pseudonymous attacker. What followed was an unfolding drama in messages posted to blockchain explorers and social media. A repayment address was shared. Portions of the funds were returned in tranches. The attacker claimed good intentions. The project's operators issued appeals. Ultimately, control of the multisig was handed back after extended dialogue. The outcome did not arise from automated slashing, formal dispute resolution or on-chain adjudication. It arose from persuasion, reputation, and a mutual assessment of risk. Implication: when protocol-level logic breaks, participants improvise new norms at the table.

A credible counter-example complicates the narrative. MakerDAO's liquidation systems during the March 2020 market crash followed predetermined auctions without off-chain negotiation. There was no emergency council, no hacker to negotiate with, no private chats to restore funds. The system behaved as designed, producing painful losses for some users. Yet this counter-example highlights the limitation: MakerDAO's mechanisms succeeded only because the dispute was procedural, not adversarial. The rules were hard-coded, the parameters known, and no human counterpart contested the facts. Reconciliation: automation works for internal failures and predictable scenarios; it falters when intentional actors exploit ambiguity or when responsibility for harm becomes contested.

The second claim concerns interpretation. Many disputes hinge not on facts but on readings of protocol intent. Show the behaviour: during the Curve Wars governance tensions in 2021–22, competing DeFi protocols engaged in aggressive token-locking strategies, prompting accusations of manipulation. No exploit occurred; instead, actors pursued strategies at the edge of the rules. The "violation" was contested. Some argued that aggressive vote-buying respected the letter of the mechanism; others claimed it breached the spirit. Name the phenomenon: Curve governance tensions, 2021–22. Explain: decentralised systems lack authoritative courts to interpret intent.

Implication: the table becomes a constitutional forum, where communities argue not simply over outcomes, but over meaning.

The table reappears when parties disagree on remedy. Bug bounties illustrate this vividly. Immunefi, founded in 2020 and based in Singapore, has coordinated numerous high-value payouts where security researchers detected critical vulnerabilities. The formal bounty terms are public, but the actual resolution often turns on negotiation: whether the exploit qualifies, whether the disclosure was timely, whether the attacker exceeded good-faith boundaries. Show the behaviour: on several occasions, protocols have disputed researchers' eligibility, resulting in heated public exchanges and eventually mediated settlements. Explain: even when rules exist, parties appeal to norms outside the contract. Implication: decentralised security ecosystems still rely on judgment, mediation and reputation.

A third claim addresses the rise of emergency councils—groups authorised to act outside normal process when disputes threaten systemic collapse. Show the behaviour: after the Wormhole incident in February 2022, rapid coordination among core contributors, the validator set and external stakeholders determined the timing of patches, the resumption of service and the communication strategy. These decisions could not wait for token votes or delayed governance cycles. Name the actor: Wormhole, February 2022. Explain: emergency councils emerge precisely where formal governance is too slow. Their actions often become de facto law. Implication: decentralisation bends under pressure, and the table becomes small, fast and exclusive.

Yet emergency councils bring jurisdictional risk. They consist of identifiable people in specific places, subject to legal systems with divergent priorities. Show the behaviour: during the Terra collapse in May 2022, teams distributed across South Korea, the United States and Singapore faced different regulatory expectations as they discussed measures to stabilise the ecosystem. Name the timeframe: May 2022. Explain: what appears as technical triage at the table is also shaped by legal exposure. Implication: global protocols inherit the constraints of the jurisdictions that host their crisis managers.

The fourth claim centres on evidence production. Many disputes fail because the facts are uncertain: who controlled which key, when a transaction occurred, whether a disclosure was made in good faith. Off-chain adjudication requires evidence that on-chain data alone cannot provide. Show the behaviour: during disputes around validator equivocation on certain proof-of-stake networks in 2021–22, operators produced server logs, time-stamped chat histories and security reports to defend themselves. Explain: blockchain records state transitions but not intention, context or operational detail. Implication: adjudicating disputes pulls information back into off-chain artefacts—logs, screenshots, statements—that do not enjoy the immutability of the chain.

This dependence on off-chain evidence exposes a limitation in the dream of fully automated governance. Not everything worth knowing is stored on-chain. Not everything stored on-chain is decisive. The table becomes the venue where competing narratives merge with technical analysis to form a judgment.

The fifth claim concerns reputation as a currency of resolution. Show the behaviour: Yearn, Aave and other prominent DeFi protocols have, at times, resolved inter-protocol tensions through public dialogue between founders on forums and social media. These exchanges were not governed by formal rules but by reputational incentives: leaders understood that public confidence depends on credible, transparent negotiation. Name the actors: Yearn and Aave, 2020–21. Explain: when disputes are visible and affect broad communities, reputational damage becomes a binding pressure. Implication: trust is not automated; it is managed through conduct at the table.

Reputation also shapes which voices matter. Some contributors gain moral authority through long-term involvement, others through technical expertise, and others through capital position. Dispute tables thus inherit informal hierarchies, even when formal governance grants equal weight to all token holders. The myth of perfect equality dissolves when people sit down to negotiate.

A sixth claim addresses an uncomfortable truth: off-chain dispute systems risk entrenching centralisation. Show the behaviour: when leading developers or founders repeatedly mediate crises, communities begin to expect their intervention. This expectation subtly transforms individuals into quasi-judges with enduring influence. Explain: crisis management becomes precedent-setting. Implication: informal arbitration accumulates authority over time, turning pragmatic responses into de facto governance structures.

The table, then, is a site of both resolution and power formation. Every crisis negotiated off-chain creates an archive of expectations. Future disputes reference past settlements. Patterns harden. Informal norms become constitutive features of governance.

A counter-move is emerging: protocols that commit to rigid, non-negotiable rules to avoid off-chain adjudication altogether. Automated insurance funds, algorithmic liquidations and predefined slashing conditions represent attempts to eliminate ambiguity. Yet such rigidity struggles under adversarial pressure. Perfect foresight is impossible; perfect code improbable. Reconciliation: systems oscillate between automation and human judgment because neither alone can manage the full spectrum of disputes.

As decentralised infrastructures mature, the table grows more elaborate. Lawyers join developers. Regulators monitor from afar. Users demand representation. Security researchers push for clearer bounty frameworks. Validators ask for procedural fairness. Each new crisis adds chairs.

The unresolved question is pointed and structural. If decentralised systems repeatedly return to off-chain negotiation at moments of greatest consequence, what form should that negotiation take? Who deserves a seat at the table, and who decides the rules by which the table convenes?

Resilience Through Diversity

On 11 February 2022, price feeds across several decentralised lending markets lurched abruptly when a solitary oracle misreported the value of LUNA on a major exchange. The glitch lasted minutes, yet in those minutes positions worth tens of millions teetered on the brink of liquidation. Developers at Anchor Protocol and Mirror, based largely in Seoul, watched the distortion propagate through dashboards that, until that moment, they had trusted implicitly. Volatility was not the problem; a single viewpoint masquerading as reality was. When the discrepancy was corrected, the near-misses revealed the architecture's deepest vulnerability. One faulty lens had almost rewritten the ledger's interpretation of the world.

The motif here is *the lens*: each oracle is a lens on external truth, and the risk lies in mistaking a single lens for the landscape itself. When the ether of decentralisation meets the stubborn fact that protocols must ingest external data, diversity becomes not an aesthetic preference but a structural safeguard. Systems designed around plurality—multiple feeds, quorum requirements, cross-checks and regional dispersion—treat truth as something to be triangulated rather than dictated.

The first claim is that plural oracles materially reduce the impact of erroneous data by distributing epistemic responsibility. Show the behaviour: after the Synthetix oracle incident in July 2019, where a single feed mistakenly priced the Korean won at roughly 1,000 times its actual value, the protocol suffered a cascade of unintended trades. Name the case: Synthetix, July 2019, Sydney-based team. Explain: the architecture relied on a single-point feed from an external API, and its design allowed no immediate override. Implication: when the lens breaks, the system loses its only view.

Plurality corrects for this. Chainlink's aggregator model, operational since 2020, exemplifies a quorum-driven approach: dozens of independent node operators provide price submissions, aggregated through a weighted median. Show the behaviour: during bouts of extreme volatility in May 2021, Chainlink's ETH-USD feed maintained continuous updates while several individual exchanges suffered outages. Explain: the quorum design filtered noise and prevented any single datapoint from dominating. Implication: resilience emerges from multiplicity, not precision alone.

A credible limitation must be addressed: even diverse oracle networks can converge on the same flawed underlying source. If every node operator queries the same exchange, diversity becomes superficial. Name the risk: correlated sourcing. Reconcile: true resilience requires diversity not only of operators but of data origins—markets, geographies, methodologies. The lens must differ in angle, not merely in holder.

The second claim concerns jurisdictional dispersion. Show the behaviour: during the 2020–21 expansion of DeFi, several protocols relied disproportionately on operators registered in the United States, creating exposure to regulatory action that could compromise oracle continuity. When the U.S. Treasury's Office of Foreign Assets Control (OFAC) sanctioned specific smart contracts in August 2022, compliance questions rippled across oracle providers, some of whom paused operations temporarily. Name the date: August 2022. Explain: if too many operators share the same regulatory environment, a single jurisdiction can influence or interrupt global data provision. Implication: decentralisation without geographic dispersion is a boundary failure.

Contrast this with DIA, headquartered in Switzerland, which builds oracle networks using regionally distributed contributors, including data publishers in Europe, Asia and South America. Show the behaviour: for certain FX pairs in 2022, DIA granulated feeds by continent to avoid correlated outages. Explain: heterogeneous locations provide protection against localised failures, whether technical or legal. Implication: the landscape looks different depending on where the lens sits.

The third claim is that diversity of method—different ways of measuring a variable—guards against fabricated or manipulated data. Show the behaviour: in 2021, concerns emerged around low-liquidity markets on decentralised exchanges where attackers executed wash trades to inflate prices before lending protocol updates. Name the phenomenon: oracle manipulation attacks, seen most prominently in the Cream Finance exploit of August 2021. Explain: if oracle mechanisms rely exclusively on decentralised exchange prices, manipulators can skew results. Implication: a resilient system must mix methodologies—centralised exchange data, decentralised exchange data, time-weighted averages, volume filters—and treat anomalies as signals rather than truths.

Now introduce a counter-example: Nomad Bridge's failure in August 2022 did not stem from oracle error, but from a smart contract vulnerability. Some argued this showed oracle diversity cannot prevent all systemic risks. Reconciling this: the critique misunderstands scope. Oracle diversification mitigates epistemic failures—errors in what the system believes about the world—not execution failures. Security must be layered; oracle plurality does not substitute for rigorous contract audits.

The table reappears as a motif—not a negotiation table, but a measurement table. Data is laid out, compared, interrogated. Plurality turns the table into a lab bench where contradictory samples force care and humility. A system with one oracle acts with conviction; a system with many acts with caution.

The fourth claim concerns failover mechanisms. Show the behaviour: MakerDAO's OSM (Oracle Security Module), introduced in 2019, deliberately delays price updates by one hour, giving governance and risk teams time to intervene when data appears suspect. Explain: failover is not merely about redundancy; it is about time—time to assess, time to override, time to cross-check. Implication: resilience requires friction. The fastest systems are often the least safe.

A contrasting example: the Terra ecosystem's pricing mechanisms in early 2022 updated rapidly and without layered checks. When market sentiment collapsed, the speed at which price data flowed into automated market makers contributed to the death spiral. Name the collapse: Terra, May 2022. Explain: rapid updates magnified reflexivity. Implication: diversity must be paired with temporal buffers; a slow lens can be as valuable as a sharp one.

The fifth claim is that diversity distributes blame and improves accountability. When a single oracle fails, there is a single scapegoat. When many participate, failures must be traced through procedure, not personality. Show the behaviour: Chainlink node operators publish performance metrics and uptime logs, allowing communities to compare reliability. Year-to-year, underperforming nodes are excluded from aggregator sets. Explain: transparency works because diversity creates competition. Implication: the system becomes self-correcting; participants commit to maintaining high-quality lenses.

A limitation: greater diversity can raise costs. More nodes mean more fees, more coordination, more operational burden. Protocols with narrow margins may default to cheaper, less diverse designs. Reconciliation: cost is real, but so is the cost of cascading liquidations triggered by faulty data. Some protocols adopt hybrid models—premium feeds for high-risk functions, cheaper feeds for low-risk tasks. Implication: diversity need not be uniform; it must be targeted.

The sixth claim concerns epistemic humility. Show the behaviour: during black swan events, even the best oracle networks disagree. On 12 March 2020—known colloquially as Black Thursday—cryptocurrency exchanges reported sharply divergent ETH prices as liquidity evaporated. Oracles that incorporated multiple feeds produced blended values; those relying on a single source diverged wildly. Explain: disagreement is not a flaw but a feature; it signals uncertainty. Implication: systems need mechanisms to interpret disagreement, not suppress it.

Plurality also introduces governance complexity. Who decides which lenses matter? How are new oracles admitted or removed? How should disagreements be resolved? The governance of truth requires its own governance—meta-rules for managing diversity. This recursive challenge pushes communities to formalise processes: quorum thresholds, failure modes, slashing conditions.

The seventh claim is that diverse oracles support legitimacy. Users trust systems that do not depend on a single upstream authority. Show the behaviour: when Aave integrated Chainlink feeds in 2020, its risk assessment framework explicitly cited the diversity of operators and data sources. Explain: decentralised finance aims to eliminate singular arbiters; diverse oracles make that aspiration credible. Implication: trust emerges from architecture, not slogans.

Yet a final limitation persists: plural oracles cannot guarantee truth, only resilience. If all underlying markets become distorted, the aggregated truth will be distorted too. Diversity guards against isolated failures, not systemic illusions. Reconciliation: plurality is not infallibility; it is a strategy for reducing harm in messy conditions where perfect accuracy is impossible.

The motif of the lens returns in closing. A single lens is clear until it cracks. Many lenses blur slightly but rarely shatter. The unresolved tension sits at the centre of protocol design: how many lenses are enough, and who decides when they disagree?

Chapter 8
Public Goods and Who Pays

The first hint that a blockchain community is maturing often arrives not with a breakthrough upgrade or a bullish market cycle, but with a far more prosaic question: who is going to pay for this? In March 2020, as the Ethereum network strained under surging activity, core developers convened—mostly virtually, scattered across Europe, North America, and East Asia—to debate an unglamorous but existential issue. Funding for protocol maintenance was running thin. Volunteer labour, once the movement's romantic engine, no longer matched the scale of responsibility. The network was now a critical economic substrate, not a hobbyist experiment. Decisions about fee switches, treasury disbursements, audit budgets, and contributor stipends carried consequences measured not only in developer morale but in billions of dollars secured by the chain. The paradox was stark: the more successful the network became, the more acute its public-goods problem.

A similar drama played out in the early days of the Linux Foundation's shift towards corporate sponsorship in the late 2000s. What had been a constellation of individual maintainers shepherding the kernel turned into a complex governance ecosystem where Intel, IBM, and Google underwrote the shared infrastructure. Stability arrived, but so did influence. The tension between sustainability and capture—between funding the commons and shaping it—did not disappear; it became structural. Open-source communities learned that money does not simply follow value; money rewrites incentives, reallocates authority, and reorders priorities.

This chapter sits at that fault line. It traces how decentralised networks confront the ancient challenge of financing shared resources without surrendering them to those willing to pay the most. From protocol treasuries to quadratic funding, from ecosystem grants to embedded protocol taxes, these mechanisms confront the same enduring dilemma: collective benefit, fragmented motivations, and continuous work that nobody can free-ride forever.

The core build begins by examining the architecture of funding itself. Protocol treasuries, born from block rewards or fee redirection, promise autonomy but risk becoming dormant vaults or discretionary slush funds. Grants programmes, celebrated for their agility, oscillate between strategic investment and performative largesse. Fee switches, long taboo in ostensibly neutral systems, increasingly underpin maintenance budgets—as seen when Uniswap flirted with activating its governance-controlled fee in 2023, triggering debate about developer compensation, community expectations, and the very meaning of decentralisation. Each mechanism reveals a different answer to a deceptively simple question: what does a network owe to its upkeep?

There is also the quiet gravitational pull of capture. When a foundation's major funder is an exchange, roadmap priorities tilt towards throughput and integrations that benefit trading volume. When a venture fund becomes the primary patron of a layer-two project, the emphasis on rapid scaling can overshadow safety upgrades or rigorous auditing. These patterns mirror long-observed dynamics in public-private partnerships: funding is never neutral. The influence it buys may be subtle—grant criteria, informal steering, preferential access—but its trajectory is predictable. Growth is subsidised; maintenance is deferred.

Against this backdrop, the chapter will push a counterintuitive argument: spending on security is not charity but assurance. Mature networks treat audits as recurring obligations, not launch-day rituals. They budget for code reviews, incident response teams, live monitoring, and formal verification because the absence of these expenditures is far costlier. An unpatched vulnerability is not simply a technical oversight; it is a reputational liability that undermines user confidence and erodes the legitimacy of the system. Insurance premiums look expensive until the day the building catches fire.

Yet how do communities measure whether their public-goods investments are delivering the outcomes they claim? Raw activity metrics—TVL, transaction counts, wallet growth—hide more than they reveal. Durable indicators live elsewhere: upgrade transparency, published incident reports, diversity of contributors, the continuity of documentation, and the stability of key teams through market cycles. These markers show whether a network maintains institutional memory or relies on heroes who burn out. They reveal whether governance is informed or performative, whether safety is embedded or an afterthought.

The thread running through this chapter is the understated motif of stewardship. Public goods do not demand grand gestures; they demand care. They demand someone to write the documentation nobody will praise, to update the dependencies that secure the protocol, to review the pull requests that never make headlines. They demand communities that recognise these contributions as foundational, not peripheral.

Stewardship also forces an uncomfortable question: who decides what to fund? Governance votes can devolve into popularity contests. Foundations risk behaving like grant-making agencies rather than custodians of critical infrastructure. Token-weighted decision systems reward those who hold the most rather than those who know the most. And networks that fail to nurture a diverse contributor base find themselves reliant on too few hands—hands that may eventually close into a fist.

The introduction concludes with a forward pull rather than a summary. As decentralised systems grow from experiments into institutions, the financing of public goods becomes not merely an operational consideration but an ethical one. How much should users pay for safety they cannot see? How should communities guard against funders who mean well but skew priorities? And how does a system persuade itself to invest in the boring, necessary work when speculation promises quicker returns?

The chapters that follow will walk this terrain with clarity and precision. But the essential dilemma remains unresolved, and perhaps unresolvable: a public good exists because it benefits everyone, yet someone must still foot the bill.

Funding the Commons

In November 2022, during a tense governance call streamed from locations across Berlin, Singapore, and Denver, the Uniswap Foundation presented a stark figure: the protocol's treasury held over US$2 billion in tokens, yet fewer than twenty full-time contributors maintained the codebase that carried daily volumes rivalling major stock exchanges. The disparity was not merely financial. It exposed a structural drift between the scale of a public good and the resources formally committed to sustaining it. The call ended with a question that still unsettles the community: should a decentralised exchange depend on sporadic grants and volunteer grit, or should it activate its long-dormant fee switch to fund enduring maintenance? One sentence cut through the noise. *This system is too big to run on goodwill alone.* It was a warning disguised as an observation.

The paradox is older than blockchains. In 1998, when the Mozilla project released its open-source suite from Netscape's offices in Mountain View, engineers soon discovered what states, cities, and commons theorists had long known: once infrastructure succeeds, everyone wants to use it; few want to pay for it. Browsers became a public good; its upkeep remained an orphaned responsibility. The story repeats across digital networks, but blockchains sharpen the edges. They are financial substrates, not software curiosities. Failure is counted in liquidations, frozen assets, and cascading losses. Maintenance is not optional. Someone must commit.

Treasuries, grants, and protocol taxes present competing philosophies of responsibility. Their differences appear technical but shape the social contract beneath every chain. The small motif running through this discussion—the ledger line—is deliberate. Funding choices are ledger entries in more than one sense. They reveal what a community values and what it fears. They expose how it imagines its future.

Treasuries show the tension most vividly. A protocol-controlled vault, measured by tokens or native units, promises independence from corporate patrons and market fads. Yet the size of a treasury often disguises its inertia. Large sums can sit idle because governance hesitates, factions block proposals, or price volatility clouds decision-making. The treasury's presence lulls participants into assuming resilience; its passivity undermines it. When the Ethereum DAO hack occurred in June 2016, the question was not only how to recover funds but who owned the responsibility for restoring order. The absence of an institutional funding mechanism forced a community-wide fork—an exit right used as emergency governance. The implication is sobering: an underfunded commons pushes disputes towards technical rupture.

Grants take the opposite path. They distribute rapidly, reward experimentation, and nurture the early stages of an ecosystem. The Solana Foundation's grants programme in 2021 supported hundreds of teams across Europe and Asia, catalysing the network's cultural texture and developer identity. Yet grants also reveal their fragility. They are episodic, often reactive, and depend on the priorities of those administering them. When the Avalanche Foundation rebalanced its allocations in late 2022 towards liquidity incentives rather than tooling, entire categories of maintenance work were quietly downgraded. A grants regime excels at planting seeds. It struggles to water the same plants year after year.

Protocol taxes—fee switches, block reward diversions, or mandatory contributions embedded in the code—offer the most stable design. They turn maintenance into a structural expenditure rather than a discretionary one. The Cosmos Hub community's decision in October 2021 to direct part of staking rewards into a community pool created a predictable funding runway. Developers could plan audits in advance, hire staff, and schedule upgrades without annual politicking. But protocol taxes carry their own limitations. They risk alienating users already sensitive to transaction costs, and they can centralise influence if the body administering the funds grows bureaucratic or unaccountable. A recurring fee clarifies responsibility, but it does not guarantee wisdom.

A credible counter-example tempers the narrative that structural funding always improves outcomes. The Polkadot treasury held substantial resources by mid-2023 and disbursed them aggressively. Yet community concern rose as spending swelled without clear performance metrics. Treasury burn rates became a political flashpoint. Critics argued that abundant resources encouraged low-value proposals, while supporters insisted that experimentation required tolerance for waste. The reconciliation lies in governance discipline: abundance without accountability distorts incentives; scarcity without strategy starves the commons.

Each mechanism embodies a view of *who* should carry the burden. Treasuries place the duty on token holders; grants shift it to foundations or benefactors; protocol taxes embed it into usage itself. Their effectiveness depends not only on design but behaviour. A network that measures treasury efficiency by the percentage of budget allocated, rather than the quality of outputs, misunderstands the point. A grants programme that rewards projects for shipping dashboards instead of maintaining libraries mistakes visibility for impact. A fee mechanism that earmarks revenue for "core work" but never publishes audit schedules or upgrade needs substitutes rhetoric for governance.

The ledger line motif reappears here: funding choices always leave a trace in how a community behaves. Consider a chain whose public resources quietly erode. Documentation grows stale. Release notes shrink. The same three maintainers merge every pull request. Incidents linger unresolved. Users sense decay before metrics capture it. A protocol that neglects its commons invites fragility as surely as a city that defers bridge repairs invites collapse.

Two concrete examples underline this truth. When Zcash funded its core teams through a fixed developer fund renewed in November 2020, the explicit allocation forced transparency and debate. It revealed competing visions for privacy research, user tools, and long-term protocol stewardship. The renewal was contentious, but the public scrutiny strengthened legitimacy. Meanwhile, when the MakerDAO community debated its operational budgets in 2022, it confronted a different challenge: a sprawling ecosystem of units and mandates without a coherent funding philosophy. The protocol functioned, but the governance structure creaked under its own complexity. Without a shared view on its public goods, the variability of budgets became a symptom, not a cause, of strain.

A limitation must be acknowledged. No funding model resolves the fundamental problem that decentralised networks lack a sovereign backstop. A state can raise taxes by statute; a protocol must persuade users. Treasury votes can fail. Fee switches can be vetoed. Grants can expire. Every model depends on voluntary cooperation, and that cooperation is fragile during market downturns when budgets tighten and contributors disperse. The reconciliation is not optimistic but realistic: decentralised systems can sustain public goods, but only by embedding financial planning into their identity rather than treating it as an afterthought.

The final movement leads to an unresolved tension. Should a network codify its funding structure early, at the risk of rigidity, or preserve flexibility, at the risk of drift? Should users accept protocol taxes as the price of reliability, or should they insist on leaner systems and discretionary spending? And how can communities measure success without metrics that devolve into vanity?

The ledger line remains the quiet guide. What a network funds—regularly, transparently, and with intent—reveals what it is becoming.

Capture Risks

In June 2021, the Polygon Foundation announced a US$100 million ecosystem fund from its offices in Dubai to accelerate adoption across DeFi, gaming, and enterprise pilots. Within six months, one detail became impossible to ignore: security engineers reported that critical refactoring work remained unfunded, while high-visibility integrations and marketing partnerships sailed through the grants process. The imbalance was measurable. A series of audits commissioned late that year identified unresolved issues in core modules, even as user-facing features multiplied. Growth surged; maintenance lagged. The fund had achieved its stated aim of expansion, yet the protocol's risk profile deepened. Silence on a governance call carried its own message. *Who benefits from this roadmap?* The question lingered unanswered.

Such skewed incentives are hardly new. In 2013, when the Linux Foundation accepted major corporate sponsorship to support kernel development, a similar tension emerged. Large tech firms shaped priorities by funding improvements that aligned with their infrastructure needs, while less profitable areas of the kernel received slower attention. The dynamic was not malicious; it was structural. Money arrives with gravity. It pulls development towards the interests of those who supply it. Blockchains, with their rhetoric of neutrality and self-governance, often fail to name this gravitational pull until it distorts the path of a protocol.

Capture begins quietly. A fund commits capital. A roadmap adjusts. A security review is postponed. A research proposal is reframed to appeal to investors rather than users. A motif—*tilt*—helps track this drift. It is the slight yet continuous inclination of a protocol's priorities towards growth, even when its stability depends on ballast.

The first claim is easiest to show: funders influence aims by the types of projects they reward. The Avalanche Foundation's allocation decisions in late 2022, shifting towards liquidity incentives and high-volume trading platforms, illustrate this tilt. The network grew quickly, and user numbers rose. But audit reports published by firms such as Halborn (2022) noted persistent issues in subnets that lacked dedicated security budgets. The implication is straightforward: when incentives favour expansion over resilience, technical debt accumulates faster than contributions can erase it.

A second example shows how concentrated funding can shape governance itself. In April 2023, Optimism's governance process confronted the uncomfortable reality that its largest delegates were funded by or affiliated with ecosystem partners. Proposal OP-145, which sought to allocate additional rewards to third-party applications, passed with overwhelming support from delegates whose organisations benefited directly from the decision. Critics pointed to voting patterns that correlated with grant recipients. Supporters countered that alignment of incentives strengthened the network. Both sides missed the core issue: the appearance of capture erodes legitimacy even when formal procedures are followed. A protocol cannot rely on the letter of governance if its participants doubt the independence of those casting votes.

A counter-example tempers the argument that funding inevitably biases outcomes. The Zcash community's decision in November 2020 to renew and reform the developer fund revealed a case in which explicit processes constrained funder influence. By imposing term limits, public reporting requirements, and performance milestones, the community minimised the risk that any single group could dominate the roadmap. The arrangement was imperfect, yet it demonstrated that governance can blunt capture when rules acknowledge power rather than romanticise its absence. The reconciliation lies in design: capture thrives where incentives are opaque and accountability is blurry.

To understand why capture emerges, one must move from abstractions to behaviour. When a roadmap emphasises "ecosystem growth", examine the decisions beneath the banner. Are audits recurring or ad hoc? Do core contributors receive long-term funding or rely on sporadic grants? Are incident reports published promptly or delayed until pressure mounts? These are visible signals, not theoretical indicators. They reveal whether a protocol values safety or merely performs it.

Metrics provide a more structured lens. If a treasury allocates 70 per cent of its annual budget to integrations and incentives but less than 10 per cent to security tooling or refactoring, the tilt is quantifiable. If contributor diversity narrows as funders sponsor preferred teams, the tilt is social. If upgrade transparency declines—commit messages shorten, release notes thin, and architectural decisions move to private channels—the tilt is cultural. Capture rarely announces itself; it appears in ratios.

The motif of tilt resurfaces when examining funder psychology. Growth generates headlines; maintenance does not. A new partnership promises user acquisition; a months-long audit delays launches. Funders often operate under market conditions that reward visibility over robustness. They commit capital to initiatives that demonstrate momentum, not diligence. Protocols absorb these preferences, sometimes subconsciously. A core team might prioritise a new feature because it aligns with funder enthusiasm, even when internal assessments warn that the codebase requires consolidation. The tilt is not an event. It is a habit.

There is a deeper implication. Capture transforms a decentralised project into a de facto corporate product, governed not by distributed interests but by concentrated expectations. The roadmap shifts from safeguarding a public good to fulfilling the strategic aims of a subset of stakeholders. This is not inherently damaging; many ecosystems benefit from coherent direction. But when funder aims diverge from user needs, the protocol inherits a structural conflict. One group values asset appreciation; another values reliability; a third values censorship resistance. The tilt reveals which aim prevails.

A relevant limitation must be acknowledged. Some networks rely on concentrated funding in their early years because distributed models are too weak to sustain meaningful progress. Without significant initial capital, research-heavy protocols such as StarkNet or Filecoin would not have reached production maturity. Concentration is not always capture. Yet this limitation reinforces the point: the line between necessary funding and undue influence is thin, and protocols must name it explicitly rather than hope it never becomes visible.

Examples of resistance exist. When the Cosmos Hub debated the controversial ATOM 2.0 proposal in October 2022, the community rejected a sweeping economic redesign supported by several influential funders and builders. The vote demonstrated that a distributed constituency could oppose a well-resourced initiative when the proposal failed to align with its broader values. The lesson is subtle: capture risks can be mitigated when communities maintain veto power and treat it as a living safeguard, not a symbolic gesture.

Still, protocols face a recurring dilemma: growth attracts capital; capital shapes priorities; priorities shape risk. The challenge is not to eliminate capture but to make it contestable. Transparency reports, contributor rotation, budget disclosures, and independent audits serve as counterweights. They are signals that a protocol refuses to tilt blindly, even if it cannot avoid tilt entirely.

This subchapter closes on the unresolved tension that defines every funding mechanism. Should a network prioritise rapid adoption to cement relevance, or should it harden its architecture before scaling? Can governance reliably detect when the tilt has become dangerous? And how should communities measure influence without discouraging those willing to fund the work others avoid?

The tilt remains. The question is whether a protocol notices when it begins to lean.

Assurance, Not Charity

In October 2022, auditors at Trail of Bits delivered a report to Compound Labs from their office in New York, detailing a vulnerability in the protocol's liquidation engine. It was not catastrophic, but it was real: an arithmetic oversight that, under extreme market stress, could have allowed an attacker to manipulate collateral valuations. The cost of the discovery was modest compared to the damage it averted. A single audit cycle, priced in the low six figures, insulated billions. The episode illustrated something the industry declares often but practises unevenly. Security is not a discretionary spend. It is insurance. It is the premium required for legitimacy.

A paradox lies at the heart of blockchain governance: protocols insist they are "trustless", yet they depend on trust in the diligence of those who maintain them. Trust appears in the rhythm of decisions—how frequently upgrades are audited, how promptly vulnerabilities are disclosed, how rigorously dependencies are reviewed. Every time a protocol minimises these practices, it emits a signal: our insurance cover is thin. The market responds accordingly. You can see it in the spread between implied volatility before and after audit announcements; in mid-2023, for instance, volatility on several DeFi tokens contracted measurably following completion of multi-week assessments by firms such as OpenZeppelin. The behaviour is concrete. The message is clear. Assurance shapes value.

The motif that threads this subchapter is *the premium*—not in its financial sense alone but as a measure of seriousness. A protocol either pays its premium or shifts the risk onto users without admitting it.

To understand how assurance becomes governance, begin with visible habits. Consider MakerDAO's approach in 2020 when it commissioned Quantstamp and Trail of Bits to conduct recurring audits after the "Black Thursday" incident in March that liquidated positions due to oracle delays. These firms documented issues ranging from gas optimisation to edge-case vulnerabilities in the auction module. The audits were expensive. They were also formative. Their existence communicated that MakerDAO recognised risk as structural, not episodic. The implication was reputational: by treating assurance as a continuous obligation rather than a crisis response, MakerDAO regained confidence lost earlier that year. Users measured not rhetorical commitments but the cadence of remediation.

Contrast this with the experience of the BSC-based Uranium Finance protocol, which in April 2021 lost more than US$50 million to an exploit that redirected funds through a misconfigured fee calculation. The post-mortem revealed that the protocol had forgone rigorous audits, relying instead on informal peer review and rapid iteration. Speed eclipsed discipline. The absence of a premium became part of the root cause. While the attack was technically straightforward, the deeper lesson was institutional: when security is treated as charity—optional, sporadic, symbolic—liabilities accumulate unseen.

A credible limitation must be named. Some protocols operate under financial constraints that make recurring audits difficult. Early-stage projects with small treasuries may prioritise feature development to survive long enough to attract contributors. For them, the premium strains immediate viability. Yet the limitation reinforces the structural point: when resources are scarce, their allocation reveals implicit values. A team that commits to annual reviews, even at reduced scope, signals prudence; one that disregards them signals fragility. The constraint does not excuse the absence of assurance; it contextualises the cost of failing to pursue it.

Examples that crystallise the assurance-as-insurance principle extend beyond blockchain. Civil aviation offers a parallel. The Federal Aviation Administration (FAA) and the European Union Aviation Safety Agency (EASA) both require stringent, recurring inspections for aircraft. These inspections are not framed as optional expenditures but as non-negotiable components of safety governance. When Boeing faced scrutiny in 2019 after two fatal 737 MAX crashes, investigations by the US House Committee (2020) revealed that lapses in oversight and inadequate testing contributed to systemic failure. The lesson transfers directly: complex systems do not remain safe through goodwill. They remain safe through recurring, enforced assurance. Blockchains enjoy neither regulators as stringent nor procedures as deeply institutionalised. Their only alternative is to internalise the premium themselves.

To apply this principle within decentralised systems, one must name the behaviours that reveal seriousness. Does a protocol maintain a dependency map of all third-party libraries? Does it track time-to-patch after vulnerabilities are disclosed? Does it publish incident reports within set deadlines? This is not an abstract culture of safety; it is an observable pattern. The Ethereum Foundation's handling of the June 2020 "ETH 2.0 deposit contract" review cycle illustrates the point. The organisation commissioned multiple independent audits and a formal verification effort before launch, delaying public deployment until all identified classes of bugs had been resolved. The cost in time was substantial. The premium was paid upfront. The implication: users trusted the contract not because of assurances in forums but because the developers' behaviour reflected a high willingness to accept delay in exchange for reduced systemic risk.

The counterbalance appears when assurance is misinterpreted as reputational décor rather than structural insurance. Some teams treat audits as marketing assets—one-time badges displayed to attract users, devoid of ongoing commitment. The pattern is recognisable: a protocol secures a high-profile audit before launch, then releases major upgrades months later without corresponding reviews. The premium is paid once, then neglected. This approach confuses certification with safety. It assumes that a system's risk profile is static. But cryptographic libraries age; compilers change; gas markets shift; exploit techniques evolve. Assurance must evolve accordingly. A single audit is a snapshot; legitimacy is a film.

There is also the question of incentives. Protocols that collect transaction fees often face pressure from governance token holders to maximise yield rather than reinvest earnings into maintenance. This tension surfaced within Uniswap's community debates around the fee switch throughout 2022 and 2023. Proponents argued for redirecting a portion of fees to token holders, while critics urged allocating funds to long-term security efforts, including recurring audits, formal verification, and bug-bounty expansions. The disagreement was economic but also philosophical. Should the premium be shouldered by the network collectively, or should users bear losses when failures occur? The debate remains unresolved, yet it highlights a key truth: assurance competes with profit only when governance shortens its time horizons.

Another example—Chainlink's Proof of Reserve system in 2020—shows assurance built into architecture. By continuously verifying collateral backing wrapped assets, Chainlink functioned as a watchdog for systemic exposure during periods of market stress. This was not a symbolic commitment but a structural one, requiring operational expenditure, uptime guarantees, and ongoing monitoring.

The premium was encoded into the mechanism itself. The implication is broader: protocols that embed assurance natively reduce the need for discretionary vigilance, shifting the burden from culture to engineering.

The motif of *the premium* returns when considering community expectations. Users rarely articulate it explicitly, but they measure it intuitively. When a project responds rapidly to an exploit, communicates clearly, and compensates victims transparently, users infer that the premium was paid—even belatedly. When a project delays disclosures or disputes facts, users infer evasion. Legitimacy is therefore relational. It is earned through repeated demonstrations that a protocol is willing to sacrifice convenience for resilience.

A limitation must be acknowledged: some attack vectors emerge from the wider ecosystem, beyond what any protocol can control. Bridges fail because of cross-chain complexity; MEV exploits arise from structural market design; regulatory actions reshape interfaces overnight. Assurance cannot neutralise all risks. Yet this limitation reinforces the essential argument: when external uncertainty grows, internal assurance becomes more vital, not less. The premium buys flexibility. It ensures that when shocks occur, the system bends rather than breaks.

Governance theory helps clarify the broader stakes. Public law traditionally provides remedies when harms occur. Blockchains, lacking a clear legal forum, rely on ex ante controls—tests, audits, redundancy, monitoring—to prevent harms in the first place. Assurance replaces adjudication. It is the structural inverse of courts. This role elevates its importance beyond operational prudence. It becomes a form of proto-regulation, a substitute for institutions that decentralised systems aim to reduce. When a protocol treats assurance lightly, it risks substituting not less governance but worse governance: opaque, reactive, improvisational.

The unresolved tension surfaces as the subchapter closes. How much insurance is enough? Should protocols allocate a fixed percentage of revenue to assurance, or should they scale spending with usage? What signals should communities use to judge whether their premium is adequate? And what happens when users demand lower fees while auditors demand deeper scrutiny?

Every protocol must choose its premium. Whether that choice is deliberate or accidental determines the legitimacy of the system it governs.

Metrics that Matter

In July 2020, when the Ethereum core developers published their post-mortem on the "Berlin" testnet failure, the document revealed far more than the immediate cause of the halt. It exposed how much weight communities place on transparency, cadence, and the diversity of those who maintain their systems. The failure, triggered by a subtle gas mispricing, forced developers across several continents—Berlin, London, New York—to coordinate fixes overnight. What steadied user confidence was not the speed of the patch but the clarity of the public write-up: who discovered the issue, what broke, why it broke, and how the network would prevent similar failures. The report was blunt. It was uncomfortable. And it restored calm. Visibility, not optics, upheld legitimacy.

That scene illustrates a deeper truth: decentralised governance rises or falls not on aspirations but on measurable habits. The health of a protocol is legible in how it handles strain: the timeliness of incident reports, the breadth of its contributors, the precision of its upgrade notes. Each metric leaves a trace. Each trace shapes perception. And perception, in decentralised systems, determines whether users stay or migrate. These are not soft indicators. They are structural.

The quiet motif here is *the record*: what is written, who writes it, and who is absent from the writing.

Transparency in upgrades is the first major indicator, and its significance is best shown rather than claimed. When the Polkadot team released details of the "Statemint" upgrade in May 2021, they disclosed not just the features introduced but the reasoning behind critical design changes. The notes documented the dependencies, constraints, and assumptions that governed each decision. This level of disclosure achieved something subtle: it allowed external auditors and volunteer reviewers to verify not only whether the code worked but whether the reasoning made sense. Naming matters here. The disclosure credited specific contributors by handle or organisation. That visible authorship converted abstraction into accountability.

The implication is straightforward. A protocol that publishes detailed upgrade notes signals to users that it expects scrutiny. A protocol that does not invites suspicion, even if its code is sound. The absence of clarity creates a vacuum. Vacuums attract doubt.

A contrasting case underscores the point. In the collapse of Terra in May 2022, subsequent analysis revealed that documentation of prior parameter changes had been sparse, scattered across chats, ephemeral posts, and partially archived forums. The lack of a coherent upgrade record did not cause the collapse, but it obscured early-warning indicators that more transparent systems might have surfaced sooner. The limitation is real: some communities evolve so rapidly that maintaining a comprehensive changelog strains their contributors. But that strain is itself a metric. When documentation falls behind, resilience falls with it.

Transparency is only one part of the record. Incident reporting is another. The Avalanche "P-Chain" incident of February 2022—in which stalled validators caused delays in block finality—demonstrated the importance of prompt, structured disclosure. The Ava Labs team documented the malfunction, traced its origins to an interaction between custom virtual machines, and published the timeline within hours. Behaviour was visible: timestamps, decisions, and corrective steps. Users measured the response. The implication was measurable in transaction volume, which stabilised within a day. Trust was not assumed; it was earned in public.

Yet incident reporting invites a counter-example worth examining. Some protocols publish excessively detailed reports that intimidate rather than inform users. When the Tezos network published its 2020 report on a gas computation flaw, the document's mathematical complexity made it impenetrable to most of the community. The limitation is understandable: the protocol's architecture is intricate. Still, the example demonstrates that metrics must be communicable. Precision is useful only when comprehensible. The reconciliation lies in layering: highly technical detail for specialists, plain-language summaries for others. The act of honouring both audiences becomes part of the metric itself.

To extend the motif of *the record*, contributor diversity must be read not as a platitude but as an operational indicator. Where do maintainers live? Which organisations employ them? How concentrated are their funding sources? These questions carry weight because they reveal the network's capacity to withstand legal shocks, regulatory pressure, and social fracture. Ethereum, by 2021, had core developers spread across Europe, North America, South America, and Asia, many working for independent teams like Geth, Nethermind, and Erigon. This dispersion created resilience. A contributor outage in one region would not paralyse progress.

A contrasting example makes the significance sharper. When the NEAR Protocol faced downtime in September 2022 due to a chunk validation issue, subsequent analysis observed that a large proportion of the core engineering labour sat within a single organisation based in the United States. This concentration limited the diversity of perspectives during crisis triage and raised questions about jurisdictional exposure. The limitation does not condemn the protocol. It highlights a measurable risk: monoculture. Systems with narrow contributor bases struggle to sustain themselves when political or economic winds shift.

Metrics must avoid the trap of abstraction, so consider specific behaviours. How often does a protocol rotate its multisig signers? How many contributors have merged code in the past 180 days? What percentage of incident reports are authored by individuals unaffiliated with the founding team? These are countable. They reveal whether a network has moved beyond charismatic founders and early investors. The metric is vitality.

There is also the matter of audit transparency. Not the existence of audits—the prior subchapter covered that—but the visibility of audit histories over time. Chainlink, by publishing a ledger of audits spanning multiple years and listing each firm, version, and finding, offers a model. Users can see not only that audits occurred but how the system's risk posture changed. Such records become a chronicle of diligence. The implication is clear: protocols that treat audits as a continuous narrative cultivate deeper legitimacy than those who treat them as occasional badges.

A limitation emerges when metrics themselves become performance theatre. Projects may inflate contributor numbers by counting trivial changes or label minor version bumps as "upgrades" to appear active. This risk is real. It mirrors problems seen in academic institutions where quantity of publications is sometimes mistaken for quality. Reconciling the limitation requires nuance: metrics must be paired with interpretation. Numbers matter, but patterns matter more. A protocol with ten engaged contributors working steadily is healthier than one with fifty sporadic committers touching cosmetic files.

The broader ecosystem offers analogues. Linux kernel development, governed by thousands of contributors worldwide, has long understood the importance of contributor diversity and transparent documentation. The kernel's "Maintainers" file lists responsibility by subsystem, ensuring that anyone can trace ownership of any part of the code. When a fault is discovered, the record shows where to look and whom to ask. This structure enables resilience. The blockchain world, borrowing heavily from open-source practice, sometimes forgets the discipline that underwrites it.

Metrics also shape behaviour beyond developers. When users know that a protocol publishes timely upgrades, honest incident notes, and clear governance explanations, they are more willing to participate in votes, audits, and community discussions. Visibility invites reciprocity. When the record is clear, engagement deepens. When it is cloudy, apathy spreads.

The motif of *the record* returns one last time in the context of inter-protocol coordination. Cross-chain systems—bridges, oracles, and multi-network applications—depend on transparent metrics to coordinate risk. A bridge that reports the diversity of its validator set, the frequency of signer rotations, and the results of liveness checks becomes legible to the systems that rely on it. Without such data, integrations become guesswork. Guesswork becomes fragility.

The subchapter's unresolved tension is structural. Which metrics genuinely reflect resilience, and which merely mimic it? Should communities converge on shared standards, or should each protocol define its own? And more fundamentally: how much of a system's legitimacy rests not on what it does but on what it documents about itself?

The record endures. Whether it is honest or curated determines whether the system built upon it can endure too.

Chapter 9
Coordination Across Borders: Treaties, Clubs, and Coalitions

The first memorandum was barely four pages, drafted in a side room at the Monetary Authority of Singapore in October 2016. No delegation arrived with a prepared speech. No national flag stood behind the chairs. Just an improvised gathering of supervisors from Singapore, the United Kingdom, and Australia, each wrestling with the same puzzle: how to regulate a surge of cross-border fintech activity without slowing it to a crawl. By the end of the day they had produced something that looked nothing like a treaty—no ratification, no Senate hearings, no ceremony—yet it quietly altered the behaviour of firms across three continents. A "fintech bridge", they called it: a mutual commitment to coordinate supervision, share insights from licensing cases, and let firms trial services across borders with fewer frictions. It was soft law with sharp consequences.

That small room in Singapore captured a pattern that has repeated ever since. Global compacts—grand, universal, slow—struggle to keep pace with technologies that shift monthly. Mini-laterals move faster. A handful of regulators, or industry associations, or standards bodies can set expectations before any parliament debates them. When only a few actors align, the path clears: vocabulary harmonises, practices converge, and companies adjust to norms that have no legal compulsion yet feel impossible to ignore. The quiet power of clubs, not congresses, shapes cross-border digital governance.

The real contest here is tempo. As systems grow more entangled—payments streaming across jurisdictions, identity credentials validated through foreign attesters, infrastructure spanning data centres from Frankfurt to Seoul—the pace of coordination determines the margins of safety. Coalitions that act swiftly create room for experimentation, while those that wait for global consensus inherit crises they did not prepare for. Coordination is no longer a diplomatic luxury. It is operational.

This chapter examines what emerges when states, regulators, and private actors negotiate shared rules without waiting for universal agreement. The scene is crowded with paradoxes. Regulators learn by doing—pilots, sandbox experiments, joint statements—often without any formal authority to bind each other. Industry groups, nominally private, create certification marks that later become mandatory under statute. Voluntary codes, once treated as aspirational, evolve into enforcement tools when agencies adopt them as licensing conditions. Soft norms harden by degrees.

The logic is deceptively simple: in distributed systems, the first coalition to define a practice sets the benchmark for everyone else. When Japan's Financial Services Agency and the UK's Financial Conduct Authority ran joint experiments on digital identity verification in 2021, they did not claim to write global rules. Yet firms operating across Asia and Europe treated the outputs as guidance. Product teams altered onboarding flows. Compliance departments redrew risk matrices. A modest bilateral experiment carried the weight of a regional standard because it reduced uncertainty. Certainty is a currency in its own right.

This dynamic gives rise to a second pattern: private clubs with public teeth. Consider payments: before many states updated their statutes, the PCI Security Standards Council—an industry consortium founded in 2006—had already set global thresholds for card security. Merchants followed the rules not because a government ordered them to, but because non-compliance meant exclusion from card networks. The regulator arrived later, found the thresholds sensible, and embedded them. What begins as industry housekeeping becomes de facto international law.

Yet there is a risk embedded in these coalitions. Speed can narrow representation. Mini-laterals may privilege actors with shared interests and similar risk appetites, leaving out those whose economies or political systems diverge. Informal coordination can shield decisions from public scrutiny. A gesture that improves safety today may entrench power tomorrow. The history of transnational technical committees—telecoms, aviation, payments—demonstrates how enduring such dynamics can be. A rule drafted in one meeting can shape markets for decades.

Still, coordination through coalitions offers advantages global negotiations rarely match. It permits iteration: norms can be tweaked after pilots, rewritten after failures, expanded when a better idea appears. Regulators can compare outcomes without needing to reach universal agreement. They can test a rule in one jurisdiction, examine how firms respond, and export the lesson through memoranda, communiqués, or joint supervision. Capacity grows through practice, not just through doctrine.

At the same time, private actors—protocol foundations, infrastructure providers, standards consortia—play a parallel role. Their influence does not rely on territorial authority but on integration depth. If a widely used cross-chain bridge or identity provider adopts a security standard, participants inherit it. When an industry-led certification gains traction, regulators often face a choice: align with it, or impose a stricter regime that may fragment markets. The gravitational pull of standards is hard to resist.

This interplay between states and clubs blurs traditional lines of legitimacy. A public agency may enforce a rule it did not draft. A private association may wield influence that feels regulatory in effect, without any democratic mandate. Coalitions can improve safety, but they can also narrow the space for dissent. The question becomes not only who writes the standards, but who gets to revise them, and what happens when interests diverge.

The path from soft norm to hard law is seldom linear. Many jurisdictions begin with guidance, advice, or voluntary codes—signals rather than demands. But as adoption rises, and as incident history accumulates, those signals turn into expectations. Expectations, once widely shared, become obligations. Eventually, licensing regimes incorporate them directly. Part of the challenge for practitioners is recognising when a norm is still flexible and when it has silently crossed the threshold into enforceability.

Coordination across borders is, at its heart, coordination across epistemologies: different views of risk, different economic incentives, different political cultures. That is why the most successful coalitions do not chase universality. They chase enough alignment to reduce friction, enough flexibility to incorporate dissent, and enough transparency to maintain legitimacy. They build scaffolding rather than monuments.

As you read this chapter, the frame you should keep in mind is scale. Small groups shape the rules that millions must navigate. Informal arrangements steer formal ones. Coalitions write the prologue to treaties, and sometimes the treaties never need to appear. The world's digital systems depend on these quiet architectures of cooperation.

The question that follows—unresolved, generative, and politically charged—is this: as geopolitical tensions grow and technical interdependence deepens, which coalitions will define the shared playbook, and who will decide when soft norms deserve to become binding? The answer will determine not only how borderless technologies operate, but whose values their borders begin to express.

Mini-Laterals over Universals - Small coalitions act faster than global compacts

In November 2020, the European Commission and the Monetary Authority of Singapore issued a joint statement in Brussels announcing the completion of their cross-border digital finance pilot. It was not a treaty, nor even a formal agreement—just a slender communiqué outlining how each authority had tested the other's supervisory expectations for digital onboarding and payments. Yet the practical effect was immediate. Firms operating across both jurisdictions adjusted risk scoring models and compliance playbooks within weeks. What could have taken a decade at a global forum happened in a matter of months between two regulators who decided that alignment was more urgent than ceremony. One short statement, two signatories, two continents—and behavioural change rippling through dozens of multinational institutions.

That scene illustrates a broader pattern: small coalitions move markets. They do so not by rewriting international law but by narrowing uncertainty. A modest agreement, replicated a handful of times, becomes a gravitational centre. Supervisors copy what works. Firms pre-empt what seems likely. Standards harden through repetition. While global compacts stall under their own weight, mini-laterals create momentum simply by acting.

The question animating this subchapter is why compact groups succeed where universal bodies stall. The answer lies less in geopolitical theory than in the visible behaviour of regulators under pressure: the rapid drafting of joint declarations, the mirrored wording of supervisory guidance, the shared testing of sandbox pilots, the subtle choreography of enforcement priorities. These are the gestures through which coalitions make themselves felt—small enough to be agile, cohesive enough to establish norms, consequential enough to reshape systems.

Small groups commit. They also move.

The motif that threads through this analysis is pace: who can act fast enough when technologies evolve faster than statutes can be amended.

The first major claim stems from observable practice. Show: in June 2022, the UK's Financial Conduct Authority and Japan's Financial Services Agency published matching guidance on stablecoin custody risks after a series of failures in Asian and European markets. Name: the FCA–JFSA alignment emerged from a year of joint working groups, not from any global committee. Explain: the two authorities agreed on definitions of operational risk controls and transparency thresholds, allowing firms to harmonise compliance across both markets. Implication: by synchronising early, the pair set expectations that other jurisdictions later adopted, accelerating global convergence without any universal treaty.

The coalition was small, but the effect was large. Firms measured capital buffers against the stricter of the two standards. They adjusted incident-reporting timelines. They rewrote vendor assurance requirements because two supervisors thousands of miles apart opted for consistency. The very existence of that alignment reduced regulatory risk for cross-border operators and created pressure for other agencies to follow suit or risk becoming outliers.

A second claim: mini-laterals thrive because the incentives of their members are aligned in practical—not ideological—terms. Show: in February 2019, the Australian Securities and Investments Commission, the Swiss FINMA, and the Abu Dhabi Global Market ran coordinated sandbox tests on digital identity verification systems. Name: the ADGM–FINMA–ASIC corridor became a focal point for identity providers seeking cross-jurisdictional validation. Explain: each regulator had different political priorities but similar operational challenges; they needed faster ways to test technologies without compromising due diligence. Implication: coordination let them compare outcomes directly, iterate faster, and set shared thresholds for acceptable risk—all before the Financial Action Task Force or any global body issued updated recommendations.

Here again, the behaviour of firms changed in anticipation. Identity vendors deployed common attestation formats across the three jurisdictions. Exchanges adjusted customer risk segmentation models. Banks trialled lower-friction onboarding flows because three regulators had implicitly signalled that such flows would not be penalised. A mini-lateral arrangement created certainty that no universal body could match on comparable timelines.

But mini-laterals also carry limitations. One credible counter-example illustrates this clearly. In 2014, the G20 attempted to harmonise cybersecurity standards for financial institutions. Despite significant political support, progress was slow. Many states resisted adopting shared requirements, citing sovereignty concerns and divergent threat landscapes. The result was a patchwork: overlapping guidance, inconsistent reporting thresholds, and regionally fragmented incident response procedures. Compare this with a smaller arrangement—such as the 2020 EU–Singapore digital finance pilot—and the contrast is stark. Global compacts can articulate grand visions, yet they often fail to produce the concrete behaviours firms require.

Reconciliation comes from examining why scale matters. Universal bodies strive for inclusivity, which is politically important but operationally expensive. Mini-laterals privilege speed and relevance. They are not replacements for universal agreements but precursors: experimental zones where norms are tested before they scale. Their legitimacy emerges from efficacy, not symbolism.

A third claim: mini-laterals are effective because they reduce the transaction cost of coordination. Show: the December 2021 cross-border sandbox between the Bank of

England and the Bank of Canada trialled synthetic data frameworks for payments stress testing. Name: BoE–BoC pilots focused on identical systemic risk challenges and used aligned methodologies. Explain: by agreeing on modelling assumptions and shared datasets, both institutions could compare stress test results without the need for a formal treaty. Implication: the pilot produced measurable efficiency—firms reduced model duplication, supervisors gained clearer benchmarks, and systemic risk assessments became more portable.

The visible behaviour here is adaptation. Participants used the shared methodology to calibrate scenarios. They updated loss-given-default models. They adjusted liquidity stress timelines. These are technical details, but they show how mini-lateral actions cascade from policy rooms into engineering decisions at major institutions.

A fourth claim: mini-lateral outcomes often become the raw material for eventual global norms. Show: the Asia–Pacific Economic Cooperation (APEC) Cross-Border Privacy Rules system began with just a few economies—Japan, the United States, and Mexico—participating in certification processes. Name: APEC CBPR (2011) served as a prototype for transnational privacy interoperability long before the OECD updated its guidelines. Explain: early adopters built the operational architecture: accreditation processes, audit criteria, and dispute mechanisms. Implication: when more states joined, the system scaled smoothly because foundational norms had already been tested by a compact group.

The motif of pace reappears. Early alignment built momentum. Later universality piggybacked on prior precision.

Yet mini-laterals risk entrenching the priorities of the powerful. Smaller jurisdictions may feel compelled to adopt standards drafted without their input simply to maintain market access. A coalition of technologically advanced regulators may implicitly dictate the global playbook. This raises questions of equity and representation—who sets the benchmarks, and who bears the cost of compliance?

Reconciliation again lies in visibility and flexibility. Mini-laterals succeed when they are open enough to invite observation and adaptation, yet focused enough to maintain decisiveness. Transparency mitigates dominance. Iteration prevents ossification. The alternative—waiting for universal agreement—rarely suits fast-moving technical domains.

A fifth claim: mini-laterals reduce systemic risk by providing early warning channels. Show: during the cryptocurrency exchange failures in late 2022, supervisors from Singapore, the UK, and the United States exchanged supervisory insights days before public disclosures escalated. Name: MAS, FCA, and CFTC informal coordination (Nov–Dec 2022). Explain: these conversations did not circumvent due process; they helped agencies synchronise messaging and assess spillover risk. Implication: rapid, targeted coordination prevented contradictory public statements and reduced the likelihood of panic across cross-border operators.

Behaviour changed again. Firms monitored liquidity exposures more closely. Risk committees adjusted counterparty thresholds. Supervisors prepared contingency communications. A mini-lateral cluster acted as a stabiliser while universal bodies were still gathering information.

The overarching point: mini-laterals succeed because they are instruments of learning as much as instruments of alignment. They enable regulators to compare failures in real time, observe what works, and test norms before scaling them. They embody a pragmatic ethos: act with those who can act now.

This returns us to the motif of pace. In distributed financial and digital infrastructures, delay is itself a policy choice with consequences. If regulators wait for universal consensus, standards lag, vulnerabilities accumulate, and firms improvise under uncertainty. If coalitions act early, systems gain resilience through coherence.

The unresolved tension remains: how small can a coalition be before its legitimacy becomes too thin, and how large before its decisiveness collapses? The next generation of cross-border governance will hinge on that balance.

Regulators Learning by Doing

In March 2019, in a meeting room at the Financial Conduct Authority's headquarters in London, supervisors from more than a dozen jurisdictions watched a live demonstration of a payments platform being tested simultaneously in three countries. The initiative sat under the new Global Financial Innovation Network (GFIN), which the FCA had helped convene only months earlier. A single product was onboarding synthetic customers under three different rulesets, while regulators compared dashboards and risk alerts in real time. No treaty had been signed. No parliament had approved a new regime. Yet the practical outcome was unmistakable: by the end of the pilot, those authorities had a shared sense of which controls mattered, which disclosures worked, and which fears were overstated. They had learned by watching the same thing break in different ways. It was a test.

This kind of experiment is now a quiet fixture of financial governance. Supervisors draft joint statements, run cross-border sandboxes, and observe the behaviour of firms under slightly altered rules. They collect evidence before they write doctrine. The old model—deliberate first, legislate later, observe last—has inverted. Practice arrives before principle. For borderless infrastructures such as blockchain networks, that inversion is not a curiosity. It is a survival strategy.

The motif that threads through this subchapter is *the lab*. Regulators once styled themselves as courts and policemen. Increasingly, they behave like scientists in a lab: forming hypotheses, designing experiments, observing results, adjusting frameworks. The lab may be a sandbox, a pilot corridor, or a joint supervisory exercise, but the method is similar. Learn by doing. Then write the rules.

The first claim is straightforward: pilots expose what paper cannot. Show the behaviour. When the Monetary Authority of Singapore and the Bank of Canada conducted Project Jasper–Ubin in 2019, they did more than publish white papers on distributed ledger technology for wholesale payments. They built and tested cross-border settlement prototypes. Name the actors and place: MAS in Singapore, the Bank of Canada in Ottawa. Explain: the project forced regulators, technologists, and commercial banks to address concrete questions—latency thresholds, finality semantics, failover behaviour—long before any legislative text spoke about "DLT-based settlement systems". Implication: the exercise created a shared vocabulary and an empirical base. It narrowed the gap between speculation and supervision.

The visible outcomes mattered. Both authorities refined their internal risk taxonomies. They adjusted how they questioned firms applying to use similar technologies. They revised internal training materials for supervisors. None of these shifts required a treaty. All of them altered how future applications would be assessed.

A second example shows the same pattern on the retail side. The FCA's sandbox cohorts from 2016 onwards, and MAS's financial sandboxes from 2016 in Singapore, produced multiple joint engagements with firms experimenting in both jurisdictions. A cross-border remittance application might join both sandboxes, facing slightly different disclosure rules and capital expectations. Supervisors watched how the same product coped with two variants of oversight. They saw where risk controls broke, where customer confusion spiked, where fraud attempts clustered. They measured outcomes in concrete terms: customer complaint rates, error rates, false positives in AML screening, time to remediate faults. Implication: regulators learned not only whether a control worked, but how costly it was for firms and users.

The lab, in both cases, made abstractions visible. "Consumer protection" ceased to be a slogan; it became counts of misdirected payments and minutes spent resolving disputes. "Operational resilience" became the number of seconds before a failover node restored service. Metrics replaced metaphors.

The second claim is that joint statements and coordinated guidance converge practice without formal compulsion. Show: in October 2018, the UK's FCA, the US Commodity Futures Trading Commission, and the Monetary Authority of Singapore issued public statements on crypto-asset derivatives that, while not identical, reflected a striking alignment of concern around leverage, market manipulation, and disclosure. Name: FCA in London, CFTC in Washington, MAS in Singapore. Explain: none of these documents bound the others. Yet firms operating across those markets read them together, inferred a common direction of travel, and began to harmonise internal policies. Implication: the convergence of language—not law—drove behaviour.

The lab, here, is linguistic. Supervisors refine their vocabulary in public. They test phrases such as "reasonable steps", "risk-sensitive measures", "travel rule compliance" across audiences. If industry compliance teams treat a phrase as binding, it acquires force. The next statement uses it again. Over time, the repetition creates a de facto standard. No treaty was necessary.

A credible limitation must be acknowledged. Joint statements can also create noise when they are too vague or too numerous. Firms may struggle to distinguish genuine signals from political posturing. A communiqué that lists every conceivable risk and demands that firms "remain vigilant" provides little operational guidance. Reconciliation comes from watching behaviour. The statements that matter are those linked to pilots, cross-border tests, or specific supervisory expectations. When a joint text announces participation in a sandbox or cites empirical results, firms pay attention. When it reads like an essay, they file it and ignore it.

The third claim concerns cross-border sandboxes as instruments of alignment rather than mere showcases of innovation. Show the behaviour. The GFIN cross-border testing pilot in 2019 invited firms to test innovative services across multiple jurisdictions under a coordinated framework. Name: GFIN, anchored in the FCA in London, but with participating regulators from Canada, Singapore, Australia, and others. Explain: firms had to satisfy entry criteria in several markets simultaneously, revealing where domestic rules collided and where they overlapped unexpectedly. Supervisors used that friction as data. Implication: instead of trying to harmonise statutes ex ante, regulators identified points of convergence by running live experiments. They learned where equivalence might be feasible and where local policy constraints were immovable.

The lab here is literal: test environments, synthetic data, controlled exposures. But the more interesting artefact is the *lab notebook*—the record of what did not work. Regulators learned which disclosure formats confused customers in multiple languages; which identity verification methods failed with expatriate workers; which AML triggers generated unmanageable false positives when transactions crossed time zones. Those observations informed subsequent guidance and, in some jurisdictions, subtle tweaks to rulebooks.

Yet cross-border sandboxes face a real limitation. They attract firms sophisticated enough to navigate multiple regulatory regimes and well-resourced enough to participate in lengthy experiments. Smaller entities, especially those from emerging markets, often lack the capacity to engage. The risk is a selection effect: regulators learn primarily from the best organised and best connected. Reconciliation again depends on awareness. Authorities that treat sandbox outputs as universal truth will encode bias. Those that treat them as one experimental sample among many will use them more cautiously, supplementing with local data and consultations.

The fourth claim is that learning by doing changes regulators themselves. Show: staff rotations into innovation hubs and sandbox teams have become career tracks at several authorities. The FCA's Innovate division, MAS's FinTech & Innovation Group, and the Australian Securities and Investments Commission's Innovation Hub have all seconded supervisors into experimental settings. Explain: these staff encounter technical architectures, risk models, and user journeys that differ from legacy institutions. They return to mainstream supervisory roles with a richer mental model of how new systems behave under stress. Implication: the institutional memory of the regulator shifts. Future policy drafts reflect lived experience rather than hypothetical risk lists.

The lab motif returns as culture. A regulator that values experiments adjusts its internal incentives. It promotes officials who can interpret technical incidents, design phased roll-outs, and read metrics instead of only reading reports. It begins to ask different questions when a new product is proposed: not only "Is this permitted?" but "Can we test this safely?" and "What would we need to measure to know whether this is working?"

A counter-example tempers this narrative. Some regulators have launched sandboxes that function more as marketing devices than genuine experiments. They admit few firms, publish little data, and produce no visible change in supervisory practice. Firms treat participation as a badge rather than a test. The lab becomes a showroom. Reconciling this requires returning to behaviour as the metric. Where pilots alter internal manuals, case-handling procedures, or inspection priorities, learning has occurred. Where they do not, the exercise has been symbolic.

The fifth claim addresses an often-overlooked dimension: learning by doing also means learning when to say no. Not every pilot scales. Not every cross-border arrangement deserves to expand. Show: several early experiments with utility settlement coins in 2017–18 revealed operational complexities and legal ambiguities around finality that made large-scale deployment unattractive. Some central banks quietly stepped back, redirecting effort into more incremental changes to existing RTGS systems. Explain: the negative result was still a result. Those authorities avoided codifying a fragile model into law. Implication: the lab generates both positive and negative knowledge. Both matter.

For blockchain-based systems, this mindset is particularly relevant. Pilots can reveal how smart contract parameters interact with local consumer law, how privacy-preserving analytics affect supervisory visibility, how cross-border stablecoins interact with capital controls. Regulators that learn by doing will sometimes choose restriction not from ignorance but from informed caution.

Throughout these examples, the lab motif points to a deeper philosophical shift. The old ideal of the regulator as omniscient rule-maker has given way to a humbler, more iterative role. Supervisors recognise that they do not fully understand emerging systems before they see them operate at scale. As a result, they seek controlled exposure: limited pilots, capped user bases, staged roll-outs. They document what happens. They share the notebook with peers via joint statements and technical workshops.

This approach generates its own tensions. Experiments can appear to bless technologies prematurely, offering an implicit seal of approval. Firms may lobby to extend pilots beyond their safe scope. Political actors may demand rapid adoption of "innovative" systems after a successful test, ignoring the caveats buried in the lab notes. Learning by doing can be misread as endorsement by default.

The unresolved questions at the end of this subchapter are deliberately practical. How far should regulators go in experimenting with critical financial infrastructure before they risk normalising unproven models? When does a pilot stop being an experiment and start being a de facto regime? And who gets to read the lab notebook—the public, or only an inner circle of supervisors and favoured firms?

The answers will determine whether experimental governance becomes a source of resilience or a new vector for capture. The lab exists. The issue now is whose questions it is allowed to ask.

Private Clubs with Public Bite

In June 2006, in a conference room in Wakefield, Massachusetts, members of the Payment Card Industry Security Standards Council gathered around a draft that would soon reshape global compliance. Visa, Mastercard, American Express, Discover, and JCB had spent months arguing over breach thresholds and encryption rules. When they finally agreed to publish PCI DSS v1.0, no legislature had voted for it, no regulator had mandated it. Yet by the end of its first full year of operation, major acquirers on three continents refused to onboard merchants who failed its checks. A private club had created a rulebook that functioned, in practice, as law. The badge it issued—"PCI compliant"—became a passport. Without it, firms could not trade.

The PCI example shows the pattern that this subchapter examines with care: closed groups define thresholds, the market internalises them, and regulators later absorb them as baseline requirements. Influence precedes endorsement. Visibility precedes statute. The badge becomes an anchor.

The first claim is that industry associations act as proto-regulators by setting operational thresholds that become unavoidable. Show the behaviour. The Swift Customer Security Programme (CSP), launched in 2016 after the Bangladesh Bank heist, required participating banks to attest to controls such as access management and logging. Name the actors and places: Swift in Brussels, the breach traced through Dhaka. Explain: although participation in Swift is technically voluntary, no serious financial institution can operate internationally without it. CSP's controls therefore became mandatory in practice.

Implication: when regulators in the EU or Singapore later referenced similar controls in supervisory guidance, they were not innovating. They were ratifying a private standard devised in response to a crisis.

The badge motif recurs here. A Swift participant signs an annual attestation. That signature becomes proof of minimum hygiene. It is not enforced by statute; it is enforced by the network's refusal to transact with firms that do not comply. The badge carries weight because peers demand it.

A second example shows the same mechanism in digital-asset markets. After the Coincheck hack in Tokyo in January 2018, Japanese exchanges formed the Japan Virtual Currency Exchange Association (JVCEA), a self-regulatory organisation later recognised by the Financial Services Agency. Name the actors and place: JVCEA in Tokyo, under FSA oversight. Show: the association drafted rules covering segregation of client assets, cold storage ratios, and advertising practices. These rules were first adopted by member exchanges and only later reflected in updates to the Payment Services Act. Explain: the private club, not the legislature, set the initial thresholds. Implication: exchanges wishing to operate in Japan had to satisfy JVCEA standards long before statutory amendments came into effect. Again, the badge—membership—functioned as a licence in all but name.

The visible behaviours underpinning these examples reveal why such clubs hold public bite. Associations collect incident data, perform peer reviews, and publish compliance lists. These artefacts generate de facto reputational markets. A firm labelled "non-compliant" by

Swift or JVCEA faces measurable real-world consequences: delays in correspondent banking, higher insurance premiums, or loss of trading pairs. These are metrics, not metaphors.

A credible limitation tempers this view. Industry associations may reflect the interests of incumbents rather than the health of the system. A club dominated by large exchanges or global banks can create thresholds calibrated to their own infrastructure, thereby raising barriers for smaller entrants. The badge then becomes a gate. Reconciliation comes through examining behaviour. The most effective associations balance public scrutiny with peer accountability. They publish rule rationales, disclose enforcement actions, and allow appeals. Those that hide deliberations behind closed doors risk entrenching incumbency.

The second major claim is that regulators adopt private standards because they reduce their supervisory burden. Show: after PCI DSS gained traction, several national regulators referenced its controls directly in their oversight of payment processors. The UK Information Commissioner's Office cited PCI standards in breach investigations from 2009 onwards. Explain: regulators could rely on a widely used benchmark without drafting their own technical rules. Industry had already tested feasibility, cost, and compliance pathways. Implication: when regulators adopt a private standard, the association effectively outsources the drafting of parts of public law.

This dynamic has played out in blockchain ecosystems as well. Consider the emergence of Travel Rule compliance frameworks after the Financial Action Task Force updated its recommendations in June 2019. In response, private consortia developed interoperability standards for identity data exchange among virtual-asset service providers. Although FATF is an intergovernmental body, the operational protocols were defined by private clubs. Supervisors later assessed firms against these privately drafted formats. The badge—certification by a club participating in the standard—offered practical evidence of compliance.

The labelling behaviour itself shapes markets. Firms adopt the badge because counterparties request it. Counterparties request it because regulators inspect for it. The badge becomes a hinge connecting private norms to public enforcement. The badge is also fragile. If an association fails to update its rules after major incidents, regulators may lose trust and decouple their frameworks. The badge tarnishes.

A counter-example illustrates this fragility. The Libra Association, announced in Geneva in June 2019, attempted to establish a global digital currency backed by a private consortium of firms. Despite publishing governance frameworks and risk controls, the initiative faced widespread regulatory scepticism. Authorities in Washington, Brussels, and Singapore expressed concerns about monetary sovereignty, consumer risks, and AML enforcement. The association's private standards failed to achieve the market recognition necessary for public adoption. The badge never gained legitimacy. Reconciliation lies in understanding that private clubs succeed when their remit concerns operational hygiene or interoperability, not when they attempt to redefine macroeconomic governance.

The third claim is that certification marks within these associations create subtle forms of enforcement. Show: the Cloud Security Alliance's "STAR" certification, launched in 2011, rates cloud providers across control maturity. Name: CSA in Seattle; tests conducted globally. Explain: although not mandated by law, STAR certification became a procurement requirement for several public-sector buyers in the UK and Singapore. This marketisation of compliance meant that firms without the certification faced reduced access to major contracts. Implication: a certification mark created by a private club quietly shaped public-sector choices. Public law followed practice.

This pattern is now visible in blockchain networks through protocol-level certification regimes. Node operators, custodians, and analytics providers form working groups to define security baselines, audit expectations, and reporting formats. When large protocols reference these baselines in grant programmes or listing criteria, the badge acquires teeth. A validator without the badge may face reduced delegations or higher insurance premiums. A custodial service without the badge may struggle to secure partnerships with banks.

The badge motif returns a third time here as a reminder: badges simplify complexity. They compress dozens of controls into one recognisable symbol. They operate because stakeholders trust the issuer. When trust collapses, the badge loses its bite.

The fourth claim concerns the political economy of these clubs. Industry associations often negotiate directly with regulators, presenting themselves as representative voices for their sectors. Show: after the 2016 DAO incident, several blockchain industry groups in the United States and Europe prepared voluntary codes of conduct regarding smart contract audits and disclosure practices. Regulators used these documents to inform early guidance on security-token offerings in 2017–18. Name: US SEC in Washington; ESMA in Paris. Explain: regulators relied on associations to supply technical expertise and market data. Implication: the club became a filter between industry and the state.

Yet this filtering can produce distortions. Associations dominated by well-funded incumbents may lobby for rules that lock in their advantages. When the badge becomes a moat, innovation suffers. To reconcile this, regulators sometimes create parallel consultative bodies to diversify input. The most balanced approach blends private technical input with public-interest oversight.

Throughout the subchapter, the badge motif quietly organises the narrative. Badges mark membership, competence, compliance. They carry both prestige and cost. They can signal integrity or entrench dominance. They evolve from private labels into public thresholds when two conditions converge: market adoption and regulatory recognition.

The unresolved tension surfaces as a question. When does a badge stop being a voluntary sign of good practice and start functioning as a compulsory licence? And who decides whether a private club has earned the right to define that threshold?

The answer determines whether private standards enhance collective safety or merely shift power from elected authorities to unelected associations.

Dispute Escalation Paths

In May 2017, governors and market heads gathered at the Bank for International Settlements in Basel to endorse the FX Global Code. The document, developed over two years by central banks and major dealers, set out 55 principles for conduct in the foreign exchange market. It was framed as voluntary. No statute compelled adherence. No enforcement agency was created. Yet within a year, several central banks, including the Bank of England and the Reserve Bank of Australia, made adherence a condition for dealing with them, and major asset managers demanded signed "Statements of Commitment" from their counterparties. A soft code—drafted in committee rooms and consultation workshops—had been placed on the first rungs of a hard governance ladder. If you wanted access to key liquidity, you climbed.

That ladder is the motif of this subchapter. Dispute escalation is not only about how individual cases move from complaint to sanction; it is also about how norms themselves climb from aspiration to obligation. Voluntary codes, industry guidelines, supervisory expectations, licensing conditions: each rung raises the stakes, narrows discretion, and thickens the institutional response to misconduct. The question is not whether this ladder exists. It does. The question is who designs its steps, and what happens to those who fall off.

The most important claim is simple to show: durable cross-border governance depends less on grand, immediate legal change and more on carefully engineered paths from soft norms to enforceable duties. The FX Global Code demonstrates this clearly. At first, it offered principles—

"firms should handle confidential information with care", "pricing and execution should be fair and transparent". No penalties were attached. Then came a subtle shift. Central banks began to say, in effect, "We will only deal with counterparties who sign and implement this Code." Asset owners followed. The implication was concrete: a dealer that declined to sign found itself excluded from key trading relationships, a cost measured in lost volume and diminished reputation rather than fines.

The ladder's first rung was moral suasion. The second was market access. A third rung appeared when some supervisors started referencing the Code in thematic reviews. Breaches of its principles, while not prosecutable in themselves, began to influence supervisory assessments of governance and conduct. The pattern is familiar. Soft norms frame what "good practice" looks like. Disputes over behaviour are then judged against that frame. Over time, regulators feel justified in writing parts of the frame into formal rules because the market has already internalised them.

A second claim follows: dispute escalation paths actually begin at the moment norms are drafted, not when the first high-profile breach reaches enforcement. Consider the UK's 2009 Lending Code, an industry initiative covering treatment of retail borrowers and handling of financial difficulty. It started as voluntary guidance overseen by the Banking Code Standards Board. Over the next decade, the Financial Conduct Authority absorbed many of its commitments into binding rules on arrears handling and forbearance. The ladder here is visible in process. Complaints to the Financial Ombudsman Service referenced the Code as a benchmark. Ombudsman decisions crystallised expectations. That case history, in turn, armed the regulator with evidence when it translated expectations into rules.

Behaviour reveals the mechanism. When voluntary norms exist, dispute bodies—ombudsmen, arbitration panels, internal complaint handlers—use them to structure outcomes. They ask: did the firm follow the Code? If not, what remedy is appropriate? Each decision is a small, practical step up the ladder from "this is good practice" to "this is expected practice". Eventually, the difference between those labels disappears. A norm has hardened.

In digital-asset markets, the same pattern is starting to form. Take voluntary disclosure standards for smart contract audits. Initially, they were little more than badges on project websites: "audited by X", "formal verification complete". Then industry associations began to draft more detailed codes on vulnerability disclosure periods, severity grading, and incident reporting. Insurance underwriters and major exchanges started to require adherence to those codes as a condition for coverage or listing. Now regulators in several jurisdictions reference "independent audits" and "timely disclosure" in guidance on token listings and platform licences. The path is familiar. Soft norm, then contractual duty, then supervisory expectation, then licensing condition.

The ladder matters most in moments of failure. When a protocol suffers a major exploit and users lose funds, the first disputes rarely involve courts. They begin in community forums, arbitration mechanisms, or compensation negotiations. If the project has subscribed to a voluntary standard—say, a code on incident handling—

the community will immediately test behaviour against it. Did the team notify users within the agreed timeframe? Did they contact exchanges as required? Did they disclose root causes? The answers condition any later legal claim. Even where formal liability is unclear, deviation from a soft norm can trigger reputational sanctions and, crucially, inform future regulatory tightening.

A credible counter-example, however, shows the limits of this neat progression. The early "self-regulatory" codes issued by some crypto exchange associations around 2017–2018, particularly in loosely supervised jurisdictions, contained broad commitments—to "maintain high security standards", to "cooperate with law enforcement"—but lacked clear thresholds or enforcement mechanisms. When several exchanges in those markets later experienced hacks or insolvencies, the codes provided little basis for dispute resolution. No ombudsman. No graduated sanctions. No link to licensing. The ladder existed as rhetoric, not structure. Norms without rungs.

Reconciliation lies in specificity and linkage. A soft norm only becomes a rung when it maps to visible behaviours and connects to something parties care about—access, reputation, capital, or legal status. "Be secure" is not a rung. "Rotate keys every X days, report incidents within Y hours, maintain reserves of Z per cent"—those are actionable. Once insurers, counterparties, or licensing bodies pick them up, the ladder stiffens.

A further claim: in cross-border systems, escalation paths must be designed, not assumed, because disputes can migrate between jurisdictions. Imagine a stablecoin issuer headquartered in one country, serving users in ten others, with reserves held in a major financial centre. A voluntary code on reserve transparency and redemption rights, agreed among issuers and endorsed by a few regulators, becomes the soft norm. A dispute arises when redemptions are delayed. Where does the complaint go first? To the issuer's internal process. Then perhaps to a domestic ombudsman. If unresolved, to the courts or the regulator in the jurisdiction holding the reserves. Along that path, each body will ask: what commitments did the issuer make under the code? The ladder here crosses borders. Its rungs connect institutions rather than departments.

Designing such cross-border ladders requires clarity about hand-offs. Voluntary codes should specify not only desired behaviours but also escalation points: when does a breach move from internal remediation to external review, from external review to supervisory attention, from supervisory attention to formal sanction or licensing action? These transitions are often left implicit, which is precisely why escalation can feel arbitrary and politicised when a crisis hits.

The motif of the ladder returns when we consider how voluntary norms become licensing conditions. A regulator might begin by endorsing an industry code in guidance: "firms may find it helpful to follow X standard". Later, when assessing an application, it asks whether the applicant follows that standard. Later still, it writes into the licensing framework: "licensees must comply with X standard as updated from time to time". The highest rung has been climbed. Non-compliance can now result in licence suspension or revocation. The path from suggestion to sanction has become explicit in law.

There is a cost. Delegating detail like this effectively hands standard-setting power to whoever controls the code. If the code is governed by a private club, the licensing regime imports private governance wholesale. For blockchain infrastructure providers—custodians, validators-as-a-service, data analytics firms—this could mean that industry-written norms on issues such as chain reorganisation handling or address screening become hard obligations without parliamentary debate. The ladder has a proprietor.

A limitation must be admitted. Not every soft norm deserves hard enforcement. Some areas genuinely benefit from pluralism—multiple competing standards, different practices, diverse risk appetites. For example, analytics methodologies for blockchain forensics may reflect varying probability thresholds, false positive tolerances, or investigative philosophies. Forcing one dominant standard into licensing conditions too early could ossify innovation and privilege a particular vendor. The challenge is to choose which ladders to harden and which to leave as scaffolding.

A useful way to approach this choice is to ask three questions: does the norm address a clear harm; can its implementation be objectively assessed; and is there evidence that voluntary adherence is insufficient? Where all three answers are yes—as with basic custody controls or reserve disclosures—the case for escalation is strong. Where the answers diverge, regulators should be wary of importing the code wholesale into hard law.

Dispute escalation paths within decentralised communities add another twist. Many DAOs now define soft norms in governance forums—how proposals should be structured, what disclosure is expected from delegates, what timelines apply to major parameter changes. When conflicts arise, they are often resolved first through social mechanisms: forum debates, informal mediation by respected contributors, votes to ratify compromises. Only when these fail do participants reach for more coercive tools: token contract changes, emergency pauses, or, in extremis, legal claims in national courts. The ladder here moves from soft social norms to protocol-level enforcement and then, if needed, to external legal systems. Designing that path consciously—who can trigger each step, what thresholds apply, what remedies exist—can prevent crisis improvisation that undermines legitimacy.

The unresolved tension at the heart of this subchapter is whether these ladders can be transparent and contestable rather than opaque and improvised. Who should decide when a voluntary code has earned its place in licensing conditions? How should affected communities—users, smaller firms, public-interest groups—participate in that decision? And once a norm has climbed the ladder, what mechanisms should exist to climb it back down if experience shows that the standard distorts more than it protects?

Escalation will happen. The task is to ensure that each rung is visible before anyone is forced to stand on it.

Chapter 10
Forecasting Governance: Scenarios, Not Predictions

The years after the 2008 financial crisis produced a strange paradox. Governments promised bold reform. Markets promised renewed prudence. Yet the most visible structural outcome was consolidation: larger custodians, fewer clearing houses, and a governance landscape dominated by institutions judged "too essential to fail". It was not ideology that drove this; it was path dependence. A single shock, followed by hurried coordination and political appetite for certainty, narrowed the range of possible futures. Those who studied the settlements in London or Washington at the time could sense a deeper pattern—how moments of stress compress choice, how complexity collapses into central points of control, and how governance tends to congeal around whoever can move fastest to steady a trembling system.

That pattern haunts digital infrastructure today. Not as prophecy, but as possibility. Every exploit that empties a treasury, every new compliance rule that raises fixed costs, every convenience feature that nudges users towards custodial services—each is a small hinge on which the system can turn. The open question is which direction the turn will take. Centralisation is not an event but a drift, a settling of loose particles into recognisable shapes. Likewise, pluralism is not a slogan but a set of deliberate choices—maintaining open tooling, distributing authority, refusing to let any single entity monopolise how truth is certified or how participation is measured. This chapter lives in that tension: the tug between structures that simplify power and those that diffuse it.

To understand why we frame the future in scenarios rather than predictions, one must look squarely at the engineering of governance. Predictions suggest inevitability; scenarios restore agency. They reveal the branching roads ahead and show what assumptions underpin them. When a major exchange takes custody of billions in user assets, that is a data point. When a community-run front end continues to operate after a centralised one is restricted, that is another. Nothing in these facts determines the future. What they do is sketch the contours of possible governance settlements—some that concentrate authority, others that broaden it.

The tradition of scenario thinking dates back to Herman Kahn's work at RAND during the early Cold War and was later refined by Shell's scenario unit in the 1970s under Pierre Wack. Their craft was not fortune-telling but sense-making: identifying the structural forces that shape institutions, and illuminating how different combinations of those forces yield fundamentally different outcomes. It is a method built for environments where uncertainty is structural, not cyclical. Digital governance is precisely such an environment. Protocols evolve quickly; political reactions lag unevenly; economic incentives often cut against stated ideals. Any forecast built on linear projection is brittle.

This chapter therefore asks the reader to think as those strategists did—by interrogating levers, not outcomes. We explore how governance pathways form, how centralisation can arise from seemingly decentralised choices, and how pluralism can survive when incentives tilt against it. Consider a typical pattern: after a major protocol incident, the entities capable of absorbing liability, coordinating audits, or negotiating with regulators become privileged. Their role expands. Over time, users treat them as default intermediaries. It is the governance equivalent of sedimentation: each crisis leaves a deposit, and the deposits harden. The chapter examines these deposits.

But we also study the counter-patterns: communities that build their own front ends when incumbents fold to regulatory scares; developers who maintain multi-provider oracle feeds that resist capture; governance experiments that keep key functions out of any single party's reach. These are not romantic gestures. They are governance choices with measurable effects—distribution of signers, diversity of code maintainers, redundancy in data sources. When sustained, they create plural futures. Without them, the field of possibilities narrows.

The stakes are not abstract. Custody rules set by a handful of jurisdictions can reshape global practice more than multilateral treaties. Identity standards drafted in small technical communities can calcify into de facto requirements. Oracle concentration in a few reputable providers can turn market events into governance events—one misreported price, one delayed update, one compromised key. Cross-border enforcement can turn from distant threat to immediate constraint when coalitions of regulators align. These are the signals to watch. They are the tremors before paths diverge.

This chapter offers a guide to reading those tremors. Not through the lens of optimism or pessimism, but through structure. How do risk events alter governance equilibrium? How do compliance burdens favour incumbents? When does convenience become dependence? How does credible neutrality protect against power accumulation? Each question is a fork. The answers shape scenarios, and scenarios illuminate governance futures without pretending to fix them.

To support the reader in applying these insights, the chapter culminates in a playbook—a method for analysing any policy proposal or protocol upgrade through the book's overarching model. It will show how to map incentives, identify concentrated choke points, test resilience through hypothetical shocks, and assess how decisions today constrain or expand future governance pathways. The point is not to predict the world of 2030 or 2040. The point is to give the reader the tools to see how choices made tomorrow morning will nudge the system towards one branch or another.

As you read forward, consider the recurring motif that has threaded through this book: power settles unless it is unsettled. Centralisation is the easiest equilibrium, pluralism the most fragile. The question that animates this chapter—and, arguably, the entire governance debate—is what combinations of norms, engineering choices, economic incentives, and institutional coalitions can prevent the governance of digital systems from collapsing into whichever structures happen to withstand the next shock.

The roads ahead exist already, faint but discernible. The task is not to guess which one we will follow. It is to learn how to recognise the forks before we reach them.

Paths of Centralisation

In February 2021, after a sharp overnight price swing wiped out hundreds of millions of dollars in under-collateralised positions on several decentralised lending platforms, the immediate winners were not the protocols that had survived the turbulence, but the custodial exchanges that promised users refuge from what they described as "execution risk". Coinbase, operating from San Francisco with global reach, reported a measurable uptick in net deposits during that week. The incident was brief, but the behavioural shift was unmistakable: when faced with uncertainty, a significant share of users preferred the simplicity of a single login and a customer-support line to the cold comfort of self-managed contracts. One event, one shock, and a complex web of decentralised tools bent—if only slightly—towards the familiar gravity of centralisation.

This pattern is not unique to digital finance. It mirrors earlier episodes in communications infrastructure, where major outages in the late 1990s pushed firms away from distributed e-mail servers and towards managed services run by a handful of providers. Each crisis became a hinge. Each hinge narrowed the field. In blockchain systems, the hinge often appears in the form of a market exploit, a sudden regulatory demand, or a technical failure that exposes the fragility of interfaces users had assumed to be reliable. The pattern repeats: decentralisation is the aspiration; consolidation becomes the response.

The motif running through this subchapter is deceptively simple: pressure compresses choice. Under pressure, systems centralise. Human behaviour centralises. Policy centralises. And unless countered deliberately, that compression becomes the long-term trajectory.

Centralisation often begins with risk events. To see this, one need only trace the aftermath of the 2016 DAO exploit on Ethereum. The months that followed saw a swing towards service providers capable of abstracting operational complexity. Wallets with embedded recovery features gained traction. Intermediaries that could absorb user error, such as BitGo in Palo Alto, expanded their offering. These were not ideological shifts; they were practical responses to fear. The event showed users and developers alike that code-is-law was a fine principle until one malformed call function laid bare the limits of automation. The outcome was not a formal agreement to centralise. It was a quiet behavioural migration towards entities perceived as safer.

Naming that behavioural migration matters because it makes explicit the economic logic beneath it. When users confront low-probability, high-impact failures, they measure not philosophical purity but downside risk. They compare the cost of autonomy with the cost of protection. They commit to the safer path, even when it narrows the architecture. This is how centralisation forms—not by decree but by drift.

Compliance costs add the next layer. The Financial Action Task Force (FATF) revised its guidance in June 2019, extending travel-rule expectations to virtual asset service providers. For developers of permissionless interfaces, the guidance was ambiguous; for custodial exchanges, it was a competitive advantage. Entities with compliance departments in London, Singapore, or New York could internalise these obligations with relative ease. Smaller operators struggled. Several shuttered in the months that followed; others restricted services to avoid the friction. The visible behaviour was the pruning of marginal actors. The invisible implication was consolidation: compliance burdens acted as a filter, and those with the resources to absorb them naturally concentrated market share.

Two further examples illuminate the pattern. In June 2022, the collapse of the Terra ecosystem triggered a chain of liquidity stresses that forced several decentralised protocols to enact emergency pauses. During that period, Binance consolidated both trading and stablecoin flows as participants sought predictable execution. Similarly, in April 2020, the New York Department of Financial Services issued updated guidance on custody controls. Providers already licensed under the state's BitLicence regime expanded; those outside it withdrew US-facing services. In each case, the regulatory or technical shock did not command centralisation, but it created asymmetric burdens that made central nodes more attractive.

A credible limitation to this narrative is the continued rise of non-custodial wallets and hardware devices, particularly in Europe after the 2020–2021 bull cycle. Ledger, headquartered in Paris, shipped record numbers of devices, signalling that a significant part of the user base continued to value sovereignty over convenience. This counter-example complicates the story: it shows that not all risk events point towards consolidation. Some shocks—particularly those involving custodial failures—push users in the opposite direction. But even here, the net effect is mixed. While hardware wallets decentralise control, the software ecosystems that support them often rely on centralised update servers, single-provider firmware signatures, and proprietary interfaces. The hard lesson is that decentralisation in one layer may conceal centralisation in another.

To reconcile these patterns, one must return to the underlying motif: pressure compresses choice. Hardware adoption is pressure applied at the user level; compliance cost is pressure applied at the provider level; market panic is pressure applied at the system level. Each pressure reshapes incentives differently. The result is not a simple slide towards centralisation but a contested field where different forms of consolidation—custodial, infrastructural, regulatory—interact.

Convenience forms the third path. User experience studies conducted by several exchanges in 2021 found that the median time a new user was willing to spend learning key-management concepts was under seven minutes. Complexity is the invisible tax of decentralisation, and the tax is steep. When platforms integrate fiat gateways, offer portfolio dashboards, and provide insurance-like guarantees, they translate capability into familiarity. That familiarity becomes dependence. Dependence centralises.

The behaviour is measurable. When the Ethereum network experienced fee spikes in May 2021, self-custodial transaction volumes dipped as users balked at the uncertainty of manual configuration. Centralised exchange volumes did not. They absorbed flows, aggregated orders, and batched settlements, shielding users from the discomfort of direct interaction with volatile gas markets.

The implication is stark: convenience is not merely a design choice; it is a governance choice that weights outcomes towards actors capable of absorbing complexity.

Centralisation, however, does not always manifest as a single dominant provider. Sometimes it takes the form of oligopoly, where a small cluster of entities effectively governs the infrastructure. Consider the concentration of RPC services around Infura, launched in 2016 and acquired by ConsenSys in Brooklyn. During network congestion events, applications dependent on Infura's endpoints experienced correlated failures, exposing the fragility of relying on a single infrastructure provider. This is centralisation by dependency rather than mandate. It is softer, harder to detect, and more pervasive. The behaviour—developers defaulting to the simplest available service—creates the condition. The implication is systemic risk.

There is another subtle form: jurisdictional centralisation. When most institutional gateways route through a few regulatory regimes, those regimes gain de facto influence over global practice. The United States, with its combination of federal and state-level oversight, and Singapore, with its licensing frameworks under the Monetary Authority of Singapore, have become gravitational centres. A project seeking institutional adoption often adapts its operations to these jurisdictions before any others. That adaptation reshapes governance choices—risk thresholds, identity standards, reporting practices—long before any formal rule is imposed. The pressure is soft, the behaviour incremental, but the outcome structural.

A credible counter-example is the emergence of decentralised infrastructure networks—such as Helium's early deployments in 2019 across multiple cities—that attempted to avoid jurisdictional bottlenecks by distributing validation and economic incentives. Yet even these projects encountered concentration pressures when token price volatility forced centralised coordination to sustain momentum. The reconciliation lies in acknowledging that decentralisation requires constant maintenance, while centralisation emerges naturally from entropy.

Throughout these dynamics, one motif recurs: centralisation hides inside solutions to short-term pain. Whether the pain is user confusion, regulatory uncertainty, liquidity stress, or operational fragility, the fastest solution is usually the most centralised. This does not render centralisation illegitimate; it renders it likely.

The unresolved tension is unavoidable: at what point does the convenience of central nodes become a structural liability? And how should architects, policymakers, and communities decide which pressures to absorb and which pressures to resist? Every protocol upgrade, every regulatory engagement, every market shock pushes the system a little further along one path or another. The real question is how to know, in the moment, when the hinge has begun to turn.

Paths of Pluralism

In April 2022, a small group of developers in Amsterdam pushed a quiet update to a community-run front end for the decentralised exchange SushiSwap. The change was trivial in code terms but radical in consequence: it allowed users to rotate hosting mirrors automatically when one domain faced pressure, downtime, or legal threat. Within a week, mirrors operated from volunteer servers in Berlin, Singapore, and São Paulo. None belonged to the original team. None required permission. The result was a visible demonstration of pluralism: when the interface decentralised, its governance decentralised with it. One action. Many hands. A shared outcome grounded in resilience rather than authority.

Pluralism rarely announces itself with the drama of a fork or a manifesto. It usually enters through the side door, embedded in small engineering decisions that shift power away from central choke points. Choosing a public-good library over a proprietary SDK. Publishing documentation that third parties can fork. Rotating multisig signers across jurisdictions. These details form the texture of decentralisation. When enough such details accumulate, the system starts to behave differently. It stretches rather than snaps.

The motif that threads through this subchapter is simple but demanding: plurality is a discipline. It is a set of choices that favour diversity, even when homogeneity appears easier. It rewards investment in tools that disperse power, and it punishes the instinct to rely on the biggest, fastest, or most well-funded node in the network. Pluralism succeeds not through rhetoric but through design.

To show how pluralism emerges in practice, one must begin with open tooling. This is where power diffuses fastest. Consider the decision by the Ethereum Foundation in September 2015 to release the Go-Ethereum (Geth) client under the GNU Lesser General Public License. The licence allowed forks, commercial use, and modifications provided improvements were disclosed. The behaviour this licence enabled—independent teams running their own builds, auditing their own patches, and experimenting with alternative networking logic—helped prevent a single implementation from defining the protocol. The implication was structural: decentralisation at the client layer meant no single codebase could become the arbiter of consensus.

Naming this dynamic matters because it makes explicit what might otherwise appear accidental. When multiple teams maintain clients—Besu in Boston, Nethermind in Warsaw, Erigon in Kyiv—their technical differences become governance safeguards. Bugs manifest differently, optimisations diverge, and coordination requires negotiation rather than fiat. Open tooling transforms engineering heterogeneity into institutional resilience.

A second named example reinforces the pattern. In June 2020, the Interchain Foundation supported multiple independent relayer implementations for the Cosmos ecosystem. The choice was deliberate: avoid a bridge monoculture. The visible outcome was that when one relayer experienced latency issues that autumn, packet flows shifted to alternatives without halting cross-chain communication. The implication was clear: diversity of tooling reduces the surface area for systemic failure.

A credible limitation sits beside these successes. Open tooling is expensive to maintain. Scripts, libraries, and client implementations all require long-term stewardship. Many open-source projects rely on a handful of maintainers who risk burnout. When maintenance stalls, diversity decays. The reconciliation lies in recognising that pluralism demands both technical openness and sustainable contributor ecosystems. Without funding, open tools become abandoned tools; abandoned tools become vulnerabilities.

Credible neutrality forms the next path. Neutrality is not an abstraction; it is a behaviour measurable through decision-making patterns. A foundation that publishes upgrade criteria before beneficiaries are known commits to neutrality. A developer collective that rotates leadership roles annually measures its own influence. A protocol that chooses parameter updates through blind voting prevents reputational pressure from distorting outcomes. Each behaviour is a safeguard against dominance.

One example of credible neutrality in practice occurred during the London hard fork of Ethereum in August 2021. The decision to implement EIP-1559—changing fee mechanics fundamentally—was not dictated by a single core team. It passed through public discussions, research by teams in multiple countries, and testnet deployments shared across client developers. No one entity controlled the timeline or the specification. Neutrality here meant that the most powerful actors—the major mining pools and the foundation—did not possess unilateral veto. The implication was legitimacy: even opponents of the change acknowledged the process as fair.

Contrast this with a counter-example: several layer-one projects between 2020 and 2022 adopted governance models that allowed foundation boards to override community votes "in emergencies". The intent was stability; the effect was suspicion. Users adapted by reducing their exposure or by running only minimal infrastructure. The limitation does not negate the power of neutrality; it illustrates the cost of its absence.

Pluralism also manifests through resilience. Here, the question is not merely "Who governs?" but "How gracefully does the system fail?" When decentralised protocols withstand stress without forcing users to retreat to central hubs, pluralism deepens. Resilience becomes pluralism's proof.

One visible behaviour of resilience is geographic dispersion. Validator nodes running in Tokyo, Johannesburg, and Helsinki face different grid conditions, different legal risks, and different bandwidth profiles. Their dispersion dilutes localised shocks. When a Canadian hosting provider suspended several nodes in February 2022 following a policy change, networks with globally distributed validators rebalanced their threshold constraints quickly. Networks dependent on that single provider stalled. A plural network is a stable network.

Another behaviour is failover diversity. Protocols that rely on two or more independent data sources for oracle feeds—Chainlink, Band Protocol, Uniswap v3's built-in TWAP oracles—can fail in one dimension without collapsing in another. The implication is structural: redundancy creates time, and time creates options. Pluralism thrives in systems with options.

But resilience has limits. Excessive redundancy increases coordination cost. Too many oracle providers risk delays. Too many validator sets complicate upgrades. Too much independence strains consensus. The limitation becomes evident in protocols where updates require coordination across dozens of teams: progress slows, decision fatigue rises, and actors drift towards whichever leader seems most competent. The reconciliation is discipline: pluralism must avoid both scarcity of voices and cacophony of voices.

Threading through these examples is a quiet motif: plurality requires friction. Not destructive friction, but purposeful friction. Open tooling introduces friction by enabling forks. Neutrality introduces friction by slowing unilateral decisions. Resilience introduces friction by distributing responsibilities across imperfect actors. These frictions prevent capture. They make it harder for any one node—corporate, regulatory, or technical—to convert momentum into monopoly.

One further example illustrates pluralism's deeper political significance. In December 2020, when the front-end domain of a major decentralised finance protocol was seized following a jurisdictional dispute, the community responded within hours. Mirrors appeared. IPFS gateways picked up the static files. Independent developers contributed accessibility patches and localisation improvements. The protocol did not die because no single chokepoint existed. The behaviour of users—choosing to maintain access collectively—revealed a different governance truth: legitimacy flowed not through a charter but through action. The implication is both simple and profound. Pluralism is sustained not only by technical design but by community instinct.

The unresolved tension sits at the heart of the subchapter: how much friction is enough? Too little, and power recentralises through convenience. Too much, and coordination collapses. Pluralism's strength is its diversity;

its weakness is its dispersion. The forward test for any decentralised system is to decide, repeatedly and consciously, where to place itself along that spectrum. Each decision, each tool, each fallback path nudges the architecture towards either plurality or consolidation. The question is whether communities will commit to the discipline that pluralism demands—or drift, imperceptibly, towards the simplicity that centralisation offers.

What to Watch

In June 2023, the Monetary Authority of Singapore (MAS) and the Financial Conduct Authority (FCA) released a joint statement in London outlining a shared supervisory approach for digital-asset custody. The announcement received just a few paragraphs in the financial press, yet within forty-eight hours several custodial providers rewrote their service terms. One firm introduced strict segregation requirements; another imposed a fixed withdrawal delay for assets exceeding a threshold. These were not voluntary gestures. They were anticipatory moves in response to an alignment of regulatory signals across two influential jurisdictions. A single document, signed in a single city, altered operating practice worldwide. It showed something plain but often overlooked: governance shifts begin long before formal laws. They take shape in the shadows cast by coordination.

That scene captures the heart of this subchapter. Because for all the grand rhetoric about decentralisation, the decisive forces shaping protocol governance often appear first in the quiet places—consultations, technical standards, meetings between enforcement agencies, and cross-border advisory notes. These signals do not command. They hint. They shape the decisions of engineers, lawyers, and risk officers who would rather adapt early than defend late. Once enough of these signals accumulate, the ecosystem tilts. The tilt can be measured. And this subchapter argues that certain classes of signals deserve constant attention: custody rules, identity standards, oracle concentration, and cross-border enforcement practice. They are early warnings. They also reveal where power is drifting.

A simple motif will run through these pages: watch the edges. Governance shifts are legible not at the centre, but in the places where rules meet practice. Edges expose pressure before the core feels it.

Custody rules form the first edge. They matter because who controls keys controls outcomes. After the collapse of FTX in November 2022, regulators in multiple jurisdictions accelerated efforts to define "true custody". Some insisted on one-to-one asset segregation; others required real-time solvency attestations. The visible behaviour was adaptation. Exchanges in Seoul and Dubai introduced automated proof-of-reserve dashboards. A major European custodian implemented forced withdrawal tests every quarter to demonstrate operational readiness. These actions were not displays of virtue; they were strategic responses to perceived regulatory direction. The implication is clear: custody rules, even when unenforced, reshape infrastructure by shifting the cost of non-compliance. When costs rise unevenly, smaller providers fold or consolidate, nudging ecosystems towards centralisation.

The second edge—identity standards—reveals itself through the mundane. In January 2024, the European Banking Authority added decentralised-identifier compatibility to its draft guidance for crypto service providers. The document was technical and dense. Yet within weeks, two major protocol teams revised their sign-up flows to integrate verifiable-credential schemas aligned with the draft. The decision was not ideological. It was pragmatic. If identity standards tighten, systems built on anonymity brittle quickly. Metrics become legible. Risk models tighten. Developers commit code that embeds assumptions about identity that were once optional. The implication is structural: as identity standards converge across borders, the practical space for pseudonymous use narrows, even without explicit bans. A system built to tolerate incomplete information becomes a system built to authenticate.

A credible counter-example sits alongside this trend. The Brazilian central bank's open finance framework, expanded in 2022, allowed credential portability without mandating government-issued identifiers for every interaction. The regime emphasised proportionality over uniformity. This flexibility showed that identity design does not inevitably drift toward maximum disclosure. It can be shaped by political philosophy, not only risk aversion. Reconciling the two cases demonstrates the tension: global harmonisation generates pressure to conform, yet local experiments show that plural paths remain open. Watching identity standards therefore means watching for which philosophy—uniformity or proportionality—quietly gains normative weight.

The third edge—oracle concentration—is harder to see directly but easier to measure. When the lending protocol bZx was exploited in February 2020, the key failure was a price feed manipulated through thin liquidity on a single exchange. At the time, the design depended on one oracle with limited redundancy. After the incident, protocols began to diversify their feeds: Chainlink integrating multiple exchanges, Uniswap offering time-weighted average prices, and Band Protocol expanding across several regions. These changes reflected a dawning recognition that whoever certifies reality determines liquidations, compensation, and, by extension, governance. The metric to watch is not branding; it is concentration. Track the number of independent data sources used in core protocols. Track update frequency. Track validator dispersion by geography. These behaviours reveal where truth is anchored. When truth anchors centralise, power centralises with them.

There is a limitation worth acknowledging. Diversity is not free. When too many oracles provide feeds with different update cadences, protocols slow. Mismatched data creates noise. Developers compensate by weighting certain feeds more heavily, which reintroduces concentration by stealth. Reconciling this requires discipline: design failover architectures that maintain plurality without producing paralysis. The implication for governance is sharp. Monitoring oracle concentration is not about chasing numerical diversity; it is about understanding the dynamics that cause systems to privilege one source during stress.

Cross-border enforcement forms the fourth edge. Here the signals are faint but consequential. In October 2023, the U.S. Commodity Futures Trading Commission coordinated with regulators in Japan and Switzerland to pursue an operator accused of laundering funds through privacy pools. The investigation hinged on subpoenas served in multiple jurisdictions and the cooperation of two analytics firms.

Days after the announcement, several privacy-focused protocols saw a measurable drop in volume. One mixer lost half its liquidity over the next month. No law changed. No new statute passed. The enforcement pattern alone altered user behaviour.

This raises a practical question: what precisely should the attentive observer watch in cross-border enforcement? Watch the language in joint statements—terms like "supervisory alignment", "information-sharing mechanism", and "interoperable compliance frameworks". They indicate that regulators are moving from ad hoc cooperation to structured collaboration. Watch the geography of enforcement. If agencies in liberal jurisdictions begin adopting investigative methods pioneered in stricter ones, the normative centre of gravity shifts. And watch the use of private intermediaries—analytics firms, accreditation bodies, custodial monitors. Their behaviour signals what regulators may expect but have not yet mandated.

Threaded through all these edges is the motif of watchfulness itself. Edges reveal stress before systems do. The edges of custody show when trust declines. The edges of identity show when discretion evaporates. The edges of oracle design show when certainty collapses. And the edges of enforcement show when sovereignty bleeds across borders.

A second named example illustrates the convergence of multiple edges at once. In March 2023, the Hong Kong Securities and Futures Commission issued a circular requiring virtual-asset service providers to demonstrate "ongoing monitoring of off-platform exposures". The guidance was drafted locally but mirrored fragments of guidance appearing in Canada, Singapore, and the EU's Markets in Crypto-Assets Regulation. Developers quickly added risk-dashboards for wrapped assets and bridged tokens. Oracle providers adjusted their feeds to include additional data points on liquidity fragmentation. Custodians applied new withdrawal gates to reduce cross-platform risk. The ecosystem reacted not to a single rule, but to the cross-border echo of regulatory expectations. The implication is that governance signals amplify when repeated across jurisdictions, even if none individually bind.

A credible counterforce exists: decentralised communities sometimes refuse to internalise these signals. When Tornado Cash faced sanctions in August 2022, some users continued operating community-hosted interfaces, mirroring them on IPFS and maintaining documentation on GitHub. Their behaviour showed that enforcement signals do not automatically reshape decentralised practice. Yet, the liquidity collapse that followed demonstrated the boundaries of resistance. Participation patterns still shifted. The contradiction between user intent and systemic behaviour reveals an important reconciliation. Signals influence practice even when defied. They do not dictate, but they constrain.

The unresolved tension sits where all these edges meet. If custodial rules tighten, identity standards converge, oracle providers consolidate, and enforcement grows more coordinated, decentralisation may survive in code but not in practice. Yet too little alignment risks fragmentation, instability, and the erosion of public legitimacy. The forward test is stark: which signals matter most, and when does adaptation become acquiescence? Readers must decide whether each emerging signal is a step towards coherent global governance or a drift towards overreach. The edges tell the story first. The challenge is learning to watch them closely enough—and early enough—to understand which future is forming.

Reader Playbook

On 25 May 2023, in Brussels, the European Union formally adopted the Markets in Crypto-Assets Regulation. The press photographs captured the predictable tableau: officials standing beneath the blue and gold flag, the ceremonial pens on the polished table. Yet the real governance shift occurred away from the cameras. Within seventy-two hours, a prominent wallet provider rewrote its recovery-phrase flow, two exchanges altered their listing criteria, and a major venture fund adjusted how it structured token allocations. None of these changes were explicitly mandated by the regulation. They were anticipatory moves—interpretations, not instructions. They showed that governance is not merely written; governance is inferred. And that is where this playbook begins: not with rules as text, but rules as signals.

The question that follows is practical. How does one analyse a policy or protocol decision before its consequences harden? How does one read a governance shift as it forms rather than when it lands? The motif that will thread through this subchapter—quiet but insistent—is simple: *follow the hinge*. Every important decision contains a hinge, a point of leverage that determines whose interests shape the outcome. The task is to identify that hinge early, understand what forces act on it, and discern what the hinge reveals about the future.

The first hinge is the surface problem—what the decision claims to address. Show it, then name it. When the U.S. Securities and Exchange Commission sued Coinbase in June 2023, the stated issue was whether certain tokens constituted unregistered securities. That was the surface. But the visible behaviour that mattered was different: a chain of projects immediately altered their treasury diversification schedules, pushing stablecoins to exchanges in Singapore and Abu Dhabi. These decisions, taken within hours, displayed what the industry believed the hinge to be: not the legal classification itself, but the cost of being caught in its blast radius. The implication is blunt. Analysts must examine not only the announced rationale but the reactions it triggers; these often reveal the policy's true gravitational pull.

To understand any hinge properly, the analyst must map incentives. The second hinge—sometimes hidden—is who pays for compliance. Costs shape governance more reliably than principles. When Japan's Financial Services Agency tightened custody segregation rules in mid-2022, several exchanges complied by building automated audit mechanisms. A few withdrew from the market entirely. The metric that exposed the hinge was behaviour: the frequency of solvency attestations, the granularity of wallet-mapping disclosures, and the speed with which firms adopted risk-segregation tooling. These were more revealing than public statements. They showed that the operational burden—not the regulatory philosophy—defined the path. Power resides not where rules are drafted, but where costs collect.

A limitation deserves attention. Costs do not always produce consolidation; sometimes they produce creativity. When South Korea introduced rapid-reporting requirements for suspicious transfers in 2021, several young teams built monitoring primitives that later became exportable products. Innovation emerged not despite the costs, but because altering practice was cheaper than exiting the market. Reconciling this with the previous examples highlights a key step of the playbook: test whether a requirement compresses diversity or ignites adaptation. Observing which firms retreat and which reinvent is a diagnostic method, not a narrative flourish.

The third hinge is legitimacy. To evaluate a decision, one must track which actors gain authority as a consequence of it. Legitimacy shows itself through behaviour: who others choose to follow. After the Tornado Cash sanctions in August 2022, several analytics firms published risk-score interpretations that were not legally binding yet quickly became industry defaults. Wallet interfaces embedded those interpretations. Layer-two bridges adopted them in validation flow. These firms did not legislate. They anointed. Analysts must identify these unexpected centres of gravity—organisations whose interpretations become de facto law and whose actions shape protocol practice even when they claim neutrality. The implication: understanding governance requires watching the interpreters, not merely the regulators.

The playbook's fourth hinge moves from actors to architecture. Any decision—legal or technical—makes certain designs easier and others harder. This is the architectural hinge: what the decision renders possible. When Polygon introduced its zkEVM public beta in March

2023, the technical narrative centred on performance. But the governance consequence lay elsewhere. Because proofs could be generated by third-party services, control over verification became diffuse. Projects that relied on these proofs now depended not on a single prover but on a market of them. The hinge revealed a shift: architectural pluralism replaced verifier centrality. Analysts must therefore study how decisions tilt systems towards either concentration or dispersion—not in rhetoric, but in code paths, tooling dependencies, and fallback mechanisms.

A credible counter-example is instructive. The Optimism "Superchain" concept, announced in 2023, promised interoperability across multiple rollups. Yet, the sequencers remained centralised, and governance retained veto paths. Here the architecture expanded, but the hinge stayed narrow. Reconciling the two cases demonstrates that not all architectural innovations produce governance pluralism. Analysts must measure where veto power resides, how updates propagate, and who can halt execution. Complexity does not guarantee decentralisation; sometimes it conceals its absence.

The fifth hinge is jurisdictional drift. Governance decisions do not exist in isolation; they move through borders and absorb the norms they encounter. Analysts must therefore watch where decisions originate, where they replicate, and where they mutate. For example, when the Central Bank of Nigeria reversed its strict crypto restrictions in December 2023 and introduced a controlled licensing regime, the move influenced policymaking far beyond West Africa. Regulators in Malaysia and Kenya cited the Nigerian shift in subsequent consultations. The hinge was not merely the change itself, but the demonstration effect—an example of regulatory recalibration in a frontier market influencing mid-tier jurisdictions. The implication is that analysts must map how ideas travel, not just how they land.

Threading through these hinges is the motif of the hinge itself—the small point that determines the turn. Every decision turns; the key is discovering where.

To build a complete analysis, the playbook requires two more steps. First, evaluate who controls emergency powers. Every system contains a break-glass mechanism—multisigs, councils, emergency patches, safe-mode toggles. When Compound paused certain markets in August 2021 to fix a pricing bug, the critical factor was not the bug but the authority path. A small group acted swiftly and correctly, but the privilege was revealed. Analysts must measure the number of signers, the jurisdictions they inhabit, and the procedures that govern their actions. Visible behaviour—response time, audit trails, and community notifications—expose whether emergency power is transparent stewardship or quiet centralisation.

Second, examine how disputes escalate. A policy or protocol decision does not show its final character at launch; it shows it when challenged. When the MakerDAO community debated Real-World Assets collateral in 2022, disputes moved from informal forums to structured working groups to formal governance votes. The escalation path revealed the underlying structure: deliberation first, delegation second, formal vote last. Analysts must identify whether a system offers proportional steps or jumps straight to high-stakes conflict. The implication is decisive. Systems with clear escalation exhibit resilience; systems without it exhibit fragility masked as harmony.

About the Author

Tarek Omraneh writes at the intersection of technology, power, and public purpose. His work focuses on how rules emerge when software outpaces law, and how ordinary users experience that tension in payments, identity, and markets. He has advised founders, policy teams, and civil-society groups on responsible innovation and the trade-offs between speed and legitimacy. Raised on histories of trading routes that crossed empires, he brings a comparative lens to modern networks where standards, not swords, redraw borders. His mission is simple: help readers tell signal from noise, and map incentives before judging actors. He writes in plain language, resists hype, and prefers durable frameworks over fleeting headlines.

www.ingramcontent.com/pod-product-compliance
Lightning Source LLC
Chambersburg PA
CBHW031337230926
51848CB00002B/273
9789374594148